TRIUMPH

The Racing Story

Mick Walker

The Crowood Press

First published in 2004 by
The Crowood Press Ltd
Ramsbury, Marlborough
Wiltshire SN8 2HR

www.crowood.com

British Library Cataloguing-in-Publication Data
A catalogue record for this book is available from the British Library.

ISBN 1 86126 684 7

This book is dedicated to a sorely missed friend and fellow motorcycle enthusiast, George Hallam.

Typeface used: Bembo.

Typeset and designed by
D & N Publishing, Hungerford, Berkshire.

Printed and bound in Great Britain by CPI Bath.

Contents

Preface

In the early days of my motorcycling career, two makes figured heavily: Ducati and Triumph. During the early to mid-1960s I owned at various times, a Tiger 100SS, a Tiger 110, a 5TA Speed Twin and a Doug Southwell six-fifty Triton. Later, I raced a Formula Cub with considerable success, including wins at Snetterton, Cadwell Park and Lydden Hill during 1968. Finally, after getting married in 1969, I owned a Tiger 90 unit three-fifty twin.

During the early 1970s, together with many other enthusiasts, I marvelled at the fantastic performances generated by the Triumph Trident (and BSA Rocket 3) triples in both Formula 750 and Production class events. These came in direct contrast to those being gained commercially by the parent company, the giant BSA Group.

After their demise, I had some dealings with the Triumph Workers' Cooperative at Meriden when, as the UK's Moto Guzzi spares importer, I was involved with the arrival onto the British market of the Co Uno (Cooperative Number One). Based on the Moto Guzzi (and Benelli) 125 Turismo this was a single-cylinder, two-stroke commuter bike. However, I was not impressed by the cooperative and, therefore, not surprised when this failed in the early 1980s.

Then, as editor of *Motorcycle Enthusiast*, I attended the official launch of the Les Harris Bonneville from a new factory in rural Devon one day in June 1985. However, the only bikes built by Harris (besides some Rotex-engined machines badged under the Matchless brand name) were kickstart T140V (five-speed) Bonnevilles with many Italian-sourced components.

But, many have forgotten the fact that, after the co-op went into liquidation, John Bloor (a successful Midlands-based property developer) purchased the Triumph name and licensed the Harris operation. Bloor had also insisted that Harris stick rigidly to the original specification, so plans for developments to update the Bonneville still further were not allowed.

Into the 1990s, and the newly created Bloor Triumph company made its entry. In contrast to the many 'white elephants' that litter recent British motorcycle history, John Bloor spoke with his actions rather than fine-sounding words that could never be transmitted to production.

Since then, the Bloor operation has grown and represents a serious challenge to the all-dominant Japanese industry, at least in the design and quality stakes. I have visited the company's Hinckley, Leicestershire headquarters several times over the last decade, and have always returned home proud to be British.

Having personal contact with many of the personalities involved in *Triumph – The Racing Story* has made my task easier than it would otherwise have been, as have the many miles I have ridden on various Triumph machines during my career. My brother Rick was also an inspiration – his list of Triumph ownership being at least the equal of mine, including a Tiger Cub, Tiger 110, unit TR6 Trophy and a T150 Trident. Special thanks to Roger Winterburn, Brenda Scivyer, Guy and Les Ethrington, Steve Lilley, Dave Woods, Bernard Hargreaves, the late Ivor Davies, Colin Dunbar and Percy Tait.

Finally, it is left to me to say to you, the reader, that I hope you have as much enjoyment in reading *Triumph – The Racing Story*, as I have had writing it.

Mick Walker, April 2004

1 Early Days

Of all the numerous British motorcycle marques, Triumph is probably the best known. Together with BSA and Norton, they dominated the scene for a considerable part of the twentieth century – and are still a big name today – with a modern, state-of-the-art plant in Hinckley, Leicestershire, thanks to the vision of current owner John Bloor. But in the days when Great Britain ruled the two-wheel world, BSA was seen as the biggest, Norton the big name in racing, and Triumph the producer of affordable sports bikes. Generally, except for its Gold Star, BSA-built commuter and touring machines, Norton produced specialist, expensive Grand Prix bikes, and Triumph offered motorcycles that the man-in-the-street could buy from his local dealer, tune, and then go racing.

From the very first Isle of Man TT in 1907 (when they secured second and third positions), Triumph have built a solid reputation for delivering the goods when it comes to speed events: at Brooklands, with countless victories and lap records; more TT successes, including post-war Clubman and Production wins; Thruxton 500-mile glory; the one-model Formula Cub racing series; success at Daytona and elsewhere in America; Formula 750 (the forerunner of the Super Bike class) with the legendary triples; and sprinting and record breaking – including gaining the World's Fastest.

In November 1883, 21-year-old Siegfried Bettmann, a German Jew from Nuremburg, arrived in London and took on agencies for a number of foreign firms, including the White Sewing Machine Company of Cleveland, Ohio, which was later to manufacture trucks and cars. Bettmann then began to export bicycles under the Triumph brand name. At first these were made for him in Birmingham, but in 1887, with a partner, Mauritz Schulte, Bettmann set up his own factory in Much Park Street, Coventry. Business expanded rapidly in 1895 with an injection of £45,000 (several millions at today's value) by Harvey du Cros of Dunlop (*see Ariel – The Complete Story*), and two years later the Triumph Cycle Company went public with a capitalization of £170,000.

The company's first motor vehicle, in 1898, was a tricycle designed and built as a prototype by the Beeston Cycle Co. Ltd; but the venture did not proceed to production. Experiments with motorcycles began in the following year, but not until 1902 did the first real model appear. Simply called the 'No. 1', this was essentially a Triumph bicycle that had been strengthened to carry an imported 239cc Belgian Minerva engine. Rated at 2¼bhp, the engine was mounted at the base of the front down-tube. This drove the rear wheel direct from the crankshaft by means of a long belt. Why a Belgian-made engine? The answer was simple: at that time the Continental Europeans were ahead of the British, and Schulte (in charge of the engineering side) wanted the best engine he could get until he was ready to produce his own.

By 1905, Schulte and Charles Hathaway (a talented designer and also Triumph's works manager) produced what many claim to have been the first completely British-made motorcycle, the prototype of which had formerly appeared towards the end of 1904. This was powered by Triumph's own engine, a 363cc (78 × 76mm) side-valve single for which the makers claimed a power output of 3bhp at 1,500rpm.

It was also said to be the first engine to have its mainshaft supported by ball bearings. Transmission was again by a long belt direct from the crankshaft to the rear wheel. Ignition was by accumulator, but for an additional £5 the buyer could specify a Simms-Bosch magneto.

To publicize their new motorcycle, Triumph took part in an ambitious test: one of the new machines was set the difficult task of covering 200 miles (320km) a day for six days. Towards the end of the attempt the frame broke. Undaunted, the company made a fresh attempt and were successful this time, covering 1,200 miles (1,930km) without any form of mechanical breakdown.

In 1906, Triumph relocated to new premises in Priory Street, Coventry, and this would be their address for the next thirty years.

Early Races

Then came the very first Isle of Man TT. Jack Marshall brought his Triumph home runner-up in the single-cylinder race, behind Charlie Collier (Matchless), averaging 37.11mph (59.7kmph). Frank Hulbert was third, with two other Triumphs finishing thirteenth and fourteenth. In 1907 the engine displaced 453cc (82 × 86mm), and was enlarged to 476cc (84 × 86mm) for the following year. The 1908 design was also equipped with a variable pulley. This provided alternative ratios, at a time when hills were viewed with horror by most motorcyclists. The pulley on the crankshaft screwed in and out to provide alternative ratios of 4:1 and 6:1, but necessitated a somewhat complicated roadside procedure, as the drive-belt had to be shortened or lengthened by means of small, detachable sections. The word 'pioneer' in motorcycling terms meant just that!

In the same year, 1908, at Brooklands, Surrey, a private one-lap race took place between W.G. Bickford riding one of the 476cc singles, and O. C. McMinnies on a Vindec (essentially an imported German Allright). McMinnies won at a speed of almost 53mph (85.3kmph), and thus gained the distinction of winning the first motorcycle race staged at the famous Brooklands track. Jack Marshall returned to the Isle of Man in 1908 and won the Single Cylinder class of the TT, averaging 40.49mph (65kmph); he also set the fastest lap at 42.8mph (68.8kmph). Sir Robert Arbuthnot was third, and a quartet of other Triumphs were placed 4th, 5th, 7th and 10th: all in all a very successful showing.

In 1909 the finishing order for Triumph was W. F. Newsome third, plus 5th, 11th, 14th and 15th. In 1910, W. Creyton was third, followed by other Triumph competitors in 4th, 6th, 7th, 8th, 11th, 13th and 15th.

Early Models

Tourist Trophy Racer

By now, Triumph's racing reputation was growing, and it was further assisted by the Coventry works building of a model based on the successful Isle of Man racer. This was marketed as the Tourist Trophy Racer, and had (as did the latest pukka works bike) a displacement of 498cc (85 × 88mm). It featured belt-drive and variable pulley (high 3¼, low 4½:1). Pedalling gear (a feature of both touring and racing models at the time) was dispensed with, and two sets of footrests were provided. That year, 1911, Triumph were the first single-cylinder machines to finish (the rules and classes having been changed), coming home 6th, 8th, 9th, 13th, 18th and 25th.

For the 1912 TT, Triumph introduced a single, but important, modification. To make gear-changing an easier task, bottom gear of the three-speed hub was suppressed. J.R. Haswell rode superbly to finish runner-up in the Senior TT at 46.41mph (74.7kmph), with other Triumphs coming home 5th, 6th, 7th, 9th and 16th.

A new frame was introduced for 1913, but the engine remained as before. Other changes included a separate oil tank (carried on the seat pillar) and a Philipson pulley in place of the hub gear. The gear-control gear was interconnected with the rear brake pedal, so that the gear ratio was lowered to its limit whenever the brake was applied. But these changes did

The very first production Triumph motorcycle, the Model 1, using an imported Belgian Minerva side-valve single-cylinder engine displacing 239cc.

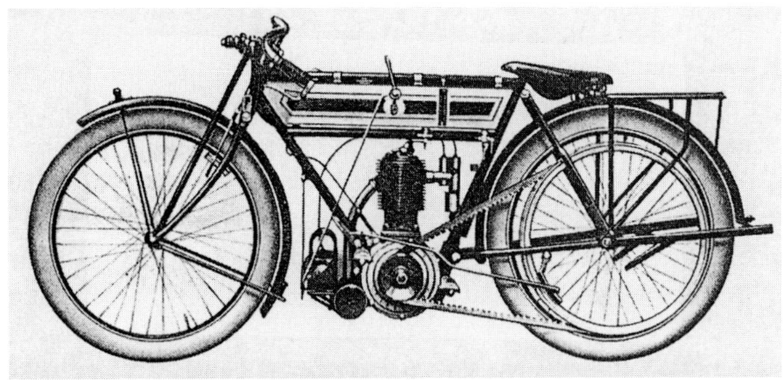

1911 Triumph 3½hp TT machine. This employed a 498cc (85 × 88mm) sv single-cylinder engine, patented variable pulley transmission, magneto ignition and Triumph-made double-barrel carburettor.

BELOW: *Triumph rider Percy Butler with the machine he rode to sixteenth place in the 1912 Senior TT, in the Isle of Man.*

not do Triumph much good, and for once the TT results were poor, with the highest finisher being placed down in eighteenth position. At Brooklands, however, J.R. Haswell won the 500cc Solo class of the Six Hour race, and in the same year a Triumph finished runner-up in the French Grand Prix – the firm's first major Continental success. Then 1914 saw a return to form in the Senior TT, with Triumph finishing 5th, 8th, 16th, 27th and 37th.

The First Twin

The first Triumph vertical twin, with a side-valve engine displacing 600cc, proved an unsuccessful experiment in 1913. The valves were housed fore and aft of the cylinder barrels, with the exhaust valve at the front. The cylinders were a monobloc casting, and the crankshaft was solid, with the throws 180 degrees apart. It also featured horizontally split, car-type crankcases and an outside flywheel.

By now, Siegfried Bettmann had become a prominent Coventry figure, being made the city's mayor in mid-1913. He had been made chairman of the Standard Motor Company (based in Coventry) two years earlier in 1911.

World War I, which began in August 1914, brought great prosperity to Triumph, who supplied more than 30,000 motorcycles (mainly the 550cc Model H single-valve single) to British and Allied forces. Motorcycles were so successful that Bettmann was unwilling to make a move into four wheels at this time. However, although Mauritz Schulte had designed many of the best Triumph motorcycles (including the wartime Model H), he 'retired' (some would say he was forced out) after disagreements with Bettmann. Schulte was given a 'golden handshake' of £15,000.

The First Car

After Schulte came Claude Vivian Holbrook, recruited by Bettmann after the war; they first met at the War Office in 1914 whilst Holbrook was handling government motorcycle procurement. Holbrook was keen to get Triumph into the automobile industry, and wanted a small car with which to compete against the top-selling Austin Seven. In 1921 he persuaded Bettmann to purchase the factory of the recently defunct Dawson Car Company, also of Coventry, and the first Triumph car arrived two years later in 1923. However, it was not until 1927 that Triumph cars took off, with the 832cc Super Seven, designed by Stanley Edge (who had assisted Herbert Austin with the design of the Austin Seven).

The 'Riccy'

One of the most famous racing Triumphs was the legendary 'Riccy'. The top end of the engine was designed by that famous authority on the internal combustion engine, Sir Harry Ricardo (1885–1974). Ricardo was a distinguished consultant engineer specializing in power units. Besides his work for Triumph he also made a considerable contribution to both motor and aviation industries during the first half of the twentieth century. He became a Fellow of the Royal Society in 1929, and was knighted in 1948.

The Riccy's official name was the Type IR. Of advanced design, there were several features that for the time (1921) were notable innovations. One of these was its four valves, two inlet and two exhaust, with a 90-degree angle between the pairs, and the inlet valves were masked, the first application of this feature on a motorcycle engine. It displaced 500cc and had pushrod (ohv) valve operation. The cylinder barrel was of steel, spigotted into the cast-iron cylinder head that was held down by five studs on a metal-to-metal ground joint. The bore and stroke measurements were 80.5 × 98mm respectively and, unlike other designs of the era, the piston was not fully skirted, but was of the slipper type (later used widely on full-blown sports and racing engines).

The Triumph company entered six of the new machines for the 1921 Senior TT in the Isle of Man. Although the race results were extremely disappointing (only one machine finished, in sixteenth place), extensive development went on and the 'Riccy' collected a large number of race

The 'Riccy' (Ricardo) Type IR was one of the most famous of all racing Triumphs; the top end of its ohv engine featured four valves, which when it appeared in 1921 was cutting-edge technology. The 499cc (80.5 × 98mm) single also used another innovation, a slipper-type piston.

After its race debut in the 1921 Senior TT, the 'Riccy' was put on general sale; this is a 1922 example and shows the various design features to good effect, including twin-port cylinder head, forward-mounted magneto/dynamo, front-wheel speedometer drive, and polished aluminium primary chaincase.

victories and speed records. For 1922, Ricardo modified the engine in considerable detail. The bore and stroke were altered to 85 × 88mm, this allowing a 25 per cent increase in valve area. The valve gear was strengthened, so that the exhaust ports lay at an angle to each other, instead of in the previous parallel formation. Dry sump lubrication replaced the original total loss system; a double-piston oscillating pump delivered oil under pressure to the big-end bearing, and scavenged the sump.

Major Frank Halford (later to become a distinguished aircraft designer, and later still, managing director of the de Havilland Engine Company) spent time at the Brooklands circuit with an experimental version of the 'Riccy' that differed in one very important respect: the cylinder head was water-cooled! The radiator for this was carried in the front part of the petrol tank. However, it was ultimately decided that the advantages provided by the water-cooling were not sufficient to justify the additional complication, and the experimental head was abandoned. Even so, Frank Halford went on to set several records with a four-valve Ricardo Triumph, including: the Flying Mile at 83.9mph (135.01kmph); the One-Hour at 76.74mph (123.47kmph); and the 50-Mile at

77.27mph (124.33kmph). In the 1922 Senior TT, Walter Brandish finished an impressive runner-up, averaging 56.52mph (90.95kmph).

The 'Riccy' was to remain in the Triumph range for the next five years, but was discontinued when the new two-valve Model TT arrived in 1927.

The Model TT

Victor Horsman was a Brooklands ace, record breaker, tuner and, later, Liverpool motorcycle dealer. He was also the inspiration for the two-valve, overhead-valve Model TT single, which effectively replaced the Ricardo Model IR (Riccy) in the Triumph racing family of machines. Long before the TT arrived the Riccy had fallen out of favour.

The engine of the TT was developed by Horsman, and it was an impressive-looking motorcycle, with its twin-port ohv head and enclosed valve gear (the latter an advanced feature for its day). Displacing 494cc (80.5 × 98mm), it featured a three-speed gearbox with a crossover drive as employed on the earlier Triumph side-valve models. The new-type front forks featured large, adjustable fabric-friction discs and a steering damper was included in the specification. One of the new TT models took part in the 1927 Isle of Man Senior TT, with Tommy Simister finishing third at an average speed of 65.75mph (105kmph). Later, in 1929, the TT became the ST, featuring enclosed, lubricated valve gear and roller-bearing rockers.

Under the influence of Claude Holbrook, Triumph was now taking an ever-greater interest in four wheels instead of two, and was manufacturing almost the complete car on site, including engines and body panels. But by 1931 the effects of the Great Depression (caused by the American Wall Street stock market crash of October 1929) were hitting Triumph hard, as they were other British companies. Motorcycle sales were down by a third, and no dividend was paid on ordinary shares, the first time this had happened for thirty years. There was certainly no cash to design, build or race competition motorcycles. The bicycle business was sold off to Coventry Bicycles, and Holbrook was in favour of selling the motorcycle side as well.

In 1933 Bettmann, now seventy years of age, resigned from the company he had founded. Outwardly, Holbrook professed everything was rosy, and on the surface all appeared healthy: Triumph had a flourishing car body-building department headed by Walter Belgrove; Donald Healey was technical director of the four-wheel division; and Triumph cars chalked up a number of competition successes. Then the old White and Poppe engine factory (suppliers to the Ariel marque and others) was purchased in 1935.

Racing Bikes in the Thirties

The Model 5/10

During April 1934, a racing version of the existing 493cc (84 × 89mm) overhead-valve, single-cylinder roadster was first shown. A trio of the Model 5/10 (as it was officially labelled) machines took part in the Senior TT in June of that year, though all retired for various reasons; after this, limited production began.

Although clearly based on the roadster, it not only featured a more highly tuned engine (cams, valves, springs, piston, exhaust and carburettor), but also a lowered frame. In addition, a special connecting rod and cylinder barrel were fitted, whilst a choice of pistons was made available for use with petrol-benzole or alcohol. The maximum speed approached 100mph (160kmph). One of the Model 5/10 bikes also took part in the 1935 TT, but again a retirement was posted. The last machines were built in 1936.

Another Twin: the 6/1

In July 1933, a new Triumph twin made its bow. Fitted with a Val Page-designed 647cc (70 × 84mm) vertical engine, it was in many ways a modern start for Triumph. Its overhead valves were operated by a single gear-driven camshaft mounted at the rear of the crankcases. The mag-dyno was gear-driven from the camshaft, with the dry sump lubrication featuring an oil tank in the crankcases. A flywheel was carried on the

Victor Horsman, leading Brooklands ace, record breaker, tuner and later Liverpool dealer, with one of his Triumphs at the Surrey circuit during the early 1920s.

BELOW: *Vic Horsman was the inspiration behind the two-valve ohv Model TT of 1927. Displacing 494c (80.5 × 98mm), it featured a three-speed gearbox, with a cross-over drive as employed on the earlier Triumph side-valve models.*

BELOW RIGHT: *In 1928 the TT became the ST, and finally the CTT (shown here). Although the top end remained similar, the bottom half of the engine was considerably changed, and given a much more modern appearance. Production ended in 1932.*

nearside (left) of the 360-degree crankshaft, and outboard of it went the primary drive, which was by double helical gears – an expensive feature, as it caused the engine to run backwards.

The machine, coded 6/1, entered production for the 1934 season. To send it on its way, one of the new six-fifties, hitched to a sidecar, circled Brooklands for 500 miles (800km) at 60mph (96kmph). After also being put through the gruelling ISDT (International Six Days' Trial), Triumph were awarded the coveted Maudes

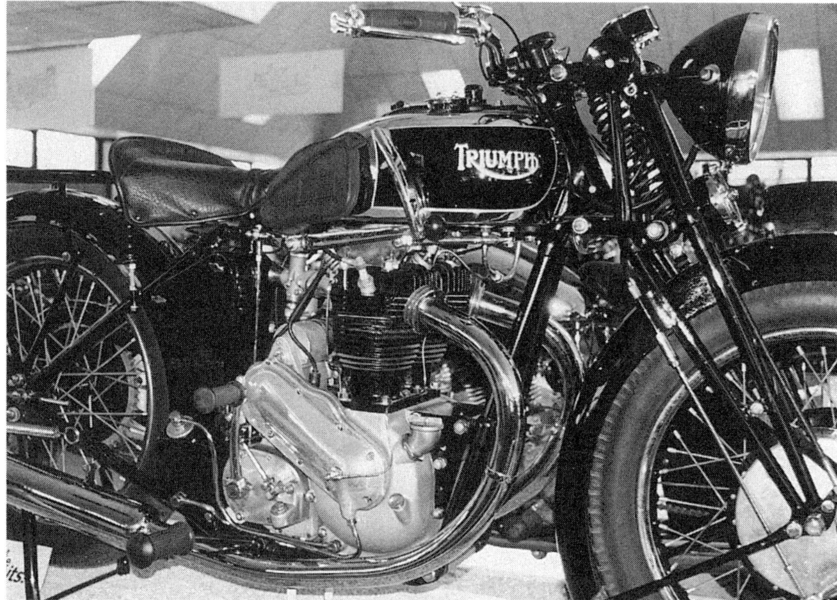

The 647cc (70 × 84mm) Val Page-designed 6/1 vertical twin preceded Edward Turner's famous Speed Twin by several years; it made its public debut in July 1933. But after winning the Maudes Trophy, sales were never more than a trickle, and it died, along with the old Triumph management, in the 1936 sale to Jack Y. Sangster.

Trophy. Production ran until 1936, although few examples were sold; however, it did have the distinction of pointing to Triumph's future direction a few years later. This was to come after a complete reshuffle of the Triumph pack, with both a new designer and a new owner.

Financial Disaster: Postwar Recovery

A catastrophic loss of £212,000 was recorded in the 1935/36 trading year, so the motorcycle division was unloaded to Jack Y. Sangster (already the Ariel boss) at the end of 1936 for an alleged £50,000. The car side continued under Claude Holbrook, who went on to preside over more financial woes until June 1939, when the Triumph car side went into receivership. Donald Healey sold it on behalf of the receivers to Sheffield steelmakers Thomas Ward and Co. Then came World War II, and the factory was taken over by the government to make, amongst other things, parts for the aviation industry. Bomb damage in 1940 (as at the motorcycle works) meant that Triumph cars was without a home. In 1944 Sir John Black of the Standard Motor Company purchased the shattered remains of the plant and the rights for the Triumph name (four wheels only) for £75,000: the Triumph Motor Co. (1945) Ltd was formed as a wholly owned subsidiary of Standard, and in 1946 launched the first of its post-war cars. The most famous of these were the TR series of sports cars, and the Mayflower and Herald saloons. In 1961 Standard-Triumph was taken over by the Leyland Group, later to become the state-owned British Leyland (BL). The last Triumph-badged car (essentially a Japanese Honda Acclaim) was built in 1984.

Jack Sangster was an astute business man. As recounted elsewhere (*see* Chapters 2 and 6), with the brilliant designs of Edward Turner he built the Triumph motorcycle company into one of the most successful and profitable in the industry. Interestingly, with Holbrook out of the way, Siegfried Bettmann returned to become a figurehead chairman of the motorcycle company following its purchase by Sangster. He finally retired in 1939, and died in 1951 at the age of eighty-eight.

2 Turner's Speed Twin

Edward Turner's Speed Twin was without doubt one of the truly classic motorcycle designs of the twentieth century. Turner moved to Triumph shortly after Jack Y. Sangster had acquired the Triumph motorcycle marque in early 1935, both having been together previously at the Ariel company. The original Triumph Speed Twin was launched at the end of July 1937, and certainly in my opinion it was, as the factory's former publicity man Ivor Davies said, 'The most epoch-making motorcycle of them all'. In most other cases the company tried to create a real impact in individual events, such as the Montlhéry demonstration for the Thunderbird, and the world speed record for the Bonneville; the Speed Twin excelled in more than one.

Edward Turner, who joined Triumph in 1936 following the Sangster takeover, was the design genius behind the Speed Twin – a model that set Triumph and himself on the road to fame and fortune.

An Entirely New Design

As with all great designs, the Speed Twin was essentially simple. Amazingly, the engine was actually lighter and narrower than the Tiger 90 single of the same era. Of course Triumph had produced a twin in the past – but not one in the vein of the Speed Twin. Edward Turner could have built a flat twin (such as a BMW or Douglas), or a V-twin (such as a JAP or Matchless), but he chose a vertical layout because it offered the prospect of the best power-to-ratio, due to the chance to design a compact unit. Other reasons, as Turner explained at the launch, included:

> ...even firing intervals, perfect cooling, and extreme rigidity, which is the essence of high power output; the engine will go into a smaller frame without loss of accessibility; the two cylinders do precisely the same amount of work, and the engine is amenable to all single-cylinder tuning techniques... This type of engine is superior to any other form of twin except on balance.

He also selected a 360-degree crankshaft. When questioned about this in 1939, the designer had this to say: 'Cranks at 360 degrees (in line) were chosen as the best all-round plot for the

The 1938 model year Triumph Speed Twin, Turner's original masterpiece, which placed the company at the very forefront of motorcycle design. It actually weighed less than the existing Tiger 90 single!

following reason – it offered the best carburation possibilities of any type, due to its even firing impulses and short induction pipes.' So why not 180 degrees (as used widely by the Japanese much later)? Turner's explanation was this:

> The answer is two-fold. First, the advantages of even firing intervals would be lost, and the carburation would be correspondingly less satisfactory. Secondly, although the primary balance would be better, a serious couple would be introduced, so that on the whole, the advantages would be outweighed by the disadvantages. And regarding balance, basically the balance of a 500cc twin with crankpins in line was slightly superior to that of a single, because, although the total weight of the parts to be balanced is the same, the stroke is less, and the counter-weighting necessary to produce the best results is slightly less than in the case of the single.

At first, Edward Turner had planned an overhead camshaft layout, but this was soon abandoned in favour of a twin-cam pushrod unit, pleasingly symmetrical, with a gear-driven camshaft fore and aft of the cylinder barrels – somewhat akin to the layout of the Riley car that Turner used at that time. Some commentators have said that the inspiration for the concept of Turner's vertical twin-cylinder engine came directly from the Riley unit. There is no denying that Edward Turner was impressed with the design of the Riley power unit, and that both had separate camshafts (inlet and exhaust) mounted on opposite sides of the cylinder block. In both cases, this had the bonus (for an ohv engine) of allowing the valves to be

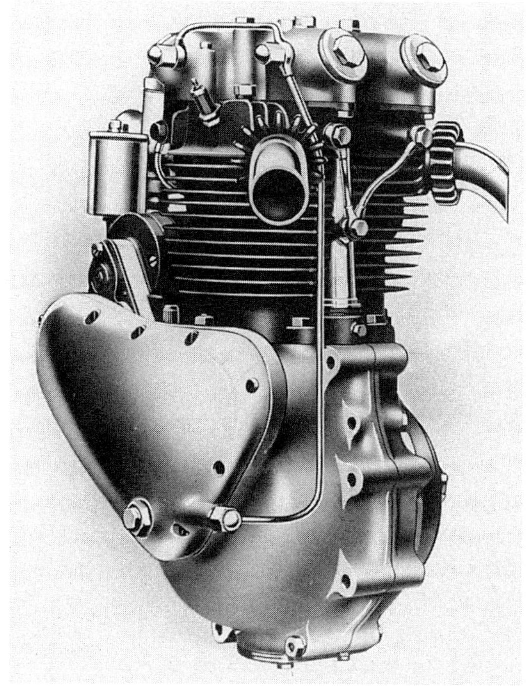

The original Speed Twin engine as it appeared in late 1937. Displacing 498.76, it shared its 63 × 80mm bore and stroke dimensions with Triumph's existing Tiger 70 two-fifty. It also set the fashion for vertical twins, which were to dominate the motorcycle world for the next three decades.

operated by relatively short pushrods, thus reducing the load on the valve gear.

As factory insider Ivor Davies revealed in his book *Triumph – The Complete Story* (Crowood, published in 1991): 'Just how true the "Riley theory" is, no one can tell now, and it is not really of any consequence – most designs are developments or modifications of something that has gone beforehand.' If the Riley provided some inspiration, the most important part of Edward Turner's design genius was his ability to utilize existing components to maximize production-cost savings. One illustration of this policy was the 498.76cc displacement of the new Special Twin that was achieved by having identical 63 × 80mm bore and stroke dimensions with Triumph's existing Tiger 70 two-fifty single. So production could be rationalized, with pistons, small ends, piston rings and circlips being common components.

Original Design Features

Even so, there were several features of the new Triumph engine that were original. One was the built-up crankshaft (the subject of a patent). A feature of this was the absence of a middle bearing. In an interview a few months after the launch of the Speed Twin, Edward Turner said 'There are good reasons… [for its absence], …since with comparatively close cylinder centres it would be difficult to provide an adequate bearing and to ensure correct alignment without adding very considerably to the cost of manufacture.' Also, a middle bearing might have involved an outside flywheel, and therefore extra width and conflicting torsion effects between the flywheel and the mass of the internal balance weights.

At the Speed Twin's launch, Edward Turner said, 'The central flywheel system has direct advantages, and the method of sandwiching it between two circular crank cheeks ensures rigidity.' The space contained between the crank cheeks and the inner periphery of the flywheel flange formed a convenient home for a centrifugal oil filter. Of a manganese molybdenum steel alloy, the crankshaft was exceptionally strong. Turner stated that '…the advantages of this steel are ample strength and rather lower cost than a suitable nickel-chrome steel.' But above everything, Turner emphasized the importance of 'the stiffness and rigidity of the crankshaft construction' to his design.

Speed Twin 1937

Engine:	Air-cooled ohv vertical twin, cast-iron head and barrel, 360-degree three-piece crankshaft, six-stud barrel; vertically split crankcases; separate engine and gearbox
Bore:	63mm
Stroke:	80mm
Displacement:	498.76cc
Compression ratio:	7.2:1
Lubrication:	Double-plunger pump, dry sump
Ignition:	Magneto
Carburettor:	Amal type 76 15/16in
Primary drive:	Chain
Final drive:	Chain
Gearbox:	Four-speed, foot change
Frame:	All-steel tubular construction, single front down-tube; duplex lower rails
Front suspension:	Girders with central spring
Rear suspension:	Rigid
Front brake:	7in drum, SLS
Rear brake:	7in drum, SLS
Tyres:	Front 3.00 × 20; rear 3.50 × 19

General Specifications

Wheelbase:	54in (1,370mm)
Ground clearance:	5in (138mm)
Seat height:	27.75in (705mm)
Fuel-tank capacity:	3.5gal (15.9ltr)
Dry weight:	353lb (160kg)
Maximum power:	26bhp @ 6,000rpm
Top speed:	90mph (145kmph)*

*Early road-test machine reached a mean (two-way) 94mph (151kmph).

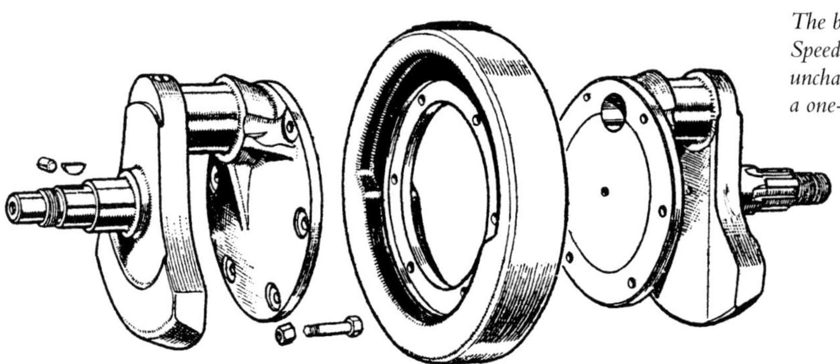

The built-up crank (three-piece) from the Speed Twin. This was to remain largely unchanged until it was finally replaced by a one-piece type at the end of the 1950s.

Interestingly it was this rigidity that he cited as the reason for the use of light alloy for the connecting rods, for although it would have been possible to produce steel con-rods of no greater weight, the additional mass of metal provided with the light alloy helped stiffen the beam to a marked degree. There was another valuable feature in that light alloy conducts heat away from bearings at a higher rate than would have been possible with steel components. The material employed was RR56 – forged and having a tensile strength of 32 tons per square inch.

A bronze bush was used for the gudgeon pin because, said Turner, 'The comparatively high coefficient of expansion of the alloy might cause excessive clearance and hammering of the bearing when hot if the cold clearance in the unbushed small end were great enough for freedom.'

Another patented construction was that of the big end. This was unusual in several respects. The con-rod of each cylinder bore directly onto the crankpin, but the steel bearing cap featured a thin lining of white metal. This design took advantage of the high heat conductivity of the light alloy, whilst the white-metalled cap acted as a safety valve because, in the event of oil failure, the metal would flow, preventing a seizure.

The big-end bolts were forged in one piece integral with the split-bearing cap (the bottom section of the connecting rod), the nuts being above the centre line of the big end instead of below. This arrangement not only saved weight, but more importantly, it enabled the diameter of the crankcase to be reduced and thus increased rigidity. A nickel-chrome steel of 100 tons tensile strength was employed for the combined cap/bolts.

A full-skirt piston design was employed. This was of conventional layout except for the internal webs incorporated to provide increased rigidity of the gudgeon pin bosses, and to conduct heat away from the centre of the piston crown (it is worth pointing out that the higher performance Tiger 100 version, introduced a few months later, not only sported a higher compression ratio – 8:1 instead of the Speed Twin's 7.2:1 – but also slipper rather than full skirt).

An iron head and cylinder barrel (both one-piece castings) were specified, the latter with a six-stud base flange that was subsequently ditched in favour of an eight-stud design in 1939, after suffering a spate of cracking.

Ball-race main bearings supported the crankshaft, the gear-driven camshafts being housed in bronze bushed tunnels front and rear of the crankcase mouth, with large radius followings in cast-iron guides, whilst chrome-plated steel tubes enclosed dural pushrods that operated forged rockers in bolt-on 'Y'-type aluminium rocker boxes. Behind the cylinder barrel sat a magdyno gear driven from the inlet cam, whilst a peg on the end of the shaft drove a double-plunger oil pump. One side of the double-plunger delivered oil to the crankshaft via a small bronze bush that existed only for the purpose of guiding lubricant into the crankshaft. Oil was delivered through the shaft to the big ends at a pressure that designer Edward Turner considered 'ample' for the needs of the big ends and pistons.

A relief valve at the end of the crankshaft permitted the remainder of the oil delivery to fill the timing gear cover to a predetermined level, after which it overflowed to the crankcase and was returned to the oil tank (a dry-sump lubrication system was employed) by the scavenger pump.

The difference between oil pressure and volume was stressed as 'important' by Edward Turner. The oil was filtered on both sides of the return pump – on the suction side via a gauze strainer, whilst on the delivery side it was through a felt filter.

The First Production Models

The original prototype engine produced a full 30bhp. The initial production examples of the new Speed Twin that arrived in late 1937 generated three or four horses less. However this, combined with its light weight (353lb/160kg; dry) was still good enough to give a top speed, with full road equipment and silencers, of 90mph (145kmph). In a road test dated 21 October 1937 *The Motor Cycle* recorded a speed of 93.75mph (150.84kmph). This was a mean (two-way) average; the best timed run 'with the wind behind' gave a speed over the quarter mile of 107mph (172kmph), which *The Motor Cycle* tester truthfully said was 'truly an amazing figure for a fully equipped five-hundred'. But one has to speculate whether this outstanding (by the standards of the era) result was not achieved by a specially prepared machine, rather than by a standard 'off-the-showroom-floor' model.

Officially coded the Model 5T, the Speed Twin's low weight was assisted by its use of existing cycle parts from the five-hundred Tiger 90 single. This meant that although the twin-cylinder engine was slightly lighter than the single (as already explained), the additional silencer and exhaust pipe (both had a single carb) meant that the weight was the same. As the Speed Twin engine was no wider – in fact it was slightly narrower – the chain line was identical, and the engine was therefore not offset in the frame.

In the general specifications for the 1938 model Speed Twin were 3.00 × 20 front and 3.50 × 19 rear tyres; girder front forks, rigid frame; 7in brakes and a 15/16in Amal Type 76 carburettor.

Priced at £77 15s with full electrical equipment and a Smith's 120mph speedometer, the new Speed Twin was finished entirely in Amaranth (dark) Red, except for exposed metal parts and chromium-plated components such as the

Vintage-racer Mick Broom with his 1939 Speed Twin, VMCC, Cadwell Park, summer 1971.

Wicksteed and Winslow

Ivan Wicksteed and Marius Winslow had been schoolboy chums, and this friendship led them to form a partnership as rider and tuner respectively during the early 1930s. This proved highly successful, and at the 1937 London Olympia show the pair approached Edward Turner on the Triumph stand for his opinion of their idea to tune and supercharge the newly released Speed Twin. Turner's reply was short and to the point: 'A very logical conclusion. Good afternoon, gentlemen.'

Turner had designed the Speed Twin to be a roadster like his Ariel Square, not a racer. However, as with the Ariel, there were those who thought otherwise, and Wicksteed and Winslow were amongst them. So, undismayed by Turner's comment, the pair went out and purchased a Speed Twin from a local dealer and got down to converting it into a Speed *Machine*. Its first outing came at Brooklands in March 1938, where it lapped at over 107mph (172kmph) in normally aspirated form with a supercharger. Next, the pair fitted a blower – and as Turner had predicted, their problems began.

Most of the trouble centred around the mixture strength and induction bias, as this had to be trial and error since there was no one else available to offer advice or guidance. It was at this point that the original design weakness of the Speed Twin became all too apparent, when the six-stud cylinder barrel broke off at its bottom flange. The solution was offered by none other than Titch Allen (years later to be the founder of the Vintage Motor Cycle Club). Titch suggested fitting a nut and bolt between the head and the tank rail, and screwing these apart until the tube bent: something of a 'Heath Robinson' solution, and one that caused considerable mirth at the time – but it worked, and has since become an accepted way of curing the problem on engines built prior to the arrival of the improved eight-stud engine.

Following the Allen 'modification', the Wicksteed-Winslow Speed Twin was raced again at Brooklands, this time lapping in excess of 111mph (179kmph). However, there were still mixture problems, the result being a seizure on one cylinder. After this outing a new induction system was produced, and further testing increased the lap speed to an impressive 121.47mph (195.45kmph).

By now, the bike's performance was such that specialized, high-speed tyres were needed. The Dunlop company supplied those, but when fitted they destroyed the handling; in fact it was so poor that the tuned Speed Twin could now only be used on the banked, outer Brooklands circuit. So standard wheels and road-racing tyres were refitted, and on 8 October 1938, Ivan Wicksteed attempted to break the 500cc lap record during the British Motor Cycle Racing Club (BMCRC) Hutchinson 100 meeting. The British weather intervened and it began raining, so Wicksteed pushed his bike to the line between races to make his attempt. After a single warm-up lap and then a flying lap to actually take the record, Ivan Wicksteed set a new lap record of 118.02mph (189.89kmph). War broke out the following year, and the Brooklands circuit was never re-opened after the conflict, so this speed stands for all time.

Even though he had been against their idea, Edward Turner could see the value of Wicksteed's performance, so the factory advertised the Brooklands' success and went so far as to provide the pair with a new Tiger 100 engine, complete with a one-off crankshaft for the blower drive sprocket. This, too, ran into the same mixture bias problems, but still managed to cover the half mile on Brooklands Railway straight at 124mph (200kmph) in 1939. Then came the war.

Turner's Views

It has been a well-recorded fact that Edward Turner was not road racing's biggest supporter over the years. Much of this was because of his dislike of what he called 'works specials' (of the type built by, say, Norton during the mid- and late 1930s). A couple of extracts from Nitor's *On the Four Winds* column in the 23 March 1939 issue of *The Motor Cycle* illustrates exactly how Turner felt on the subject:

> That the TT has done more than anything else to assist and inspire design was a point Mr Edward Turner, managing director of Triumph, made at a lunch for riders and others concerned in the recent certified test (the Maudes Trophy attempt carried out by the factory earlier that month). He mentioned that, as producers of fast sporting motorcycles, Triumph were often asked why they did not show more interest in the TT. The reason was that the races no longer formed an attractive proposition for manufacturers. In recent years they had forced the production of a type of machine no longer practical for ordinary use. In, say, 1926 and 1927 the position was different, for at least 60 per cent of any given machine was on standard lines. Today the machines were special from wheel to wheel, and there was nothing that could be translated into production machines. 'I do not say the TT should be banished,' Mr Turner continued, 'I consider that there should be races for the stock-type machines. For our part we should be prepared to support such races, and I believe that others would do so, too.' From this Mr Turner passed on to other types of events: 'Trials and scrambles,' he said, 'do not demonstrate the ultimate reliability of the product; the one thing that does is the ACU certified test.'

Of course, post-war Triumph did seem to support (though often at arm's length) events such as the Clubman TT and production-type racing events for series-production machines, thus reflecting Turner's beliefs, which, as can be seen from this 1939 piece, he had held for a long time.

wheel rims, the exhaust and the majority of the petrol tank.

The Road Test

The Motor Cycle road test of October 1937 has been referred to in terms of the Speed Twin's performance, but this only tells a small part of the story. The importance of the original Speed Twin in the evolution of the Triumph twin-cylinder range makes it necessary to bring the reader a flavour of just what a big impact this revolutionary design made when it was introduced. The following extracts give an excellent outline of the tester's opinions:

> So versatile did the engine prove that the machine was equally at home in the thickest traffic or on the fastest main road. Much of the joy in driving the model comes, however, from the delightful way the machine will zoom from 30mph to 60, 70 or 80mph at the will of the rider without his having to touch any control other than the twistgrip. Some idea of the model's performance when the gears are used can be obtained from the fact that 74mph [119kmph] was reached in a quarter of a mile from a standing start. On the open road the machine was utterly delightful. Ample power for all conditions was always available at a turn of the twistgrip, and the lack of noise when the machine was cruising in the seventies was almost uncanny. The acceleration available would rapidly bring the machine back to a high cruising speed. Thus it was found that large mileages were tucked into the hour without the rider consciously hurrying, and long runs were accomplished with less mental effort than usual.

For the tests 'the steering damper was tightened down'. Generally the steering and handling on the road were judged to be 'excellent'. The only criticism was that the rear wheel had a tendency to 'hop on uneven surfaces', and 'with the bike's low centre of gravity, it felt more like a two-fifty than a five-hundred from the point of view of ease of handling'.

Considering that later, larger displacement Triumph twins were noted for vibration, the following comments regarding Turner's original twin were significant: 'A high degree of balance has been achieved' and 'apart from a slight period around 60mph [96kmph] in top gear, the engine is perfectly smooth and sweet. It may even be said that the period is only noticeable because of the exceptional smoothness of the engine at all other speeds, and at no time was vibration sufficient to cause any discomfort.'

A tell-tale feature of the pre-war Speed Twin (and Tiger 100) engines was the triangular-shaped casting on the crankcase for the Lucas magdyno assembly. Post-war this was deleted.

Another bone of contention with some British bikes was the none-too-small matter of oil tightness. Again, the original Speed Twin appears good in this respect, the October 1937 tester saying:

> At the conclusion of the test, which included hundreds of miles of really hard driving, the Triumph was as clean and smart as at the beginning, and apart from a very slight seep of oil from the rear end of the primary chain case, not a spot of oil had leaked from any of the joints of the power unit.

Evolution of the Species

Elsewhere in this book I have included an evolution box showing the major changes, updates and modifications throughout the life of the 500 (and 650) Triumph twins. But even this is not the full evolution chart for the Triumph vertical twin-cylinder family: later still, from the beginning of the 1970s, came the larger displacement 750. As for the original 500 series, this (albeit in updated unit-construction guise) ran right through until the final model, the TR5T Adventurer, was discontinued in 1973. This means that the five-hundred ran for a total of thirty-seven years and was built in an amazing variety of guises: touring, sports roadster, road racer, scrambler and trials. Its use was even greater, with virtually every form of motorcycle speed being undertaken by a 500 Triumph twin at some time or other.

As for the Speed Twin itself, it was destined to influence the evolution of both touring and sporting motorcycles more than any other design, before or since. In fact, the vertical twin concept held sway until 1969 when Honda brought out its first four-cylinder series-production motorcycle, the legendary CB750, ushering in the era of the Superbike. But Turner's compact twin-cylinder formula was still to be seen for many years thereafter, with the Japanese themselves building similar bikes.

Although much of Triumph's racing success was obviously achieved by more highly tuned and powerful engines, without the Speed Twin it is unlikely that any of this would have happened. The motorcycle is, therefore, a pivotal part of this story.

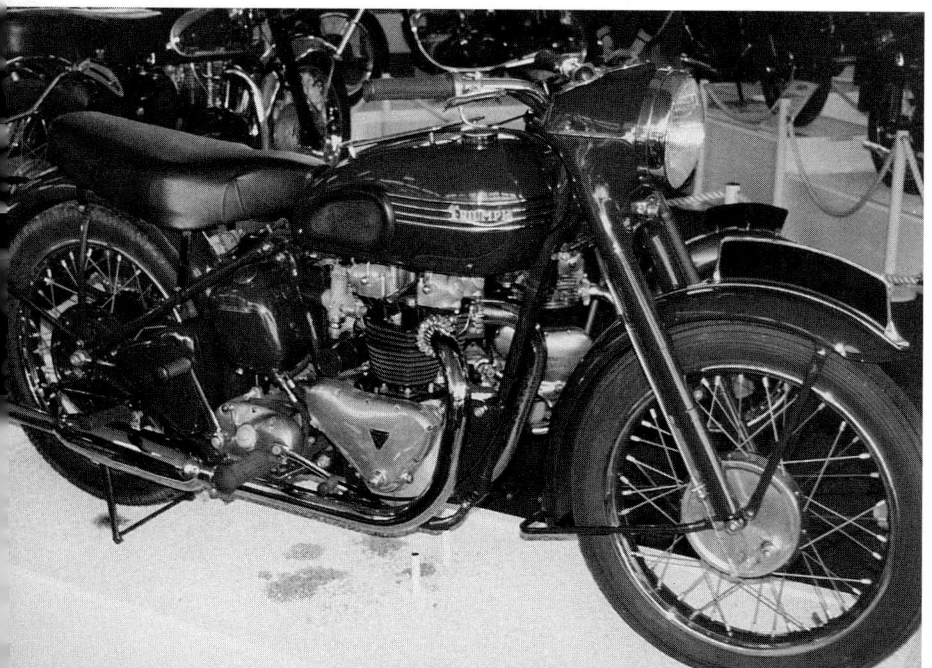

ABOVE: A 1946 5T Speed Twin engine, with front-mounted dynamo.

Post-war Speed Twins had telescopic forks rather than the pre-war girders. Also the patented Triumph (Turner designed) sprung hub was a cost option for many years, before swinging-arm rear suspension arrived in the mid-1950s. This machine dates from the 1953/4 period.

3 Grand Prix

Edward Turner was not a fan of motor racing (as discussed elsewhere), but just after the end of World War II, Irishman Ernie Lyons persuaded the Triumph boss to authorize a 'quick engine' for the latter to use in the 1946 Senior Manx Grand Prix. Lyons had been successful in his native Ireland on grass tracks and short circuits, but talking 'Triumph supreme' Turner into a racing programme was much more difficult. However, Lyons succeeded.

The man chosen to oversee the project was F.W.S. (Freddie) Clark, a tuner of considerable ability who had joined Triumph in 1937. He had ridden pre-war at Brooklands, and held the all-time lap records for the 350 and 750cc classes at the famous Surrey venue. Clark had achieved these feats in 1939 on a dope-burning Tiger 80 single and an over-bored (503cc) Tiger 100 twin, reaching speeds of 105.97mph (170.53kmph) and 118.02mph (189.92kmph) respectively.

From Racer to Production Motorcycle

Held in dismally overcast conditions with heavy rain and thick mist around various sections of its 37.73-mile (60.7km) circuit, the 1946 Senior Manx Grand Prix was nonetheless watched by a vast gathering of spectators – many observers believe it to have been the largest crowd in TT or Manx GP history up to that time. The appalling weather did not seem to affect Ernie Lyons, and he repaid the faith shown by Edward Turner by winning convincingly by 2min 13sec from the experienced Norton rider Ken Bills. Lyons' average speed of 76.74mph (123.47kmph) might appear somewhat low until one realizes that even staying on the road was difficult in the awful conditions. In addition – and hidden from the prying eyes of the press at that time – was the fact that the front-frame down-tube of Lyons' bike had actually broken! So his performance was even more outstanding.

Lyons' machine was probably illegal, as works entries were not strictly allowed in the 'amateur' Manx races. This one had been specially constructed by Freddie Clark in the Triumph development shop, and it had already been race-tested in no less an event than the Ulster Grand Prix a few weeks before its Manx victory, in August

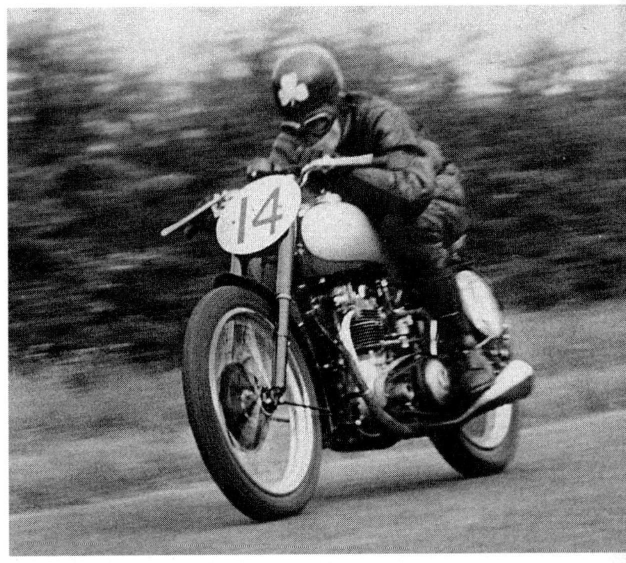

Ernie Lyons with the prototype Grand Prix making their debut during the Ulster GP in August 1946. The following month Lyons and the Triumph won the Senior Grand Prix in the Isle of Man.

A previously unpublished photograph of Lyons' machine in the Ulster paddock, showing details of the first prototype of what was to emerge as the Grand Prix over-the-counter 'customer' racer.

Origins

The origins of the Grand Prix racer can be traced to an Air Ministry requirement for an easily transportable generator set. It was this design that was to lead to the motorcycle upon which Ernie Lyons secured a surprise victory in the first post-war Isle of Man race, the 1946 Senior Manx Grand Prix, and the subsequent Grand Prix racer. Triumph's design chief Edward Turner undertook the task of producing an engine suitable for the Air Ministry's requirements. The complete generator less the dynamo was created in a mere three months, and even with a full testing programme, production began within six months of the contract being issued.

It would be easy to dismiss the power unit as simply a modified Speed Twin, but in fact it was far more than this. True, the engine was still a parallel twin and broadly similar in its external appearance, but few component parts from the motorcycle engine would fit the generator kit. To start with, the cylinder head was reversed. In addition, unlike the then current Speed Twin (or, for that matter, the Tiger 100) the cylinder head and barrel assemblies were largely of silicon alloy rather than cast iron. A high-expansion iron casting formed the valve seatings and the spark-plug bosses around which the alloy cylinder head was cast. Similarly the aluminium cylinder block had iron liners.

A flange-fitting BTH magneto was driven off the exhaust (not inlet, as on the Speed Twin/Tiger 100 engine) camshaft pinion. The inlet camshaft pinion drove a governor, mounted relative to the timing chest, in the former location of the dynamo on the production motorcycle power unit. Carried in a white metal-lined steel bush, the timing side mainshaft was directly connected to it by means of a steel driving centre for the magnesium alloy fan employed for cooling the engine and the dynamo. This driving centre had on its outer face the dog for the cranking handle needed for starting purposes.

On the other side of the engine, on the drive-side mainshaft, was fitted a flexible disc coupling, to which was connected the dynamo armature spindle. Alongside this coupling was a ratchet mechanism so that a cover plate could be removed from the drive-side crankcase casting and a kick-starter crank and segment unit fitted, thus providing an alternative means of starting.

Surrounding and supporting the dynamo was a light alloy casting that above, carried the combined fuel and oil tank, and below, formed legs to which were bolted rectangular-section feet. At the other end of the unit the feet attached to triangular brackets on the fan body. The tank embodied compartments for 3gal (14ltr) of fuel at the top, and 5pt (2.84ltr) of oil in the base.

(continued oveleaf)

Origins *(continued)*

Triumph was not responsible for the manufacture of the dynamo. However, it is worth noting that it had an output of 200 amps at 30 volts. The high armature speed of 4,000rpm (the governed speed of the engine) meant that adequate cooling was essential. Turner and his design team thus had cooling of both the engine and the dynamo as a major consideration. They achieved this by employing a fan with a displacement of 400 cubic feet per minute, rather more than half of the cooling draught being directed over the cylinder block and head by means of the fan blades and cover assembly, thus ensuring that at no time was the cylinder head temperature higher than 120°C. For the dynamo, a duct led air from the fan to its component parts, including the armature and its windings. To aid the cooling of the lower half of the engine, the oil pump was of a very high capacity – almost double that of the Speed Twin engine!

A second, vitally important requirement of this generator set was that the governor should do its job really well; the specification demanded no greater variation in engine revolutions than plus or minus 5 per cent on switch-over from full power to open circuit or vice versa. It should also be remembered that compared to most stationary engines, the Triumph unit featured an extremely light flywheel, and the figure of only 2.5 per cent variation that normally occurred was a high tribute to Triumph's ingenious governor device. As previously mentioned, this governor was driven by the inlet camshaft pinion, the spindle carrying a conical ball flinger device that was operated by centrifugal force.

The Triumph generator set was an extremely capable device, being able at the time of its introduction to start one of the world's most powerful aero engines: the massive Bristol Centaurus radial unit. As a journalist of the day wrote: 'The Triumph generator unit is doing sterling work in all parts of the world where the RAF flies.'

That it was also to spawn a racing motorcycle is even more amazing, and probably unique in the annals of motorcycle history.

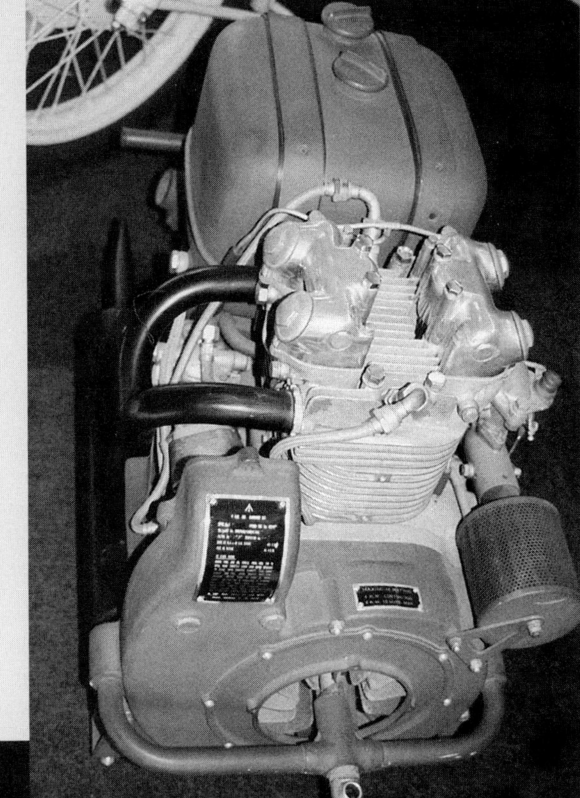

ABOVE: The wartime Triumph generator set, powered by an all-alloy, five-hundred twin-cylinder engine that was later to form the basis of the post-war Grand Prix racer.

LEFT: The cylinder head and barrel – note the squared-off pinning and straight ports – are both features of the Grand Prix power unit.

The production Grand Prix engine from the official Triumph launch in January 1948. Note the BTH TT racing magneto, twin parallel carburettors and all-alloy components – head, barrel crankcases and timing cover.

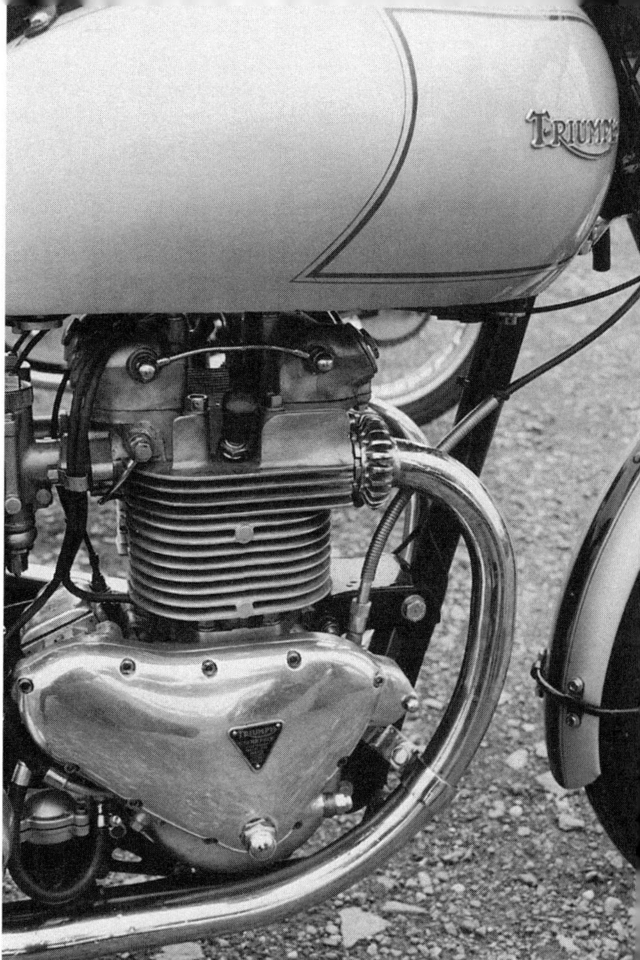

The Grand Prix engine with the exhaust camshaft-driven rev-counter cable clearly showing in this view. Producing 40bhp to 7,200rpm, it could propel the machine to speeds approaching 120mph (193kmph). However, reliability was only marginal, particularly if the maximum recommended rpm was exceeded.

1946. Besides its special tuning, the Manx GP-winning machine, although based on the series production Tiger 100 model, employed the light-alloy cylinder barrel and head from a wartime generator unit, and also an experimental Edward Turner-designed sprung rear hub.

Lyons' success was also instrumental in Triumph building a production version, sold as the Grand Prix – although this did not happen for almost eighteen months: it was January 1948 when Triumph announced that a replica of Lyons' victorious machine was to be offered to the general public. Some might ask why it took so long for the factory to make a move, but it is important to realize that the immediate post-war era was one of intense production pressures, when it seemed that however many motorcycles were built, there were nowhere near enough to meet demand. This demand came from the transport-starved masses both at home and abroad. In fact, in line with other British motorcycle manufacturers in the late 1940s, most of Triumph's production went for export, and potential British customers had to make do with either pre-war models or ex-War Department machines.

Triumph also took the opportunity to test their racer in the shape of the works development bike, campaigned successfully by M.D. (David) Whitworth during the course of the 1947 season. Notable performances included the Belgian Grand Prix: in this race Whitworth was leading on the second lap, but crashed; however, he remounted and finally finished

David Whitworth was one of the Grand Prix model's most successful riders. Here he is receiving the winner's trophies for both the 350cc (Velocette KTT) and the 500cc (Triumph) races at the Grand Prix de Bruxelles, 22 June 1947.

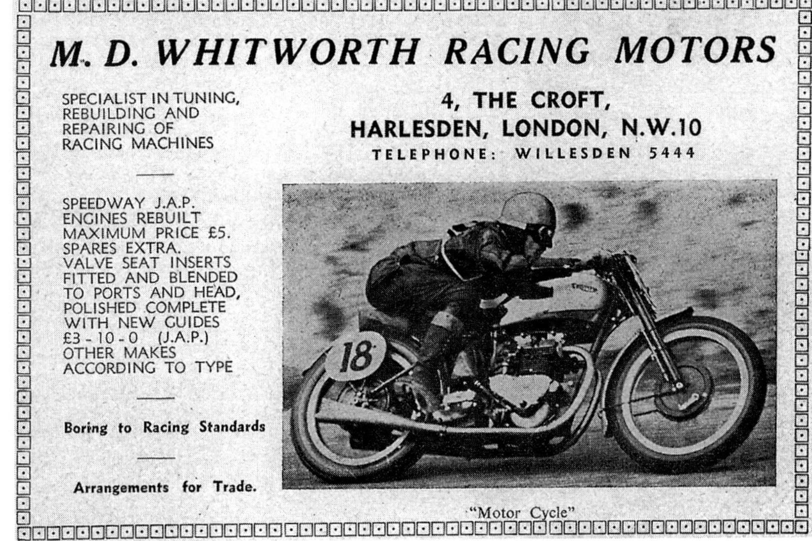

An advertisement for M.D. (David) Whitworth Racing Motors of Harlesden, North London, ca. 1950.

fourth. Then in the Dutch TT he came a magnificent third. Added to the successes in the classics, Whitworth also won the Circuit de la Cambre in Belgium.

Technical Specification

Another reason for the delay was that Freddie Clark had left Triumph to join the London-based AMC group in January 1947, and although the Grand Prix engine was based on the standard production 498cc (63 × 80mm) Tiger 100 and shared the same bore and stroke dimensions, it had a completely isolated set of components. Each Grand Prix motorcycle was hand built and specially tuned and tested. Triumph claimed 40bhp at 7,200rpm on the low-grade 'pool' petrol of the day, with maximum speed around 120mph (193kmph); with empty tanks it weighed 310lb (140kg).

As previously mentioned, both the cylinder and head were in aluminium, each cylinder bore being equipped with a cast-iron liner. Unlike the later twin-carburettor production Triumphs, the Grand Prix had parallel-mounted, rather than splayed 1in (25mm) Amal Type 76 instruments. Although the 'ex-factory' compression ratio for the low-octane fuel of the time was only 8.3:1, higher domed pistons (of either 8.8:1 or 12.5:1) suitable for use with petrol benzole or methanol respectively, were available upon request. More robust connecting rods, of a special forging in RR56 aluminium, were able to function without the conventional white-metal shells – thus the big ends functioned without liners. The lower halves of the big ends were also made of RR56.

Built up, and with the usual Triumph bolted-on central flywheel, the crankshaft looked standard. The crank members, however, were manufactured of case-hardened, nickel-chrome steel of somewhat different section from that used in the standard Tiger 100. This was specially hardened on the big-end journals and at the main bearings, which comprised double-lipped rollers – distinct from the ball bearings used on the series-production models – and were chosen because of their greater load-carrying capacity.

The crankcase was almost standard, but had undergone slight variations in machining to make it suitable for the Grand Prix. However, it should be stressed that the GP engine could never be described as bullet-proof; in fact as one journalist remarked, it was 'grenade-like', certainly if over-revved.

A BTH racing magneto was specified, together with manual ignition control. Special camshafts provided a higher valve lift of longer duration; these had been developed in conjunction with a tuned exhaust system featuring a separate exhaust pipe and megaphone assembly on each side of the motorcycle.

Considerable efforts had been made to keep down the weight of reciprocating parts, yet at the same time ensure their greatest possible strength. To this end, duralumin pushrods were employed, together with specially lightened and hardened tappets, with hard chrome faces. The tappet-guide block was manufactured from RR56 alloy.

ABOVE: Close-up of a genuine BTH racing magneto, as fitted to the Grand Prix Triumph.

LEFT: A view showing the parallel exhaust pipes of the Grand Prix, and also the standard issue Triumph valve-inspection covers.

Lubrication was of the dry-sump type, by means of large-bore plunger pumps, and was therefore quite orthodox; but the oil tank held over a gallon and featured a special venting tower to take care of frothing at high engine revolutions. A Yokes oil filter was adopted and fitted in the return side of the system.

Nickel-chrome high-tensile gears were used in the gearbox, the ratios of which, with a twenty-three-tooth engine sprocket, were 4.78, 5.24, 6.88 and 8.26:1. Alternative engine sprockets were available, providing a higher or lower set of close ratios.

As it was intended purely for competition use, no kick-starter was fitted. The clutch was a special GP-only component, having additional spring pressure to accommodate the high engine torque. There were nine plates: five plain and four lined, the latter with special Ferodo inserts.

The large Smiths rev counter was driven off the pinion that on a standard Triumph twin would have driven the dynamo and the drive passed through holes in the front engine plates.

The steel tube frame was of a brazed-up full-cradle design with forged lugs. The front forks followed conventional Triumph practice, and were oil-damped teledraulics, except that the springs were more suitable for high-speed racing use. Both wheels had Dunlop 'welled' alloy rims. Both brakes were of 8in (203mm) diameter, the front a single-sided conventional drum, whilst the rear was incorporated with Turner's patented sprung hub.

Tyre sizes 'as sold' were 3.00 × 20 ribbed front and 3.50 × 19 studded rear. Light alloy mudguards were fitted, and a steering damper, saddle and mudguard pad were all original fitments. The wheels were balanced, and the exhaust header pipe nuts were locked to small holes drilled in the cylinder block. The fuel tank was manufactured from the series production tooling, but with the knee-grip recess deleted, thus increasing its capacity by a small amount.

Finished in an attractive silver sheen with dark blue lining, black frame and forks, and bright, chrome-plated exhaust system, the 1948 British market catalogue price for the Grand Prix was £342 18s, including £71 18s purchase tax.

The Grand Prix 1948 Model

Engine:	Air-cooled ohv vertical twin, alloy head and barrel, 360-degree three-piece crankshaft, six-stud barrel; vertically split crankcases; separate engine and gearbox
Bore:	63mm
Stroke:	80mm
Displacement:	498.76cc
Compression ratio:	8.3:1 (8.8 or 12.5:1 optional)
Lubrication:	Double-plunger pump, dry sump
Ignition:	Magneto
Carburettor:	Two × Amal Type 76 1in
Primary drive:	Chain
Final drive:	Chain
Gearbox:	Four-speed
Frame:	All-steel tubular construction, single front down-tube; duplex lower rails
Front suspension:	Telescopic, oil damped
Rear suspension:	Patented Triumph sprung hub
Front brake:	8in drum, SLS
Rear brake:	8in drum, SLS
Tyres:	Front 3.00 × 20; rear 3.50 × 19

General Specifications

Wheelbase:	55in (1,398mm)
Ground clearance:	6in (152mm)
Seat height:	29.75in (750mm)
Fuel-tank capacity:	4.25gal (19ltr)
Dry weight:	314lb (142kg)
Maximum power:	40bhp @ 7,200rpm
Top speed:	120mph (193kmph)

Post-War Successes

No doubt remembering the performances of Lyons and Whitworth, nine Grand Prix models were entered for the 1948 Senior TT in the Isle of Man. Seven bikes actually started the race, ridden by such notable riders as Bob Foster, Freddie Frith, Albert Moule and racer/journalist Vic Willoughby – though the latter only made it to Quarter Bridge on the first lap, less than a mile! But one by one they all retired, except Norman Croft who finished twelfth, averaging 76.05mph (122.36kmph). Things were better in September's Manx Grand Prix, when five Triumph GPs came home in the first twelve, including the winner Don Crossley, with an average of 80.62mph (129.72kmph). The other Triumph results were Reg Armstrong 4th, Arthur Wheeler 5th, C. A. Stevens 7th, and T. P. Crebbin 11th.

One Friday evening at the end of September 1948, the company held a special dinner in Kenilworth, Warwickshire, in honour of its Manx Grand Prix success, and for the three Triumph riders who represented Great Britain in that year's International Six Days' Trial: Allan Jefferies, Phil Alves and A.F. Gayner; Triumph boss Edward Turner stated that 'the aim in marketing the Grand Prix model was to provide enthusiastic riders with a machine capable of winning events in which those riders were likely to compete.' He went on to reveal 'the satisfaction felt over Manx GP successes', also saying:

> Since it was decided to introduce the racing model about two years ago, I have often wondered whether the policy of providing such a model has been right. However, in spite of the many worries encountered, numerous successes have come to the GP model, and I am certain that those successes were welcomed and appreciated by the riders of standard Triumph machines all over the world.

Norman Croft with his Triumph Grand Prix, which he rode in the 1949 Swiss GP at Berne.

BELOW: In the early post-war years the British short circuit scene was frequented by a mixture of purpose-built racers (from Norton, AJS and Triumph), plus a collection of one-off specials, or as here, converted roadsters such as this Ariel Red Hunter single, followed by a Triumph Grand Prix.

As a memento of his Manx GP victory, Don Crossley was presented with a silver cigarette case (this, of course, being in an era when smoking was fashionable). Besides Edward Turner, other speakers at the dinner included Allan Jefferies, H.G. Tyrell Smith and R.G. Shimwell, the South African Triumph importer, who dwelt on the great value of competition successes to the sales of British machines overseas.

Other 1948 successes gained by the Triumph production racer were Freddie Frith's at Shelsley Walsh hill climb, and David Whitworth's continued excellent showing in Continental European events, including several victories in Belgium. In addition, Whitworth ended the season with a notable victory at Ansty airfield near Coventry, finishing in front of AJS riders Reg Armstrong and Bill Doran, also Maurice Cann (Moto Guzzi) and Harold Daniell (Norton). The then unknown J.P. Hodgkin won the prestigious Folbigg Trophy at Cadwell Park in October, beating George Brown (Vincent) and Les Graham (Matchless). Sid Barnett was fourth on another Grand Prix. *Motor Cycling*'s chief tester Charles Markham rode Crossley's Manx GP-wining Grand Prix model at Ansty, and was impressed by 'the machine's speed, handling over the bumpy surface and the powerful brakes'.

The Racing Bike is Axed

Up to the appearance of the Featherbed Norton in 1950 (works) and 1951 (private), the Triumph Grand Prix remained a competitive, if often unreliable bike. It was certainly fast, with excellent acceleration, but even compared to the plunger-framed 'Garden Gate' Manx Norton, its handling was not really good enough – and the arrival of the Featherbed Manx simply made things worse. Although Triumph said that maximum power was produced at just over 7,000rpm, the GP engine would go up to 8,000, which considering its long-stroke dimensions was simply tempting fate. At the higher figure virtually anything could go 'pop', and the results were often spectacular – and expensive – including split crankcases, broken connecting rods and dropped valves.

The performance in a straight line was very good, however, and so, with pukka Manx Nortons hard to find and expensive, the Triumph

ABOVE RIGHT: J. W. Raubi with his Grand Prix model taking part in the New Zealand Hamilton 100, ca. 1952. The majority of Grand Prix models went for export, many to British Commonwealth countries.

A Grand Prix at Brough Airfield, East Yorkshire, in the summer of 1954; although no longer new, this example is in standard mint condition. However, by then it was no match for the latest breed of Featherbed dohc Manx Norton singles.

ABOVE: *VMCC (Vintage Motor Cycle Club) action at Cadwell Park in 1969. The VMCC pre-dated the classic scene and was for many years the sole source of 'old timer' racing, where machines from yesterday could be raced and viewed.*

LEFT: *This photograph dates from the early 1980s and was again taken at a VMCC meeting, this time at Donington Park; it shows a nicely restored (but eminently usable) Grand Prix.*

remained competitive at all but international level until the early 1950s. No exact production figures remain in existence for the Grand Prix model, but it is believed that at this time it was between a minimum of 150 and a maximum of 200 examples being manufactured; certainly it remained in the company's catalogue into 1950. By the end of that year, however, it had been axed in favour of a factory-supplied race kit for the production T100; this, Triumph felt, had the advantage of absolving them from any mechanical problems encountered, no matter how the owner abused or looked after his racing mount. The official factory line, in any case, stated that: 'The 1951 Tiger 100, modified with the aid of the kit (costing some £35), could be made into a more potent machine than the pukka racing Grand Prix.'

Regarding that final statement we can only speculate as to whether this was really true, or simply a lame excuse for not wishing to develop its racing model any further.

4 Tiger 100

The 1939 model year Tiger 100, with detachable end-cone silencers, girder forks and rear-mounted magdyno.

BELOW: The original six-stud, pre-war Tiger 100 engine with the option (at the extra cost of £5) of an aluminium-bronze cylinder head.

Even though the Speed Twin (*see* Chapter 2) was the design that really got the Triumph twin-cylinder series started, it was its more highly tuned brother, the Tiger 100, that put the factory on the road to racing success. Advertised as 'the £80 sportster' (£82 15s with speedometer), the Tiger 100 was launched a year after the Speed Twin, in the autumn of 1938. Technically the main changes compared to its older brother were polished ports and internals, and forged slipper pistons boosting the compression ratio to 8:1. For an additional £5, there was the option of an aluminium-bronze cylinder head.

In all but one area Edward Turner had things right first time with the Speed Twin: its one weakness was a tendency for the six-stud crankcase barrel joint to lift and/or break – and this showed up only when using maximum performance for long periods or when attempting to tune the engine for racing. It was, as one commentator said, 'A classic case of designing light and only strengthening up the parts that need it.'

By the time the first Tiger 100 rolled off the Coventry factory's production line, this weakness had been attended to, the result being a much more robust assembly held down by eight instead of the original six studs. The newcomer was finished, like the Tiger singles of the day (*see* Chapter 6), with a chromed fuel tank (of larger capacity than the Speed Twin), with silver sheen panels lined in black. The rear

Tiger 100 1938

Engine:	Air-cooled, ohv vertical twin, cast-iron head and barrel, 360-degree three-piece crankshaft; separate engine and gearbox
Bore:	63mm
Stroke:	80mm
Displacement:	498.76cc
Compression ratio:	8:1
Lubrication:	Double-plunger pump, dry sump
Ignition:	Magneto
Carburettor:	Amal Monobloc 76 1in
Primary drive:	Chain
Final drive:	Chain
Gearbox:	Four-speed, foot change
Frame:	All-steel tubular construction; single front down-tube; duplex lower rails
Front suspension:	Girders with central spring
Rear suspension:	Rigid
Front brake:	7in drum, SLS
Rear brake:	7in drum, SLS
Tyres:	Front 3.00 × 20; rear 3.50 × 19

General Specifications

Wheelbase:	54in (1,372mm)
Ground clearance:	5in (127mm)
Seat height:	27.75in (705mm)
Fuel-tank capacity:	4gal (18ltr)
Dry weight:	353lb (160kg)
Maximum power:	34bhp @ 7,000rpm
Top speed:	100mph (160kmph)

of the tank was recessed slightly at the sides so that the knee-grips were kept to a comfortable width. The mudguards were also finished in silver sheen with black lining; the frame and forks were black. The headlamp and exhaust system were finished in bright chrome plate. The silencers were shaped like megaphones (in contrast to the Speed Twin's flat Burgess-type) and featured detachable end caps. The carburettor, still an Amal Type 76, was increased in size from the $^{15}/_{16}$in (23mm) of the Speed Twin to 1in (25mm), and the main jet size was larger too, at 160 instead of the cooking model's 140. The Tiger 100 could achieve 100mph (160kmph), and each bike came with a performance certificate.

In March 1939, Triumph made an attempt to win the coveted Maudes Trophy once again. For this the ACU selected a Speed Twin (supplied by Bryants of Biggleswade) and a Tiger 100 from Sheffield dealers Horridge & Wildgoose. These were given their PDI (pre-delivery inspection) at the Triumph works under ACU supervision. The plan was to set them off from Coventry to visit John O'Groats, Land's End and Brooklands, but because of snow in the north of Scotland, the route was shortened slightly to 1,806 miles (2,906km), this being covered at an average speed of 42mph (68kmph).

Forged-type pistons of slipper design were employed on the 1939 Tiger 100.

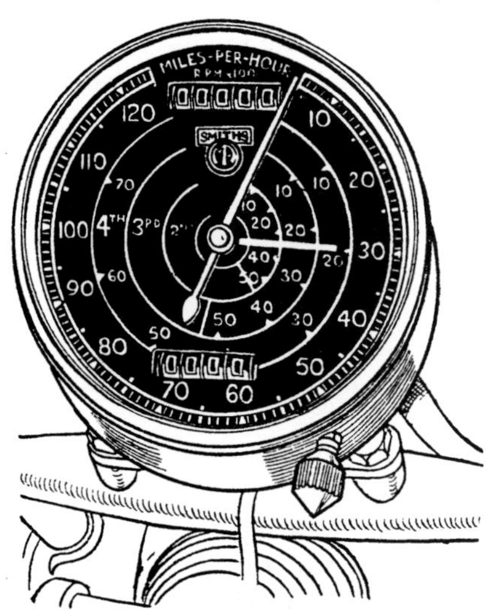

RIGHT: Another 1939 model feature was this combined rev counter and speedometer on the Tiger 100, plus Tiger singles.

After the public highway section of the test was completed, the performance testing was undertaken at Brooklands circuit in Surrey. Both the machines were ridden for six hours each – the Tiger 100 by Ivan Wicksteed and David Whitworth, and the Speed Twin by Freddie Clark and Allan Jefferies. The Tiger 100 averaged 78.5mph (126.3kmph), with a best lap of 88.46mph (142.33kmph); the Speed Twin achieved 75.02mph (120.70kmph), and 84.41mph (135.82kmph) respectively.

Although no major mechanical problems presented themselves, the oil pipe to the pressure gauge on the Speed Twin fractured at Brooklands: it was hammered flat by the mechanics to prevent oil pumping out – a crude but effective cure! In addition, and also at Brooklands, the Tiger 100 picked up a stray nail in its rear tyre, losing five minutes while the wheel was changed. The Speed Twin had a spark plug fail, but this was almost at the end and was thought to have happened because it was running low on fuel, which caused detonation and subsequent overheating.

Other factories made attempts to win the Maudes Trophy (then of enormous prestige), but Triumph ultimately came through victorious. Unfortunately they were not told officially until November, and by then Great Britain was at war and the 'victory' seemed of little consequence when set against the much greater happenings on the international front as the country switched over from peacetime production to the war effort.

Modifications to the Design

In spite of the war, the Triumph Engineering Company was still able to announce, in October 1939, that both the Speed Twin and the Tiger 100 had 'undergone certain modifications in order to keep them right up to date'. The most obvious of these was an arrangement of check springs on the girder front forks, and the steering head angle of the Speed Twin had been changed to that of the Tiger 100. The Speed Twin had also borrowed another feature from its more sporting brother in the shape of the larger fuel tank with recessed knee-grips.

Internally there had been further changes: first of all, both twins now featured fully skirted light-alloy pistons, form-ground to compensate for expansion – a feature that had been incorporated in most Triumph models for several years. The lubrication system of both twins had also been modified. This centred around the method by which the oil was led into the drilled crankshaft. Lubricant was now pumped into a small cylindrical chamber that lay in line with the crank. In this chamber was a shallow bronze piston with a tubular extension of smaller diameter that was found within the drilled crankshaft and formed the main oil lead thereto. Oil pressure, however, built up in the cylindrical chambers, pressing on the head of the bronze piston and forcing its skirt against the end face of the bronze crankshaft bearing. By this means any excessive loss of pressure through the crank bearing was avoided – an important factor, since it had been decided to increase the supply of oil thrown from the big ends to the cylinder walls.

The Military 3TW Model

At the time war broke out, Edward Turner was preparing to launch a new twin, the Tiger 85 – essentially a 350cc version of the Tiger 100, even to being finished in the same livery. Instead, he designed and built the military 3TW model. This used overhead valves, and had a three-speed gearbox unit built in with the engine. There was a duplex primary chain, dry sump lubrication, single carburettor and a Lucas alternator: a first for the motorcycle industry. Initially the engine was an all-alloy affair, but later an iron head and barrel were specified due to aluminium shortages caused by the need to reserve this material for use in the aviation industry.

There is no doubt that the 3TW was much superior to virtually every other British military motorcycle of its era. However, as described in Chapter 6, the Luftwaffe's blitz one night in November 1940 destroyed Triumph's factory in

Priory Street, Coventry, and put a cruel end to the 3TW. Instead, after first relocating to an old chapel in Warwick and later to its new purpose-built factory at Meriden, Triumph were forced to build a military version of the Tiger 80 three-fifty single.

Post-War Developments

Even before the war was officially over in Europe, the 1 March 1945 issue of *The Motor Cycle* carried the headline 'The First of the New', with the sub-heading 'Triumph Announce Their Immediate Post-War Programme: Four Vertical Twins and a Three-fifty Single: Telescopic Front Forks, Separate Dynamos and Automatic Ignition Controls on the Twins: Rear Springing Optional'.

When asked how long it would take to get into production with them, the factory spokesman replied: 'We will be ready to deliver within a month to six weeks of normal business being sanctioned by the authorities, and this applies to the main range – the twins – as well as the single.'

As for prices, the official answer was that these 'could not be indicated at the present juncture', but they would be strictly competitive and as reasonable as the firm could make them. The cost of manufacture, it was pointed out, was 'at least 45 per cent above pre-war, and there is the unknown quantity of Purchase Tax, which is expected to be 33⅓ per cent'.

Technical Changes

Of the four twins, the most noticeable feature was the introduction of the new telescopic forks. *The Motor Cycle* commented, 'These slim-looking straight-line forks give the machines a new and most appealing appearance – a decidedly rakish appearance.' With some 6in (152mm) of movement and a fork tube diameter of 1¾in (34mm), the new forks were hydraulically damped. Triumph sources were quoted as saying 'with the greater rigidity of these front forks in comparison with the girder type and the lower unsprung weight, there is a marked improvement in roadholding at high speeds'.

The figure for the unsprung weight was no less than 52lb 12oz (24kg). This included the wheel, headlamp, mudguard, number plate, speedometer and so on. In the case of the new telescopic fork arrangement the unsprung weight was 37lb 7oz (17kg), a saving of 15lb 5oz (7kg). When the 31lb 5oz (14kg) of the wheel and mudguard were subtracted, it was found that the unsprung weight with the new fork was 6lb 2oz (2.8kg) against 21lb 7oz (9.7kg), a truly impressive reduction.

A neat arrangement was provided for the front brake cable. Immediately above the hand adjuster on the brake drum there was a long, tubular distance piece running just behind and parallel to the offside (right) fork leg; as the forks operated this tube slid in a small bushing attached to the fork cover tube. Thus there was no unsightly loop.

Although no details were released at the time, rear springing was 'to be available on all models as an option'. This actually meant the patented Turner-designed spring hub (*see* separate panel). It has to be said, however, that this was not one of Edward Turner's better inventions; in fact it turned out to be one of the least successful, and was largely responsible for giving Triumph the reputation of being poor in roadholding and handling.

An easy way to spot a pre-war or post-war Tiger 100 (or Speed Twin) engine is that post-war the magdyno at the rear of the cylinder block was abandoned in favour of separate instruments – the magneto at the rear of the block and the dynamo at the front. This means that the small triangular 'plate' section of the crankcase on the pre-war engine was deleted.

The magneto, produced by Lucas or BTH, incorporated a centrifugal-type advance and retard mechanism in the drive. By this arrangement the contact breaker points opened with the armature in the optimum position relative to the poleshoes, irrespective of the timing of the spark as regards the engine. In other words, the magneto developed during the war resulted in a very fat spark at low speeds, and was a big improvement over pre-war magneto performance.

Turner's Sprung Hub

Vaguely mentioned pre-war and then put to one side when the old Coventry factory was destroyed in 1940, Edward Turner's infamous sprung hub made a highly publicized entry when Irishman Ernie Lyons won the Senior Manx Grand Prix in late summer 1946. In typical 'positive publicity' prose, *The Motor Cycle* described Turner's invention as combining 'ingenuity, simplicity, neatness and effectiveness'. However, it was not the advance it was made out to be.

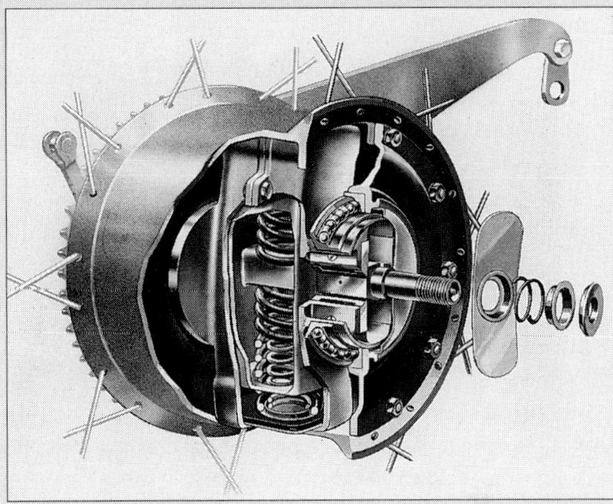

The patented Turner-designed Triumph sprung hub, showing the internal components.

Externally, the new wheel was instantly noticeable thanks to its massive aluminium-alloy hub shell, some 9in (230mm) in diameter. Straight ten-gauge spokes butted to eight gauge carried a conventional wheel rim. Enclosed within the hub shell was the springing mechanism.

A nickel-chrome steel rear wheel spindle was shouldered to fit the standard Triumph frame ends. This spindle supported a steel plunger guide of curved rectangular section, which enclosed the suspension springs. These springs, one above the spindle to take the rebound and two below – an inner and an outer – to take shock, curved in harmony with the plunger guide in which they operated.

Embracing the guide with its springs, and matching its curve, was a plunger guide box manufactured from heat-treated 'Y' alloy. This box was in two halves, married and dowelled for accuracy, and was free to move up and down under control of the springs in an arc that conformed with that formed by a radius from the centre line of the gearbox sprocket. At the top and bottom of the guide box were synthetic rubber buffers. The plunger box carried two large diameter ball races on which the hub shell ran. The wheel therefore moved in an arc, with the box, as allowed by the springs.

These bearings had in fact been developed by Triumph themselves. Each race comprised twenty-nine caged 5⁄16in-diameter steel balls running in cups stamped in case-hardened mild steel and ground to an accuracy of 0.0002in. The inner cups were fitted on the plunger guide box and the outer cups in the hub shell; on the offside (right) of the shell was a detachable plate, behind which were fitted shims for bearing adjustment.

Fitted vertically in the bearing bosses of the plunger guide box were replaceable cast-iron slipper pads. These took up the thrust of the wheel spindle, on which were mounted self-aligning slipper blocks in case-hardened mild steel. The spindle, and therefore the plunger unit, was correctly aligned and prevented from turning by means of a series of flats on the nearside (left), carrying an anchorage lever that fitted into a lug on the frame.

Fitted over the ends of the bearing bosses of the plunger guide box, and shrouding the slipper mechanism, were rubber diaphragm seals; although static, these accommodated eccentricity as the guide box moved relative to the spindle.

The rear wheel sprocket was an integral part of the 8in-diameter (203mm) brake drum, retained on the hub shell by eight studs. The brake plate supported 1⅛in-wide (28mm) shoes operated by a single cam in the conventional manner, and was screwed on to the nearside (left) boss of the plunger guide box.

Integral with the brake plate, the torque arm extended to the pivot bolt of the brake pedal (in the same position as before), to which it was attached by means of a short link. Compensation for the difference in centres between the arc of the rear wheel movement and an arc from the brake-pedal pivot was obtained by this link, and by allowing the plate to float on its threaded mounting. A conventional rod with a hand adjuster connected the pedal with the brake cam lever.

All parts of the springing mechanism were lubricated by grease, but there was a certain amount of friction between the stationary plunger guide and the moving plunger guide box. So although lubricant separated the surfaces, friction remained and provided an invariable damping value, as was intended by Turner in his design.

(continued overleaf)

Turner's Sprung Hub *(continued)*

Lubrication was effected by way of a nipple, countersunk and thus protected, in the end of the spindle on the offside (right). Grease was forced along the middle of the spindle and emerged through holes in the slipper blocks; it lubricated these sliding surfaces and entered holes in the slipper pads to reach reservoirs at the rear of the pads. From these reservoirs, the grease was forced through holes – one from each reservoir and thus two for each bearing – in the bearing cups. A further hole led from the front offside (right) reservoir to the guide box, which was packed with grease on assembly at the factory.

The sprung hub provided a maximum 2in (50mm) of movement.

At the time, journalists praised the unit; *The Motor Cycle* wrote:

> In combination with telescopic forks, [the bike] was found during a road test by a member of staff to give excellent control at high speeds and increased comfort at low speeds. Rear wheel braking is markedly improved, not only by the sprung hub, but also by the larger brake.

But in practice – and in service – the patented Triumph sprung hub was not so impressive. To begin with, in the author's opinion it was too complex a device, and it also allowed the rear end of the machine to gyrate in a similar way to a swinging-arm frame with worn bushes. The swinging-arm frame ultimately proved much superior to either Turner's 'sprung heel' or existing plunger designs, so the Triumph device was in fact obsolete almost before it hit the streets. Then there was the need for constant lubrication, and the problem of the effect that worn components would have, thus further affecting the handling. In racing use its limits were cruelly exposed. The design was probably Edward Turner's weakest.

However, it is important in any Triumph racing story, given that it was standard format on the Grand Prix over-the-counter racer, and also fitted to many of the tuned early post-war twins that flew the Triumph flag in racing events during the late 1940s and early 1950s. The fact also remains that machines equipped with the sprung hub won major events, including the Manx Grand Prix and the Clubmans TT.

It is also worth mentioning that the sprung hub was modified in several ways during 1950. The most important of these saw a change from the original cup and cone bearings to conventional ball races with integral oil seals.

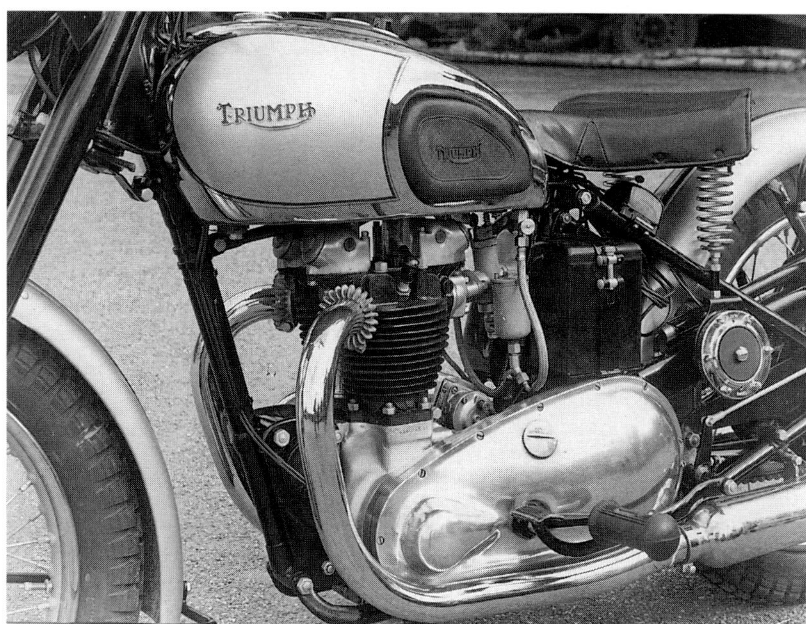

A 1947 Tiger 100 with iron head and barrel, front-mounted dynamo and telescopic front forks.

The automatic advance was standard on the latest Tiger 100, so as far as sports machines of the era were concerned, its handlebar controls duly comprised clutch and front brake levers, dipswitch and twist-grip throttle. There was no valve lifter, no advance/retard lever for magneto control – nor even a choke lever for the carburettor, the latter taking the form of a small plunger on top of the mixing chamber of the Amal carb. As a result of the transfer of the dynamo to the front of the engine, the carburettor was much more accessible.

Another noticeable change to the Tiger 100's specification was that it now shared the Burgess-type 'flat' silencers with the Speed Twin. The reasons for the move, Triumph sources stated, were that the Speed Twin type were 'less prone to damage and less susceptible to corrosion due to condensation'.

Among changes that were not so obvious at first glance was the introduction of drilled oil holes through the head and cylinder block, eliminating the previous series of six banjos that Triumph said had been 'liable to oil leakage'. In addition, a mechanical breather had been fitted to the inlet camshaft, improving conditions surrounding water retention through condensation, and thereby adding longer life to the ball race bearings. An improved oil relief valve was also fitted.

The crankshaft's central flywheel had had its periphery increased in width, thereby adding to its inertia, and on the Tiger 100 the pistons had reverted to being of the slipper type, but with the compression ratio decreased to 7.75:1 (the Speed Twin was now 7:1).

As before, besides the higher compression ratio, all moving parts were polished, and each engine received individual tuning and was tested on a Heenan and Froude brake. A certified test card was supplied with each bike.

Marketing the New Model

Compared to the 1939 price list, the one published in September 1946 showed that the price of the Tiger 100 had risen to £167 12s 10d (of which £35 12s 10d was the new purchase tax); this did not include either the cost of the speedometer or the new sprung hub rear suspension. However, the price rise did not discourage customers, and in 1947, Triumph sales zoomed ahead to such an extent that it was almost impossible to purchase a new model (and certainly not the top-of-the-range Tiger 100) on the home market – virtually everything was going for export in those early post-war months. Because of this huge demand, production numbers were all-important and changes minimal.

Except for purpose-designed, factory-built machines costing vast amounts of money, plus the over-the-counter twin-cam Manx Norton single, the Tiger 100 was probably the best engine for racing – hence the reason for Triumph launching its purpose-built Grand Prix model. Even though the austerity caused by the recently ended war was still affecting many countries, a large number of the early post-war production Tiger 100s were put on the track. Why? The following extract from *The Motor Cycle*, dated 14 April 1949, paints the picture:

> Even today, ten years after its introduction, the Tiger 100 remains a firm favourite. The engine, the famous 498cc Triumph vertical twin, has become the forerunner of the design that is accepted as the modern trend for the present day. The honour thus accorded the design is well merited, since the machine's high, tireless cruising speed, its outstanding reliability and its mechanical quietness have earned the marque a worldwide reputation. Under test, the 1949 model proved to have all the qualities of its famous forbears, plus a few new ones. It established itself as the fastest five-hundred and the second-fastest machine (the other being the 998cc Vincent V-twin) to be road-tested by *The Motor Cycle* post war.

The 1949 Model Year Specification

When the 1949 model year Triumph range was announced in October 1948 the most noticeable changes were the deletion of the tank-top instrument panel and the introduction of the headlamp nacelle. With the top of the fuel tank now clear of instruments it was given four tapped holes and, initially as a cost option, a chromium-plated parcel grid; the latter proved very popular, and became a standard fitment.

The oil pressure gauge was axed, mainly because owners were forever contacting their dealer or the factory when their particular engine ceased registering the full 50psi as it had done when fresh out of the showroom. Of more importance from a racing viewpoint was the solution, because in its place came a tell-tale plunger fitted in the pressure release valve on the timing cover. At the same time a small change was carried out to the breather duct, and all models were fitted with the same type of oil tank.

With the adoption of the sprung hub the speedometer could no longer be driven from the rear wheel. A drive point was therefore taken from the end of the gearbox layshaft, this being adopted for all models, including the Tiger 100.

The TR5 Trophy

At the London Earls Court show, in November 1948, the new TR5 Trophy model was introduced. Based on the machine that the works team had been riding in trials, this had gained a trio of gold medals and the team award in that year's ISDT – hence the Trophy tag.

The Trophy was an instant hit amongst clubmen, who could ride it to work in the week and for their weekend sport take part in trials, long-distance events and even clubman-type race meetings. The engine was based around the Speed Twin/T100, but with the light-alloy cylinder barrel and head from the generator engine, still with the cooling shroud bosses in the rather square fins. It was equipped with standard camshafts, low-compression pistons and a single carb to produce a modest 25bhp at 6,000rpm. However, it could soon be tuned to easily exceed this figure. Very soon a whole series of components was offered so that owners could 'ring the changes' (as one journalist described it) on such items as gearing, camshafts, pistons and other tuning goodies. The standard TR5 Trophy was able to exceed 80mph (130kmph), but with T100 pistons it was considerably quicker. At the other end of the scale the factory trials models were detuned and ran on lowly 4.5:1 pistons to provide walking-pace punch. Like the other models in the range, the Sprung Hub was a cost extra above the 1949 model price of £195 11s 8d price (which rose to £200 13s 3d in October 1949).

The next real development came with the new six-fifty twin, the 6T Thunderbird, which came about largely due to American requests (*see* Chapters 5 and 9).

1950 Australian Senior Clubman's Victorian TT winner Ernie Jones (46), followed by J. Russell, both riding Tiger 100s. Note the open megaphones on Jones' machine.

Updates for the 1951 Season

Triumph Engineering Ltd not only produced the TR5 Trophy and its pukka race model, the limited production (and expensive) Grand Prix at £342 18s (including taxes) in October 1949, but followed this up with a comprehensive race kit for the Tiger 100 sportster for the 1951 season. This came in conjunction with news of a new head and cylinder block for both the Tiger 100 and TR5 Trophy.

Both the new assemblies were gravity die-cast in aluminium alloy, and this allowed the finning to be much more closely pitched. The new head featured inserted valve seats in cast iron, and its holding down bolts screwed into plugs within the cylinder barrel manufactured from the same material. The superior cooling resulted from the increased finning area and from the use of aluminium as opposed to cast iron. These changes and benefits allowed the compression ratio of the Tiger 100 to be increased to 7.6:1. The exhaust ports were also splayed out in the same manner as the outgoing iron engine. Larger inlet valves were fitted and the internal breathing improved. All of this resulted in an increase in power output to 32bhp. It is worth noting that the new head and barrel was also specified for the Trophy, but with the use of a lower 6:1 ratio. The exhaust pipes were redesigned to fit the new head, and on all machines a new front brake with a cast-iron drum was used. Larger bore fuel taps were also adopted to prevent any chance of fuel starvation at speed, and the five-plate clutch was given reduced-rate springs.

The 1951 model Tiger 100 was equipped with a new dual seat as standard, with the toolbox relocated to a new home just below it and above the upper chain stay; it was for this model that Triumph brought out its race kit.

The Race Kit

The 1951 race kit (costing £35 that year) was extremely comprehensive; as can be seen from the accompanying official Triumph factory photograph, it consisted of the following components:

Tiger 100 1951 (commencing engine number 100NA)

Engine:	Air-cooled, ohv vertical twin, close pitch fin alloy head and barrel, the latter with cast-iron steel liners, Duralumin pushrods; Stellite-faced cam followers, stronger (6T-type) con-rods; vertically split crankcases; separate engine and gearbox
Bore:	63mm
Stroke:	80mm
Displacement:	498.76cc
Compression ratio:	7.6:1
Lubrication:	Double-plunger pump, dry sump
Ignition:	Magneto
Carburettor:	Amal Monobloc 276 1in (or race-kit twin carbs, *see* below)
Primary drive:	Chain
Final drive:	Chain
Gearbox:	Four-speed
Frame:	All-steel tubular construction; single front down-tube; duplex lower rails
Front suspension:	Telescopic oil-dampened
Rear suspension:	Patented Triumph sprung hub Mark II
Front brake:	7in drum, SLS
Rear brake:	8in drum, SLS
Tyres:	Front 3.25 × 19; rear 3.50 × 19

General Specifications

Wheelbase:	55in (1,397mm)
Ground clearance:	6in (152mm)
Seat height:	31in (787mm)
Fuel-tank capacity:	4gal (18ltr)
Dry weight:	355lb (161kg)
Maximum power:	32bhp @ 7,000rpm in road trim; 42bhp race kit
Top speed:	102mph (164kmph) in road trim; 120mph (193kmph) race kit

NOTE: Tiger 100 race kit catalogued for first time including twin carbs, high compression (8.25:1 petrol/ 9.5:1 high octane) pistons, hi-lift cams, etc.

TOP: A 1951 Tiger 100, with close-fin alloy motor and optional sprung hub.

ABOVE LEFT: The 1952 Isle of Man Senior Clubman's TT: the winning machine of Bernard Hargreaves.

ABOVE RIGHT: Bernard Hargreaves after winning the 1952 Senior Clubman's TT. He averaged 82.45mph (132.66kmph) on his Tiger 100.

LEFT: Factory tester and road racer Percy Tait with a race-kitted, sprung-hub Tiger 100 during a very wet race in the early 1950s.

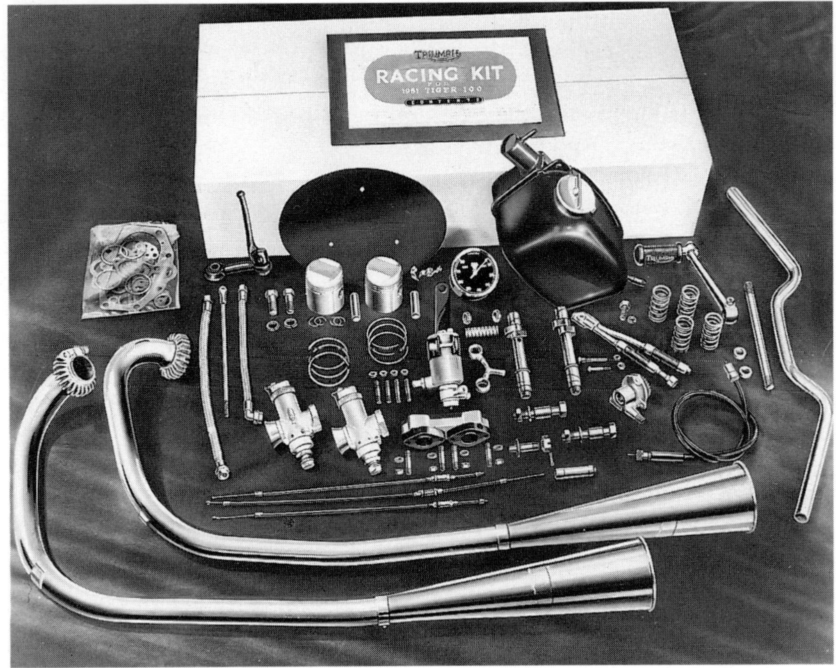

Official factory race kit for the Tiger 100: this is the 1951 version. It included cams, pistons, twin carburettors, racing exhausts, rev counter, handlebars, number plates and larger 1gal (4.5ltr) oil tank.

- Pistons complete with rings, gudgeon pins and circlips
- Carburettors complete with induction stub and remote float chamber
- E3134 camshafts
- External oil pipes
- Gasket set
- Rev counter, cable and drive gearbox
- Valve springs
- Larger capacity oil tank
- Number plates
- Handlebars
- Complete exhaust system including megaphones
- Levers
- Throttle and choke cables
- Rear set foot controls

In the 13 September 1951 issue of *Motor Cycling*, Dennis Hardwicke presented a three-page article entitled 'From Roadster to Racer', in which he outlined for readers the task of converting a standard Tiger 100 into a road racing machine, using the factory-supplied kit. The work was undertaken at 4,000 miles (6,450km) with workshop equipment 'consisting of a vice and the usual hand tools possessed by the average private owner'.

Hardwicke went on to state 'The instructions in the excellent book supplied with the kit were followed throughout and only minor differences were encountered.' One of these consisted in removing the engine-shaft shock-absorber nut, which, he said, 'is recessed in a cup. The problem was overcome by trimming 1/16in (1mm) off the outside of a 1/16in (16mm) Whitworth socket spanner with the aid of a borrowed lathe.'

After making up a suitable crankcase support for working on the bench, engine dismantling began. Stripping to the point where removal of the cylinder barrel assembly 'exposed two set screws inside the mouth of the crankcase, was quite straightforward'. But no right-angled screwdriver was available so, following a works tip that he remembered, the end of an ordinary screwdriver was ground to 'approximately 45 degrees', which enabled the screws to be removed half-a-turn at a time.

Another problem encountered was in splitting the crankcase halves. It was finally solved by 'dipping the case in a bucket of boiling water for a short time, after which the offending bearing came away from its socket. Minor burrs on the mating faces of the crankcase halves were removed with a fine file and a scraper', and all parts were thoroughly washed in petrol. The flywheel assembly was then replaced and the new racing camshafts substituted for the standard components, not forgetting the rotary breather valve, with the crankcase halves being drawn together with the engine bolts at strategic points, 'assisted by judicious taps applied with a wooden mallet'.

Hardwicke tested the camshafts; these spun freely, but not so the crankshaft. Once again he found that 'the application of heat was necessary before the drive-side bearing would go fully home in its housing'.

After the bottom end was finally completed, attention was given to the cylinder head. All parts were cleaned and refitted, using the racing components where supplied. Next, the racing pistons were fitted. Before bolting on the cylinder head, a timing disc was attached to the drive-side mainshaft. No depth gauge being available, top dead centre was checked by bolting a steel strip across the open tops of the cylinder bores.

The flywheels were rotated clockwise until the pistons touched the strip and the reading noted; then anti-clockwise until the pistons again touched – halfway between the two readings was obviously TDC (top dead centre). Next, the disc was adjusted accordingly, in relation to its fixed pointer. The strip was then removed, and the cylinder head assembly bolted down tightly. Finally, the camshaft pinions were pushed on to their keyed shafts, but without their locking nuts. At this stage Hardwicke gave readers a word of caution, saying: 'These pinions are a tight fit on the parallel-ended shafts, and it may be necessary to obtain two special extractors from the factory.'

He then went on to explain that care had already been taken 'to check that the tops of the valve stems were absolutely flat and smooth, this being essential if accurate valve timings were to be achieved'. The workshop used by Hardwicke boasted a dial indicator 'of the single type used in the Triumph experimental department; this was bolted rigidly to the head with its plunger button resting on the inlet valve spring collar.' The indicator being set to zero, tappets were adjusted until there was no clearance, but leaving the rocker just free. A similar procedure was followed with the exhaust valves.

Handbook instructions were followed – with the exhaust valve 0.020in open, the timing disc reading should be 48 degrees before BDC (Bottom Dead Centre). With the inlet valve 0.020in open, the reading should be 28 degrees before TDC. Hardwicke pointed out:

> If the initial settings are wrong, the camshaft pinions must be removed and replaced suitably, remembering that one tooth on the pinion represents approximately 14 degrees of crankshaft rotation, whilst one keyway in the pinion – there are three – represents approximately 2½ degrees of crankshaft rotations. The task is a little tricky, and it requires patience to achieve optimum results, after which the pinion nuts should be fitted and tightened and the timing rechecked.

From that point onwards, reassembly proved relatively easy. Once the correct height of the racing-type remote float chamber was ascertained, a line was scribed on it using the top of the clamp as a guide, for future reference. As a 'precaution', the stock synthetic rubber oil pipes were replaced with stronger reinforced ones, all pipes being carefully lined up to cause minimum stress.

Testing the Racer

The standard exhaust pipes and silencers, together with number plates and licence disc, were left in place in order that a 'few road miles could be covered before the machine was taken to the Motor Industry Research Association's test track at Lindley, near Nuneaton'.

Hardwicke, helped by 'a well-known racing man', put on the two small-bore racing header pipes and megaphones. Then, 'two quick laps of the three-mile circuit were completed and the nearside carburettor setting altered to bring it into synchronization. Plugs were changed and the racing man set off for a plug check'. This proved that the carburation was virtually spot on, so the two men were able to put in several laps 'with intent'.

Standard ratio 'prevented full use being made of the engine'. Even so, the best run (with 7,600 to 7,800rpm on the rev counter) showed a speed of 109.2mph (175.7kmph). Gear changes 'were made as close to 7,000rpm as possible, but sometimes it was a little difficult to catch up with the rev counter, especially in second gear'. The same bike had recorded a top speed of 96mph (154kmph) during the road test carried out a few weeks earlier in road trim, so the race kit had added an additional 13mph (21kmph) in top gear.

It is also important to point out that low-grade 'pool' petrol was used, and no doubt 80-octane fuel would have provided better results. No spare engine sprockets were available to check the 'impression that a slightly higher top gear – say, 4.9:1 – would have been beneficial, not only in preventing over-revving in top, but also increasing the top speed.'

The Clubman's TT

With its speed and reliability the Tiger 100 was, it seemed, a perfect bike for the recently introduced Clubman's TT, which for 1951 adopted new rules. Previously the races had been for 350cc (Junior) and 1,000cc (Senior), with the latter class the preserve of the Vincent V-twin. However, a change in the rules to a 500cc (Senior) meant that not only could the Triumph twin take part, but so could other popular sports models, such as the Norton International, AJS and Matchless twins, the BSA B34 Gold Star and the BSA Star Twin.

Pre-war Brooklands star Ivan Wicksteed was the favourite. Everyone agreed that barring a blow-up he would win on his Tiger 100, and, true to form, he led the race from the start, dominating the event. But, as *The Motor Cycle*'s race report of 14 June 1951 outlined:

> Sitting pretty, it seemed, and determined not to risk anything, he rolled back the twistgrip too far. He was thus overtaken on the final lap of the 150.92-mile [242.83km] race by I.K. Arber's Norton International. Wicksteed – who set the fastest lap, at 81.06mph [130.42km] – was runner-up, with another Tiger 100, ridden by G.J. Draper, third.

A year later, Bernard Hargreaves took his Tiger 100 to victory in the Senior Clubman's TT. Setting the fastest lap of the race at 83.05mph (133.62km) from a standing start on Lap 1, Hargreaves did not make the mistake of easing off as Wicksteed had done twelve months before. Of the ninety-five bikes entered, seven were non-starters, with Triumph and Norton strongly represented. The only problem Hargreaves experienced was that his machine's offside (right) rear wheel spindle nut was lost at the end of the first lap. After this the handling was not as good, but he was still able to hang on to the lead, a position he was able to retain until the end. After the race *The Motor Cycle* reported:

> The engine of B.J. Hargreaves' Triumph had been running at an ideal operating temperature; the plugs showed precisely the correct mixture – neither lean nor rich – and carbon deposit was black and soft except in the exhaust valve heads where it had a mild, reddish tinge. Particularly pleasing was the fact that all engine joints were as near absolutely oil tight as makes no difference. Although the offside nut of the rear wheel spindle had been lost early on during the race, the wheel had not moved in the frame and the chain adjustment was correct; similarly, the adjustment of the primary chain was just right. The 'home-made' rev meter bracket had fractured across one of the mounting-bolt holes.

The Tiger 100C

Spurred on no doubt by Bernard Hargreaves' Senior Clubman's TT victory, Triumph introduced the Tiger 100C, a limited production, high performance model costing £233 16s 8d, whereas the standard Tiger 100 retailed for £223 12s 3d when the 1953 model range was announced in September 1952. *The Motor Cycle* said, 'An attractive proposition for the Clubman racer, the new Tiger 100C model embodies most of the equipment that is provided in the racing conversion kit available for the Tiger 100 or the Trophy model.'

The newcomer's specification included the Amal Type 76 1in (25mm) carburettors with remote float chamber, special pistons, racing camshafts, 1gal (5ltr) oil tank, small-bore exhaust system, racing valve springs, rev counter, racing handlebars and rear set footrests. In addition, the 'C' version sported a twin-pull twistgrip (whereas the racing conversion kit had a single-pull twistgrip with a junction box with twin cables from a box on the carburettor).

For the 28 May 1953 issue of *The Motor Cycle*, racer/journalist Vic Willoughby selected at random a Tiger 100C engine being assembled at the Triumph factory, followed it through the production phase, and finally ran it on the road before taking it to the Snetterton circuit in Norfolk to compete in the meeting held there on Saturday 2 May 1953. Before his arrival the bike had been fitted with the racing exhaust system: 180 main jets (instead of the standard 150 size) and racing spark plugs. Lighting equipment was removed, and finally racing number plates were added. Willoughby began his race report by saying:

> It was four years since I had competed at an airfield, and the opposition was considerably stronger than that which would normally confront a clubman's racing machine. Nevertheless, the Triumph put up an excellent show and was not approached by any other standard clubman racer. Throughout the meeting, it was headed only by expertly ridden Featherbed Manx Nortons, Maurice Cann's 496cc Gambalunga Moto Guzzi, and the twin-cylinder Pike BSA.

The morning practice session showed that the standard twenty-two-tooth engine was too large for the circuit, and a change to a twenty-one-tooth sprocket enabled the engine to achieve 7,000rpm in top gear; but Willoughby found that 'at this engine speed, a high frequency vibration proved troublesome'. These vibes resulted in the splitting of a weld at the base of the fuel tank, and made it difficult for

1953 Tiger 100C

Engine:	Air-cooled, ohv vertical twin, close pitch-fin alloy head
Bore:	63mm
Stroke:	80mm
Displacement:	498.76cc
Compression ratio:	8:1
Lubrication:	Double-plunger pump, dry sump; 1gal (4.5ltr) oil tank with qd cap.
Ignition:	Magneto
Carburettor:	2 × Amal Monobloc 76 1in, with single, centrally mounted remote float chamber
Primary drive:	Chain
Final drive:	Chain
Gearbox:	Four-speed, foot change
Frame:	All-steel tubular construction; single front down-tube; duplex lower rails
Front suspension:	Telescopic, oil-damped
Rear suspension:	Patented, Triumph sprung hub Mark II
Front brake:	7in drum, SLS
Rear brake:	8in drum, SLS
Tyres:	Front 3.25 × 19; rear 3.50 × 19

General Specifications

Wheelbase:	55in (1,397mm)
Ground clearance:	6in (152mm)
Seat height:	31in (787mm)
Fuel-tank capacity:	4gal (18ltr)
Dry weight:	362lb (164kg) in road trim
Maximum power:	40bhp @ 7,000rpm (with racing exhaust)
Top speed:	120mph (193kmph) with racing exhaust

Willoughby to keep the throttle wide open for the length of the Norwich Straight. He also found that '...on the curves the prop stand grounded on the left, while the right-hand megaphone clip was soon wiped off.' So the prop stand was removed and a new clip was fitted, with its bolt above the exhaust pipe.

At first Vic Willoughby had been 'apprehensive concerning the clutch'. However, these fears proved unfounded, as at no point on the circuit was it necessary to come off the megaphone and slip the clutch. Furthermore, he found the task eased by being able to make all upward gear changes 'quite cleanly' without the clutch, 'such was the closeness of the gear ratios'. In the matter of engine power, Willoughby was 'delighted to find that the Triumph enabled me to scrap with the riders of the pukka racing machines of nearly twice its cost.' But he also discovered that '...its steering and braking at very high speeds ... were not quite up to the same high standard.'

In the 500cc heat the Triumph finished close behind Maurice Cann's Moto Guzzi, which in turn was behind the Nortons of John Surtees, Mike O'Rourke and P. Harrison. In the final, an unfavourable starting-grid position proved a handicap, and although John Surtees won the race 'from the worst start, I was, of course, not able to match the speed of his famous Norton, the power of his large Italian front brake or his personal prowess.' But only Manx Nortons and the Pike BSA finished in front of the Willoughby Tiger 100C.

The 1,000cc heat brought him third, behind the Nortons of O'Rourke and R.H. King, whilst in the final of the same event he was able to scrap closely for the entire race with the Norton of well-known Yorkshireman Denis Parkinson, eventually finishing fifth. Willoughby ended by saying:

> Certainly the Tiger 100C gave me an afternoon's great fun. Its performance as a clubman's racer in such distinguished company proved that it could amply fill the sporting role as well as the touring one. In the less severe competition of clubmen's races it is a potential winner, with the inestimable advantage that it can be ridden to and from the course.

Important Changes for the Pre-Unit Tiger 100 Series

A major development in the history of the pre-unit Tiger 100 series came in October 1953, when the 1954 model range was announced. This concerned the swinging-arm frame that it was to share with the recently launched 650 T110 (*see* Chapter 5). Whilst the all-alloy engined 32bhp at 6,500rpm came from the standard Tiger 100 (the twin-carb T100C model was dropped at the same time), the new frame made a considerable difference in both

Barry Sluce of the Canberra MCC on one of the very first of the swinging-arm Tiger 100s during the Mount Druitt 24 Hours production machine race in Sydney, Australia, ca. *1954.*

1954 Tiger 100
(commencing engine number 44135)

Engine:	Air-cooled, ohv vertical twin, close pitch-fin head and barrel, 360-degree three-piece crankshaft (increased dimensions and featuring 1⅝in diameter con-rod journals)
Bore:	63mm
Stroke:	80mm
Displacement:	498.76cc
Compression ratio:	7.5:1 (8:1 for USA, or on request)
Lubrication:	Double-plunger pump, dry sump
Ignition:	Magneto
Carburettor:	Amal Monobloc 276 1in
Primary drive:	Chain
Final drive:	Chain
Gearbox:	Four-speed
Frame	New type: single front down-tube cradle with swinging-arm rear suspension
Front suspension:	Telescopic, oil-damped
Rear suspension:	Swinging arm; twin Girling shock absorbers, early models 110lb rate springs; later 126lb springs
Front brake:	New 8in cast-iron drum with alloy air-scooped brake plate; SLS operation, single-sided
Rear brake:	7in integral drum/sprocket, SLS operation. Now with journal ball bearings in place of adjustable taper roller bearings
Tyres:	Front 3.25 × 19; rear 3.50 × 19

General Specifications

Wheelbase:	55.75in (1,416mm)
Ground clearance:	5in (127mm)
Seat height:	30.5in (775mm)
Fuel-tank capacity:	4gal (18ltr)
Dry weight:	385lb (175kg)
Maximum power:	32bhp @ 6,500rpm (single carb, road trim)
Top speed:	101mph (162.5kmph) (single carb, road trim)

NOTE: Twin Amal-type 76 carbs with remote float chamber (as a 1953 Tiger 100C) available as a cost option.

appearance and the riding experience. It also benefited from improved braking, thanks to a new 8in front brake developed for the six-fifty sports model. The twin-carb race kit was still available for those wishing to race the new swinging-arm Tiger 100.

During 1955 a further change was made to the Tiger 100, and all the other 500 and 650 twins, with the introduction of larger main bearings. These modified engines are easily recognized by the additional bulge on the timing side under the crankcase. At the same time the design of the big ends was changed, and a change was also made to conventional shell-type bearings. This later design of crankshaft will retro-fit the earlier engine, but it requires the use of a difficult-to-source bearing, the dimensions of which fill the requirements, but can cause problems by being overloaded.

Other changes for the 1955 model year included an increase in compression ratio to 8:1 for both the Tiger 100 and the Trophy, which, together with hotter cam profiles, increased the power (in road-going guise) to 33bhp at 6,500rpm.

When the 1957 range was announced at the end of October 1956, the main news was that on all the twins the front forks had, as *The Motor Cycle* said, 'been considerably cleaned up', and a twin-carburettor option was made available as an ex-factory fitment for an additional £9 6s on top of the 1957 model Tiger 100's £255 8s 10d purchase price (including taxes).

In April 1957 *Motor Cycling* carried out a road test of the latest T100 with the twin-carb option. They began by saying:

> On the broad valuation that, in the motorcycling world, better performance and improved specification represent progress, then the current Triumph Tiger 100, faster than ever, completely modern in design, yet less in price by £4 than its predecessor six years ago, demonstrates strikingly the headway made by Triumph Engineering Co. Ltd since 1951. …The 1957 model is equipped with the new splayed inport, light alloy head, twin carburettor – Amal 376 Monobloc of 1in and 210 main jets –

ABOVE: *The three-rider team of Bob and Barry Sluce and Brian Woodyatt with the Tiger 100 that was the outright winner of the Mount Druitt 24 Hours race. After an accident that put Woodyatt out of the running, the Sluce brothers rode as a two-man team for the final eleven hours of the event.*

Roy Barber's 1954 Tiger 100 at the VMCC Snetterton race meeting, 26 August 1985. This machine has twin, rubber-mounted Amal Monobloc carbs and a wide fin 'Delta' alloy head, introduced from 1957 onwards.

1957 Tiger 100 (optional twin carburettors)

Engine:	Air-cooled, ohv vertical twin, with splayed port 'Delta' alloy head with increased diameter inlet valves, hc pistons, racing (E3134) camshafts and 'R'-type tappets, racing inner and outer valve springs, bronze valve guides. Second chrome piston ring dropped
Bore:	63mm
Stroke:	80mm
Displacement:	498.76cc
Compression ratio:	9:1
Lubrication:	Double-plunger pump, dry sump
Ignition:	Magneto
Carburettor:	2 × Amal Monobloc 376 1in with 219 main jets
Primary drive:	Chain
Final drive:	Chain
Gearbox:	Four-speed
Frame:	Single front down-tube cradle with swinging-arm rear suspension
Front suspension:	Telescopic, oil-damped
Rear suspension:	Swinging arm; twin Girling shock absorbers
Front brake:	8in cast-iron drum, alloy air-scooped brake plate; SLS operation, single-sided
Rear brake:	7in integral drum/sprocket, SLS operation
Tyres:	Front 3.25 × 19; rear 3.50 × 19

General Specifications

Wheelbase:	55.75in (1,416mm)
Ground clearance:	5in (127mm)
Seat height:	30.5in (775mm)
Fuel-tank capacity:	4gal (18ltr)
Dry weight:	375lb (170kg)
Maximum power:	36bhp @ 6,500rpm in road trim
Top speed:	105mph (169kmph) in road trim

The 1957 Tiger 100: by now the machine had found its forte in Production races for standard roadsters.

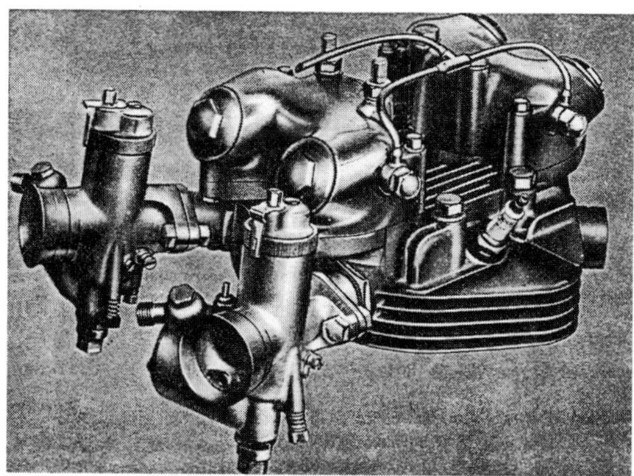

The 1957 twin carburettor (Amal Monoblocs), splayed HAD 'Delta' alloy cylinder head.

and E31/34 camshafts, and has proved to be good for 105mph [169kmph] in road trim.

One of the few British-made 500s capable of 'topping the ton' anywhere and at any time when conditions permit, the twin-carburettor T100 is, nevertheless, no longer the specially prepared track model of six years ago, but a pleasant, albeit slightly mettlesome, high-stepping thoroughbred, as quiet and well behaved in town as it is on the open road. Furthermore, being better value for a lower retail price, obtained over a six-year period of steadily rising costs, is indeed a rare achievement in these times.

By 1957, and with the continual and ongoing development of both Norton and Matchless full-blown racers (the Manx single and G45 twin respectively), the use of a converted Tiger 100 in standard guise for open class events was coming to an end, although a growing number of riders were putting the Triumph engine into

Rival British Vertical Twins

In motorcycling terms, at least during the first half of the twentieth century, there was always a 'Great' in front of Britain, an accolade earned by some truly great achievements, with great marques, great men (both designers and riders) and great bikes. During this period, Great Britain largely ruled the world's motorcycle industry, much as it had ruled the oceans in the previous century due to its control of sea power. World War II did not stop this trend, at least not in the early post-war years. When hostilities ended in 1945, the British economy was at a low ebb, and in the first four or five years of peacetime virtually every kind of manufactured goods, including motorcycles, went for export.

In 1950 Britain had a thriving motorcycle industry with a long list of manufacturers, including AMC (AJS and Matchless), the BSA Group (BSA, Triumph, Sunbeam and Ariel), Douglas, Norton, Panther, Royal Enfield, Velocette and Vincent, not to mention scores of smaller marques such as Cotton, Dot, DMW, Excelsior, Francis Barnett, James, New Hudson, Scott and Sun. But Edward Turner's 1937 500 Speed Twin had given Triumph a lead in the development and production of the ohv vertical twin-cylinder type. A few months later the more sporting Tiger 100 followed, and in September 1949 the 650 Thunderbird arrived in a blaze of publicity.

Triumph's rivals had attempted to respond, with very mixed results. BSA probably made the most successful challenge, and in the early post-war years produced first the 497cc Star Twin, followed by the 646cc A10 Golden Flash, then more sporting versions such as the A7 Shooting Star (500), and the Road Rocket, Super Rocket and Rocket Gold Star (all 650s).

Unlike its Triumph and BSA rivals, Norton was slow to develop new models after the war, even though on the Grand Prix circuit it was often unbeatable during the same period – in fact, many questioned whether the company was neglecting its production side in order to seek glories on the track. The first Norton twin – and in fact its first new model post war – was the Model 7 of 1948; this, like the later Dominator 88, used a 497cc pre-unit engine. It was not until 1956 that the larger 597cc 77 and 99 models arrived; later still came the 647cc 650SS (1962) and 745cc Atlas (1964).

AJS and Matchless were both part of the AMC (Associated Motor Cycles) group, and from 1948 offered the Model 20 (AJS) and the G9 (Matchless). AMC badly needed a twin-cylinder following the Triumph lead in 1937. The heart of the AMC 'modular' twin (essentially the Model 20 and the G9 were the same motorcycle, and coined the phrase 'badge engineering' in the two-wheel industry) was the basic layout of the British ohv vertical twin-cylinder formula, with both pistons moving together dictated by the magneto, then considered mandatory. However, the AMC variant was different in that it had a third, central main bearing between the two crankshaft throws. It also sported separate heads and cylinders, and gear-driven camshafts fore and aft (the latter shared by Triumph).

The Model 20/G9 displaced 498cc, which, as with its main rivals, saw steady enlargement over the lifespan of the South London company. The first increase came with a special USA-only 550cc version (1954–55), before its engineering team enlarged the motor to 593cc for the 1956 season. In 1958 came a bigger 646cc engine size, before the last AMC vertical twin, the 745cc. The latter was something of a cheat, as in fact it was a Norton engine, AMC having swallowed up the Birmingham marque during the early 1950s, before moving Norton to AMC's Plumstead headquarters in 1962.

Royal Enfield's first effort at producing an ohv twin in Speed Twin mould was its 495cc 500 Twin, announced in late 1948. As with other British parallel twins of the era, the crankcases split vertically and the valves were pushrod-operated. The last of the 500cc Enfield twins was the Meteor Sports Twin, production of which finally ceased in 1963. The first of the larger Enfield twins, the 692cc Meteor, arrived in 1952, with the performance version, the Constellation, running from 1958 until 1963; but although the Redditch company boasted '700cc 50bhp', the Constellation was not a very reliable motorcycle. Its replacement, the 763cc Interceptor, was much better in this respect, and ran from 1962 until the early 1970s. The Interceptor and the Norton Atlas were the largest displacement British twins of the 1960s. All RE twins featured separate barrels and cylinder heads.

Famous for its legendary Square Four, Ariel was another British manufacturer to build a series of vertical twins. After the war, firms such as Ariel needed a twin as a priority to compete with Triumph, and in this, Ariel possessed a couple of advantages: first, it already had not only the Square Four, but also the high performance Red Hunter range of singles, so suitable components for the chassis already existed. Secondly, an initial design study by design chief Val Page had been carried out during the conflict so that Ariel had a running prototype as early as 1944.

(continued overleaf)

Rival British Vertical Twins *(continued)*

Val Page had copied Triumph's 499cc engine size and, when Ariel launched its 'new' bike in November 1947, there were actually two versions: the KG tourer, and the more sporting KH Red Hunter. The latter was later produced with an all-alloy engine (KHA), which was a match for all the other five-hundred twins of the era, except for Triumph's ultra-sporting Tiger 100. In 1954 the company introduced the FH Huntmaster; this employed what amounted to a lightly retouched BSA A10 engine, and thus shared the latter's 646cc displacement.

Apart from the vertical twins listed above, the majority of the other British post-war motorcycles of 500cc and above were singles, the exceptions being the Vincent 998cc V-twin (production of which ended in 1955), and much later the BSA and Triumph triples of the late 1960s and 1970s.

In retrospect, BSA and Norton came nearest to equalling Triumph, but in the author's opinion never quite managed to – although for a time Norton benefited from their race-developed Featherbed frame. By the 1960s, however, Triumph had caught up in this respect as well. Both on the street and on the race circuit Triumph thus ruled supreme from the late 1930s until the late 1960s.

The 'Banbury Mafia'. Left to right: Rod Gould (9 – BSA Gold Star), Tim White (23 – Tiger 100) and Bruce Cox (38 – Triumph Special) pose in the Silverstone paddock, in the summer of 1961. Gould became a World Champion and later team manager, whilst Cox went to the USA and was a co-promoter of the Anglo-American race series.

a Norton chassis to create a Triton special. Therefore the Tiger 100 and the 650 Tiger 110 were to be seen in Production racing events such as the Thruxton marathon (*see* Chapter 11).

So the pre-unit Tiger became much more of a roadster than a racer in the last few years of its life, before it was replaced by the unit construction T100A model for 1960. It is, however, worth mentioning that for 1958 it received the 8in full-width front brake and 'slickshift gearbox'. In 1959, its final year, all 500 and 650 pre-unit engines gained a new crankshaft. It was finally discontinued in June of that year. Having evolved over some two decades since making its bow for the 1939 season (just prior to the outbreak of war), the Tiger 100 had become a legend both on and off the racetrack. Nevertheless, although the name was to live on into the 1960s, the unit model was a different bike for a different era.

5 The 650 Arrives

November 1949 saw the arrival of the new six-fifty Triumph, the 6T Thunderbird. The factory organized a publicity stunt at the French Montlhéry circuit near Paris, and in this photograph the three riders seated on the bikes are, from left to right, Alex Scobie, Len Bayliss and Bob Manns. Triumph boss Edward Turner is on the extreme left.

In late September 1949, Triumph Engineering Ltd launched a 650 twin in a blaze of publicity: the first three production models were taken to the Montlhéry circuit, just south of Paris, where they proceeded to cover 500 miles (800km), ending the display with a flying lap at over 100mph (160kmph). Named the Thunderbird, the newcomer was described as follows:

> A machine designed primarily for sustained high speeds on the vast, smooth highways of America, South Africa and Australia [Great Britain's three principal export markets at the time], with an engine developing 34bhp at 6,000rpm and a total weight of little more than the famous 500cc Speed Twin. Truly a mount to whet the interest of every enthusiast!

The Montlhéry Test

The banked Montlhéry Autodrome was chosen because, since Brooklands had not reopened after the end of the war in 1945, no suitable venue was available in the British Isles. The three machines (and a spare) were ridden to France, each with full road equipment and, as *The Motor Cycle* said in their report of the venture in their 29 September 1949 issue, 'were subjected to the most severe standard machine test held post-war'.

It could have backfired, had any of the three bikes failed, but Edward Turner, his engineering team and publicity men were confident that the job could be done – and were proved right, with the test being entirely successful. The three bikes covered 500 miles (800km) each, at an average lap speed of 92.23mph (148.40kmph), 92.48mph (148.8kmph) and 92.33mph (148.56kmph). Even taking into consideration stops for refuelling, rider changes and, in one instance, replacing a fuel tank, their averages for the whole 500 miles were 90.30mph (145.29kmph), 90.93mph (146.30kmph) and 86.07mph (138.48kmph). Then, in a fitting climax to the proceedings, the bikes set off to do one last high-speed flying lap at 100.71mph (162.04kmph), 100.71mph and 101.78mph (163.76kmph). A truly fantastic achievement.

The riders were all members of Triumph's own staff: J.L. (Len) Bayliss, S.B. (Bob) Manns and Alex Scobie, plus works trials stars P.H. (Phil) Alves and Allan Jefferies (the latter also a well-known main dealer from Shipley, Yorkshire). In addition the organization had been left to H.G. Tyrell Smith and Ernie Nott, whilst the famous sidecar driver Harold Taylor was in attendance on behalf of the Auto Cycle Union as official observer.

The exercise had actually begun a couple of days prior to the test session, when the trio of machines, equipped with panniers, had left the Meriden works, near Coventry. With no motorways at the time, they proceeded to ride through London en route to Folkestone where they took the ferry crossing to France, then travelled south to Paris, and so to Montlhéry. On arrival the bikes were stripped of their panniers, given a preliminary gallop around the circuit, checked over, and then took part in the test itself. As *The Motor Cycle* report said:

> For the purposes of the test, several slight departures from production standard were made. For example, out of consideration for the safety of the riders (and on Dunlop's advice), racing tyres were fitted. So that the riders could adopt the racing crouch comfortably, racing-type tank pads, small Trophy-style saddles and fixed rearward footrests were used. Because of the position of the offside footrest, it was not, unfortunately, possible to use the kick-starter, so push starts were employed.

Also for the duration of the test, KLG racing plugs were fitted, and the standard 190 main jets were replaced with 210 items on the Amal Type 76 carburettors; and because the horn bracket on one of the bikes had fractured in practice, the horns were removed from all three machines. Extra strong clutch springs and 25-tooth engine sprockets were fitted (as compared to 24-tooth on home-market machines). The compression ratios were 7:1 (standard), whilst the fuel was the then low 72-octane (pool) quality.

The Montlhéry track was constructed in the early 1920s, and the surface was of concrete, not tarmac. It measured 1.583 miles (2.547km) to a lap, with steeply banked curves at each end. George Wilson of *The Motor Cycle*, who tested one of the machines around Montlhéry briefly at the conclusion of the test, described it thus:

> The track has immense width, so much so that when you take a machine round for the first time you hardly know where to point it! Because of the bump at the bottom, circling the track at speed is a job that is arduous in the extreme for both rider and machine.

I would concur with this, having visited Montlhéry myself: the track surface alone is quite a challenge, and its severity is much increased by the banking, which increases in steepness the higher you go. The total height is probably well over 100ft (30m).

Test Day

On the morning of the test, the French sky was grey and loaded with cloud, but there were still a few breaks that occasionally revealed patches of blue sky. My friend, the late Len Bayliss – himself a racer of no mean repute, and later, in the 1960s and 1970s, a dealer in Coventry – shared many of his memories with me; sadly he died some years ago. He recalled what a 'tremendous experience' it all was, as the trio of machines 'circled hour after hour with the clock-like precision of a military operation'. Each rider was kitted out in white overalls over racing leathers and wore a white crash helmet, except for Allan Jefferies. This added an air of professionalism.

It was during one of Len's stints on the No. 3 bike (each carried racing-type numbers on their headlamps) when the tank problem occurred – it had split. As the day wore on, *The Motor Cycle* reported: 'The sun rose higher and higher above the clouds. The day became unbearably hot – and still the machines carried on. Stops for refuelling and changes of driver came and went. If the machines were being overworked, they showed no sign of it.' In fact the only other problem they encountered was a loose chainguard when Jefferies was riding. At the end of the three bikes' 500 miles *The Motor Cycle* had this to say:

> There was negligible external oil on the engines. Exhaust pipes, in fact, were only slightly discoloured near the port. Lights were still working on two of the machines, but had ceased to do so on the third; on that one also the ammeter needle had come away from its pivot. Rear chains were badly stretched; but primary chains and tappets required no adjustment whatever.

When the three bikes had been checked over and the rear chains adjusted, each did a flying lap flat out, at the speeds quoted earlier; the riders for this task were Bayliss, Manns and Scobie. When George Wilson got his chance to ride one of the bikes on the completion of the proceedings he was decidedly enthusiastic about the new model, commenting:

> On the second circuit I was clocking 100mph [160kmph] on the straight past the pits, and the engine felt to be working no harder at 100mph than my own Speed Twin engine is at 75–80mph [120–130kmph]. Acceleration is far and away superior to that of my five-hundred, and is definitely of the racer variety.

Technical Features

But what of the new Thunderbird's technical features, and how did it differ from the long-established five-hundred twins, the Speed Twin and the Tiger 100? Bore and stroke were 71 × 82mm, against 63 × 80mm of the smaller unit, giving 649cc. Factory graphs revealed that the Thunderbird engine developed the same power at 4,000rpm as the Speed Twin did at 6,000rpm. At 6,000rpm, the six-fifty engine produced 34bhp – 7bhp more than the Speed Twin at similar engine speed. But the biggest advantage was not to be found in the sheer horsepower at high engine revolutions: instead, it was that the largest twin had a flat torque curve, and superior low-down pulling power. This was also why the pre-unit six-fifty

The new 650 Thunderbird making its public debut at the London Earls Court Show in November 1949.

1950 6T Thunderbird

Engine:	Air-cooled ohv vertical twin; cast-iron head and barrel; 360-degree three-piece crankshaft; vertically split crankcases; separate engine and gearbox
Bore:	71mm
Stroke:	82mm
Displacement:	649cc
Compression ratio:	7:1 (optional 8.5:1)
Lubrication:	Double plunger pump, dry sump
Ignition:	Magneto
Carburettor:	Amal Type 276 1in, 170 main jet
Primary drive:	Chain
Final drive:	Chain
Gearbox:	Four-speed
Frame:	All-steel tubular construction; single front down-tube; duplex lower rails
Front suspension:	Telescopic, oil-damped
Rear suspension:	Rigid or optional (extra cost) Triumph Sprung Hub
Front brake:	7in drum, SLS
Rear brake:	7in (rigid) or 8in (Sprung Hub) drum, SLS
Tyres:	Front 3.25 × 19; rear 3.50 × 19

General specifications

Wheelbase:	55in (1,400mm)
Ground clearance:	6in (152mm)
Seat height:	31.5in (800mm)
Fuel-tank capacity:	4gal (18ltr)
Dry weight:	385lb (175kg)
Maximum power:	34bhp @ 6,300rpm (in road trim, with 7:1 comp ratio)
Top speed:	102mph (164kmph)

Triumph engine was to prove so popular in sidecar racing circles for many years.

Though inertia stress was considered less likely because the given power was achieved at lower engine revolutions than the 500 engine, the 650 was given stronger connecting rods. These were light-alloy, H-section stampings in hiduminium RR56, and were almost identical in design with the rods found in the Grand Prix engine (*see* Chapter 3). The lower half of the big-end eye was a white-metal-lined steel forging, and the assembly was held together by a pair of 100-ton tensile strength nickel-chrome big-end bolts. In journal diameter and proportion the crankshaft was of identical dimensions to those of the five-hundreds, but with the throw of the crank increased by 1mm to give the 82mm stroke. The material used in the crankshafts was manganese-molybdenum, with a tensile strength of 55 tons.

The layout and design of the cylinder head and barrel assemblies followed that of the Speed Twin, and both the head and barrel were of special cast iron. The valves were of different material: austenitic G2 for the exhausts, and silicon-chrome steel for the inlets. When asked why he had used different materials, Edward Turner replied:

> Well, of course, each has an entirely different job to do. The exhaust valve works at cherry-red heat and calls for the use of an austenitic steel that contains very much less ferrous metal. In brief, the requirement for the exhaust valve is a metal that retains its tensile strength at elevated temperatures.

There is no doubt that a larger carburettor or twin carburettors could have been specified for the original Thunderbird when it was launched in late 1949. Instead, a 1in (25mm) Type 76 Amal (similar to that on the Tiger 100) was fitted. The induction manifold in the head conformed to Speed Twin practice, except that it had longer-bore passages. Edward Turner went to considerable pains to point out that a larger carb gave increased top-end power, but that 'this is not only unnecessary, but undesirable!' One has to remember that at this stage, Triumph's main thoughts were with the touring motorcyclist rather than the racer.

Notable differences on the 650 were the use of external oil pipes with three banjo unions at the front and rear of the cylinder barrel/head, the centre one attached to the pushrod tube,

Although not designed as a racing motorcycle, the Thunderbird engine was nonetheless widely utilized for both solo and sidecar competition, before being superseded for speed by, first, the Tiger 110, and eventually the T120 Bonneville. Even so, many Thunderbird engines were 'racerized', even after these later models had been released, many in Norton Featherbed frames.

whilst the crankshaft ran a double-lipped roller bearing on the timing side, but retained the ball race on the drive side.

At the same time all the Triumph 500s and the new 650s were given a redesigned gearbox, intended to provide easier engagement of the intermediate gears. On the 650 the clutch was given an additional plate because of the increased level of engine power/torque.

Except for the substitution of an SU carburettor in place of the Amal, the Thunderbird carried on unchanged, and without a more highly tuned version being available from the factory. This was because Edward Turner and his team felt that the sporting rider was adequately catered for by the Tiger 100 five-hundred.

The Sports 650: Tiger 110

However, in October 1953 a sports version of the 650 twin made its bow at the Paris Salon. Again, as with the Thunderbird, the Tiger 110 owed its existence largely to the demand from the export markets, America in particular. In fact, a tuned version of the 6T Thunderbird had been under test in both Europe and North America for several months before being displayed in France.

It was the first Triumph twin to be marketed with swinging-arm rear suspension. This was controlled by a pair of Girling-made units with pre-load adjustment. In addition the Triumph design team had taken the opportunity to 'clean up' by combining oil tank, battery box, air filter and toolbox into a single assembly above the gearbox. The seat was new and of the stepped twin-level type, whilst the valanced rear mudguard was supported by extensions of the rear subframe.

Although based on the Thunderbird and still employing a cast-iron cylinder head and block, the Tiger 110 engine was considerably more powerful, producing 42bhp at 6,500rpm, with full silencing. This additional output was

The original Tiger 110. Making its debut towards the end of 1953, it featured a swinging-arm frame, a large 8in air-scooped front brake, and a 117mph (188kmph) top speed. This 1954 production model has both head and barrel in cast iron.

thanks to high-compression pistons, higher lift camshafts, modified porting and a bigger carburettor (an Amal Type 289) – 1⅛in with a 200 main jet. It is worth noting that from 1955 onwards, a switch was made to the new 376 Monobloc.

The Paris Show bike featured a 7in front brake, but the production Tiger 110 had a powered 8in unit that was ribbed, and featured an aluminium brake plate and air scoops. The result was a fast and tractable motorcycle that could easily exceed 110mph (177kmph). Some examples could reach almost 120mph (190kmph) with only the substitution of a larger main jet – and that was with full silencing! With excellent fuel economy, the Tiger 110 was to become an excellent choice for Production class racing and endurance events (*see* Chapter 11).

Main Problems

The bike had two serious faults. The first concerned the handling, which was over-light and, as road testers and racers of the day discovered, could be a real problem on uneven road surfaces where the unbraced swinging arm caused high speed weaving. The other concerned the damaging effects of high frequency vibration. This was discovered in the 6T Thunderbird machines during preparation at the Montlhéry high speed test in 1949; in the more highly tuned Tiger 110 it was more troublesome, and in extreme cases, components such as tanks (both fuel and oil), brackets and exhaust components could fracture.

For normal road use the iron cylinder head was not a problem, but for continual high-speed use (racing, for example) it was a drawback, as was the weight. So at the end of 1955 a new

Tiger 110x, 1954	
Engine:	Air-cooled ohv vertical twin; cast-iron head and barrel; E3325 cams; 360-degree three-piece crankshaft; vertically split crankcases; separate engine and gearbox
Bore:	71mm
Stroke:	82mm
Displacement:	649cc
Compression ratio:	8:1
Lubrication:	Double-plunger pump, dry sump
Ignition:	Magneto
Carburettor:	Amal Type 289 1⅛in
Primary drive:	Chain
Final drive:	Chain
Gearbox:	Four-speed
Frame:	All-steel tubular construction; single front down-tube; duplex lower rails
Front suspension:	Telescopic, oil-damped
Rear suspension:	Swinging arm, twin shocks
Front brake:	8in cast-iron drum with alloy air-scooped brake plate, SLS operation, single sided
Rear brake:	7in integral drum, SLS operation
Tyres:	Front 3.25 × 19; rear 3.50 × 19
General specifications	
Wheelbase:	55.75in (1,416mm)
Ground clearance:	5in (127mm)
Seat height:	30.5in (775mm)
Fuel-tank capacity:	4gal (18ltr)
Dry weight:	395lb (180kg)
Maximum power:	42bhp @ 6,500rpm
Top speed:	117mph (188kmph)

light alloy cylinder head of entirely new design was introduced for the 1956 model year. This new cylinder head was known as the Delta type. It was designed to dispense with the external oil drain pipes that were a feature of the 650 from the first Thunderbird models. Instead, as with the latest five-hundred Triumphs, the oil drained directly into the pushrod tubes and then ran from the crankcase to the underside of the cylinder head, not the rocker boxes. The new Delta head was die-cast with cast-in austenitic valve seats and redesigned rocker boxes; its use allowed the compression ratio of the Tiger 110 to be raised to 8.5:1 (from 8:1).

Another reason for the introduction of the new alloy head was the overheating experienced by T110 owners. For example, it was a reported fact that on long, fast runs the engine oil actually *boiled*, causing the iron head to distort, leading to a myriad of oil leaks, blown head gaskets and, of course, an instant loss of power. Another problem on the Tiger 110 and other Triumph twins of the period was loss of rocker caps, causing oil loss and poor carburation. Also the heads were still eight-stud on the early 650 twins, and were prone to cracking between the valve seat edge and the studs; these cracks often caused no trouble, but the tendency continued until nine, and ultimately ten studs were used on later Triumph twins.

All the above faults meant that in the first years of the Thruxton Nine Hours, and later 500 Mile Endurance Race, the Tiger 110 was not able to maintain its performance over the full distance of such events. Instead, the BSA Gold Star proved the winning bike. (A full catalogue of the Tiger 110's experiences, results and retirements in the Thruxton marathon is recorded in Chapter 11.)

Important Changes for 1956

Besides the introduction of the Delta alloy head for the T110 for the 1956 model – which helped cure the overheating if not the cracking – all the twins (both 650s and 500s) had a couple of important changes. The first concerned the introduction of shell-type big-end bearings in place of the previous white-metal variety. These were supplied by Vandervell and were of the babbit metal, steel-backed, thin-wall type. Connecting rods with larger big-end eyes were needed to accommodate the new shells; the new rods were heavier, thus requiring an

The Thruxton endurance race (then called the 9 Hours) was first held in 1955. This photograph, of Triumph T110 rider Percy Tait, was taken at the event the following year, in 1956. This machine has a single carb, alloy head.

adjustment of balance weights to retain the necessary balance factor.

In the gearbox, for all twins, the layshaft bushes, previously bronze, were now in sintered bronze to assist lubrication. At the same time the composition of the clutch shock-absorber rubber was changed and the clutch plates modified, the driven plates now being solid instead of pierced, and the drive plates featuring bonded-on Neolangite segments.

An attempt was also made to rectify suspension failings. A modified hydraulic bump stop in the front forks was intended to prevent bottoming under heavy braking. At the rear, the Girling shock absorbers were equipped with 100lb rate springs. The frame's headstock had the top ball race changed to the type already employed on the bottom race, and the lock stops became adjustable. But the over-weak swinging arm and its wear-prone bushes were not attended to – these bushes needed frequent greasing or they would seize, being difficult to remove!

Changes for the 1957 Season

The most visible change to the entire Triumph range for the 1957 season was the introduction of the now famous 'mouth organ' tank badge. However, from a racing viewpoint the introduction of the twin-carb option on the five-hundred Tiger 100 that year was far more important, as it prompted a demand – again from American customers – for a twin-carburettor Tiger 110. Eventually this led to Triumph's most famous model, the Bonneville, a couple of years later.

Otherwise there was a further series of detail changes that not only gave the models more showroom appearance, but, more importantly, attempted to rectify some of the Triumph's failings, in particular of the Tiger 110. The front brake (still 8in) was modified, and the spokes became straight and butted; the rear wheel spokes (a former weak point) were increased in size. From engine number 08563 the rear suspension units were uprated with 110lb springs; and in an effort to curb the dreaded rear-end weave, the former rubber-bushed eye-bushes were switched from rubber to a rubber-bonded metallic type. The silencer support stays (another fracture-prone component) were increased in strength, whilst the fuel tank was modified to reduce stress.

In the Tiger 110 and the TR6 engines, the oil drainage from the valve pockets in the cylinder head was improved, and the compression, on home-market models, was reduced from 8.5:1 to 8:1.

To reduce oil leakage from the gearbox, new sleeve gears with bushes to suit were fitted, with the mainshaft high-gear bush extended through the primary chaincase oil-retainer plate into the chaincase itself to divert the oil into there, with the chaincase's oil-retainer disc plate of larger bore to suit. Unfortunately, these measures were still not fully successful.

The vane-type clutch shock absorber was modified once more, now featuring a new mix of rubber.

1958: Success at Last

In 1958 it was very much a case of success at last, when Dan Shorey and a youthful Mike Hailwood scored a famous victory in the Thruxton 500 Miler (*see* Chapter 11), proving that finally Triumph's six-fifty sportster was reliable as well as fast. For example, the problem with the cracking head was addressed by redesigning the cylinder head: the valve sizes were decreased, thus providing more metal between the valve seats and the holding down studs, and the pistons were reshaped to match. This had the effect of slightly restricting performance.

Then there was the 'slickshift' gearbox – in the author's opinion a sales gimmick – which many owners simply disconnected! A more useful innovation aimed at countering the continuing problem of oil leaks from the aforementioned gearbox was a sealing rubber sleeve fitted between the boss of the kick-start lever and the gearbox end cover. Within the engine itself, all the pre-unit engines now embodied a garter-type seal in the drive-side crankcase half – improving breathing and preventing oil transfer between the case and the primary chaincase.

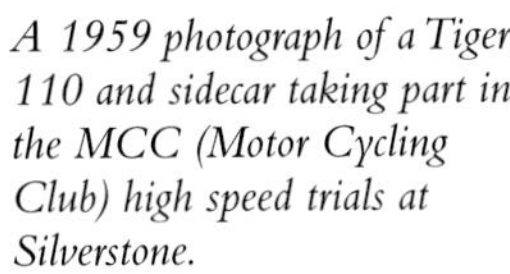

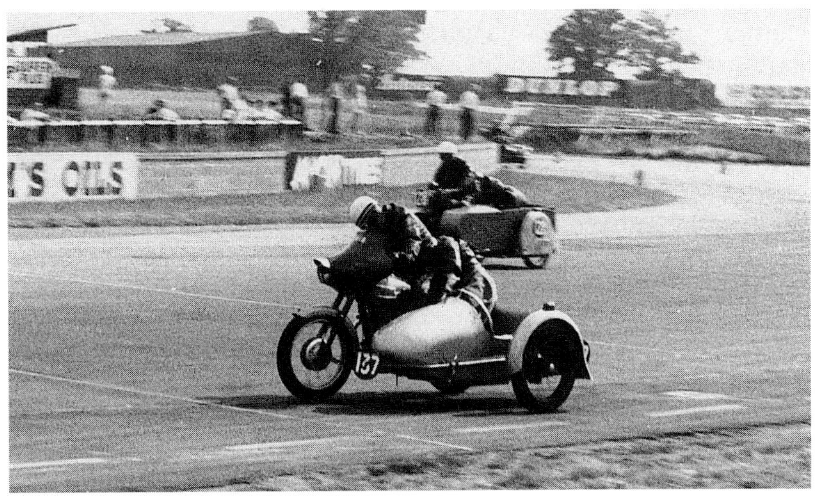

A 1959 photograph of a Tiger 110 and sidecar taking part in the MCC (Motor Cycling Club) high speed trials at Silverstone.

Although only listed as a kit, it was possible to buy a twin-carburettor head and carbs for the Tiger 110. In fact, the Shorey-Hailwood machine was so equipped.

Another introduction for the 1958 model year was a full-width 8in front brake drum (shared with the Tiger 100) similar to the smaller 7in hub fitted a year earlier on the Speed Twin.

The front forks on all pre-unit twins, save the TR5 and TR6 Trophy models, now featured new sliding members with more substantial brazed-on lugs to support a more deeply valanced front mudguard, thereby dispensing with front stays.

The Tiger 110's exhaust was also modified with a slight bend to achieve an upward tilt to the silencers.

It was now obvious to Edward Turner that his design, which had begun with the 500 Speed Twin over twenty years before, was being pushed to the limit by ever greater power demands; and it was equally obvious that the call for a twin-carb six-fifty from the all-important American market could not be ignored any longer. Turner was against this move, and felt that what was really needed was to redesign the six-fifty to become a stronger motorcycle, and at the same time, incorporate unit construction. He had done this with the smaller 350 and 500cc models, making a start with the Twenty One series three-fifty twin, introduced for the 1958 season. The bigger design was to take another four years, and involved Turner, Doug Hele and Bert Hopwood; but in the interim came the pre-unit T120 Bonneville, the story of which is told in Chapter 7.

With the new Bonneville, the Tiger 110, along with the Thunderbird, was relegated almost exclusively to the public highway rather than the race circuit.

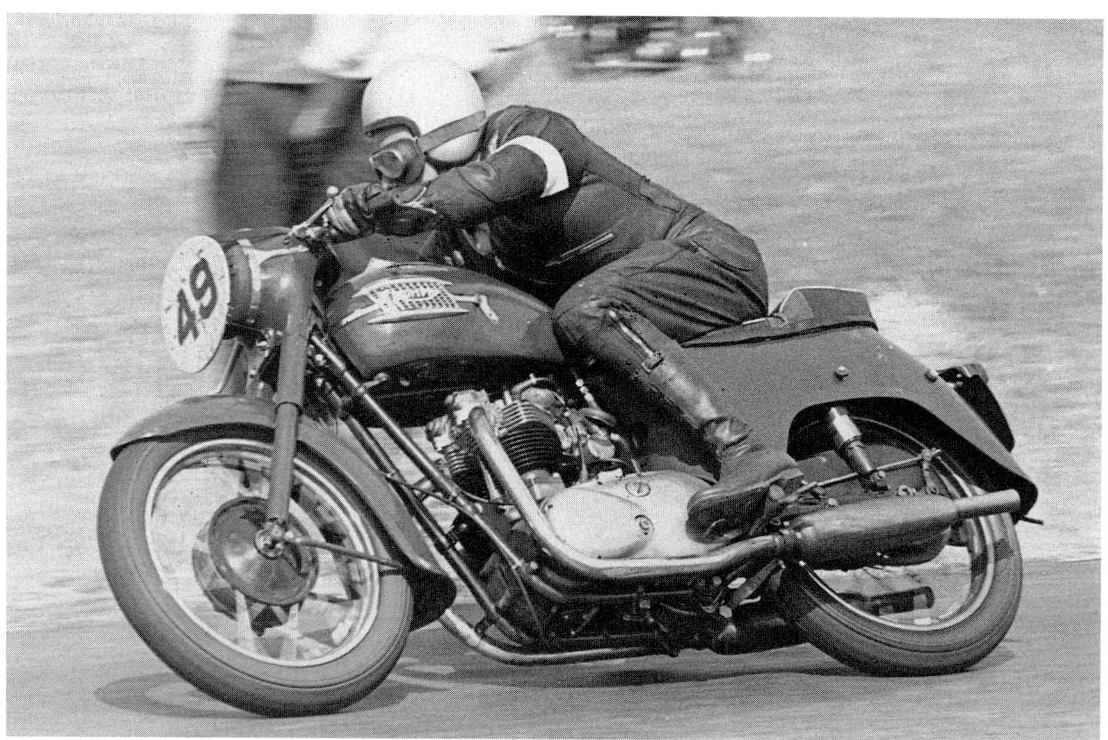

Dennis Peacock with his 1961 'Bathtub' Tiger 110 during the 1962 Thruxton 500-Mile race, in June of that year.

6 Singles

The early history of Triumph racing was very much about single-cylinder machines. To many people, the 'modern' Triumphs mean the twins and the triples, but in the period immediately before the outbreak of World War II and in the early post-war period, many competitors used single-cylinder Triumphs – plus, of course, the well-known Formula Cub racing class of the 1960s.

Turner's Influence

It is evident throughout this book that one man stands above all others in any history of Triumph racing: Edward Turner. As recounted in Chapter 3, Turner had been discovered by Charles Sangster, head of the Ariel factory. Later, Turner joined Triumph under Charles' son Jack Y. Sangster, who had purchased the motorcycle side of Triumph in the mid-1930s, when the company had hit the financial rocks after over-extending itself on its four-wheel side. Following this, the bike and car arms were entirely separate.

To oversee his new purchase, Jack Y. Sangster chose Edward Turner. Triumph's existing chief designer Val Page then left to join BSA (and subsequently Ariel). Turner was a designer who invariably produced what was wanted; in particular he appreciated the importance of power-to-weight ratio, and kept the weight down right from the drawing-board stage. If anything broke on test it was strengthened, otherwise it remained as it was, and this ensured light machines with decent performance.

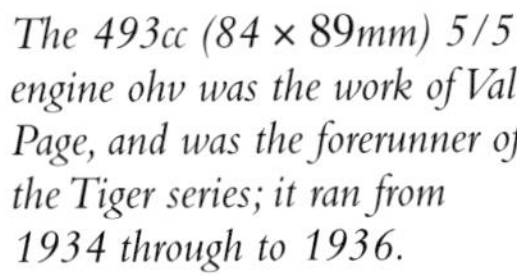

The 493cc (84 × 89mm) 5/5 engine ohv was the work of Val Page, and was the forerunner of the Tiger series; it ran from 1934 through to 1936.

Turner was someone who got things going quickly. He was a tough man to work with, but this was partly because he did not waste time, a characteristic he demonstrated right from the beginning. Thus Jack Y. Sangster purchased Triumph early in 1936, and Turner took charge shortly thereafter – and what he did was both simple and effective. Essentially, he took the existing overhead-valve singles that had been created by Val Page, and equipped them with tuned engines and additional brightwork such as chromed tank panels, together with metallic silver paintwork for the remaining body parts. They were called the Tigers 70, 80 and 90: the

ABOVE: The 1937 Tiger 80 three-fifty: based around the Page design, it was 'updated' by Edward Turner, his first task after joining Triumph.

A restored 1937 Tiger 80 Sport, with low-level exhaust.

two-fifty (249cc – 63 × 80mm) was the Tiger 70 which put out 16bhp at 5,800rpm and could achieve a guaranteed 70mph (112kmph) – hence the '70' tag. Likewise the Tiger 80 (343cc – 70 × 89mm) put out 20bhp at 5,700rpm, and the five-hundred Tiger 90 (493cc – 84 × 89mm) put out 28bhp at 5,800rpm.

The new models were introduced in the early summer of 1936, well before the traditional autumn unveiling of the next year's model range. From 1937 there were some major changes with new frames, forks and gearboxes, and from January of this year the range of Tigers was extended to include special competition versions. These bikes were intended largely for trials use, so the fittings were altered to suit, as were the gearbox ratios and state of engine tune. The Turner touch worked wonders, and before long, enthusiastic sporting-minded riders turned to the Tiger singles in droves, making the series one of the most popular of the immediate pre-war British motorcycles.

In March 1937 Triumph gained the prestigious Maudes Trophy for a one-off Standard Production Test carried out at Donington Park, near Derby. Three Tigers – a 250cc, a 350cc and a 500cc – were chosen from the stocks of various agents. The machines were despatched to Donington, briefly run in, and then put through their paces, which included a three-hour high-speed test. The five-hundred Tiger 90 covered eighty-four laps at an average speed of 54.4mph (87.5kmph); the three-fifty Tiger 80 completed eighty-nine laps, averaging 57.4mph (92.3kmph); and finally the two-fifty Tiger 70 reeled off seventy-nine laps at an average of 50.72mph (81.6kmph). In addition, maximum speed tests were undertaken at the famous Brooklands circuit near Weybridge, Surrey. Here the Tiger 70 achieved a flying lap of 66.39mph (106.82kmph), the Tiger 80 reached 74.68mph (120.16kmph), and the Tiger 90, 82.31mph (132.44kmph).

Although intended largely by the factory to be a roadster or trials mount, the Tiger series also found favour in other areas of motorcycle sport, including grass-track scrambles and road racing.

1937 Tiger 80

Engine:	Air-cooled ohv single with vertical cylinder; timing gears; cast-iron head and barrel; vertically split crankcases; separate engine and gearbox, roller-bearing big-end
Bore:	70mm
Stroke:	89mm
Displacement:	343cc
Compression ratio:	7.5:1
Lubrication:	Double-plunger pump
Ignition:	Magneto
Carburettor:	Amal type 76 1in 150 main jet (160 from 1938)
Primary drive:	Chain
Final drive:	Chain
Gearbox:	Four-speed, foot change
Frame:	All-steel tubular construction; single front down-tube; duplex lower rails
Front suspension:	Girders with central spring
Rear suspension:	Rigid
Front brake:	7in drum SLS
Rear brake:	7in drum SLS
Tyres:	Front 3.00 × 19; rear 3.25 × 19
General specifications	
Wheelbase:	52.5in (1,333mm)
Ground clearance:	6in (152mm)
Seat height:	28.5in (724mm)
Fuel-tank capacity:	3.25gal (14.8ltr)
Dry weight:	320lb (145kg)
Maximum power:	20bhp @ 5,700rpm in road trim, with silencer
Top speed:	80mph (130kmph) in road trim

War Intervenes

Then came World War II. Edward Turner designed the purpose-built 3TW, a lightweight ohv with a unit construction 350 twin-cylinder ohv engine. But just as production was speeding up after a massive War Department contract had been won, the company suffered a major setback: on the night of 14 November

1940, some four hundred German bombers raided Coventry, with the city centre as their target. By the next morning much of the area had been reduced to a smoking ruin, including Triumph's Prior Street works, located in the centre, right next to the cathedral. At that time the factory was usually active both day and night, but the night shift had taken to the shelters when the air-raid sirens had sounded, so not one life was lost. In the rest of Coventry it was a different story: 554 people had been killed, and many more were seriously injured. Seventy-five per cent of the city's industry had been either destroyed or severely damaged, as had over 46,000 houses. There was no water, gas or electricity.

As for Triumph, they had no factory, tools or machine stock, and that meant the end for Turner's 3TW three-fifty overhead-valve twin. The company found a new, temporary home at an old foundry in Warwick, some 7 miles away, and Edward Turner moved to BSA in Birmingham until mid-1943; production did not resume at the 'Cape of Good Hope' in Warwick until June 1941. But the 'Tin Tabernacle' could never be more than a short-term answer to Triumph's production needs, and so in July 1941, after government approval (needed because of the war) the directors, headed by Jack Y. Sangster, sanctioned work to begin on a brand new factory on the main A45 trunk road between Coventry and Birmingham in the village of Meriden. Today this site would be called 'green field', and that is exactly what it had been, previously only inhabited by sheep or cattle.

By March 1942 some machinery had been installed on the new site, and by the end of that year series production was under way at the Meriden works. It had also been decided that the new production facilities would concentrate upon a single model only, this being the 343cc 3HW ohv single, essentially a military version of the civilian Tiger 80.

By the end of the war in 1945 a total of 49,700 motorcycles had been built for the Forces since 1939, a truly remarkable figure when one takes into account the interruption caused by the destruction of the original factory. Although production of the Tiger 70/80/90 singles did not survive the war, many of the surviving two-fifty Tiger 70s were used in all branches of motorcycle sport in the austerity period of the late 1940s and early 1950s. The Triumph works even prepared a number of Tiger 70s for both trials and road racing, which was unusual, given that they were no longer available as a current model. On the tarmac, besides the race-kitted Tiger 70s, there were also a number of specials using the Triumph cycle parts and the 499cc ohv JAP engine.

The Surtees Tiger 70

The most famous rider to straddle one of the Tiger singles in the immediate post-war era was without doubt John Surtees. This was right at the beginning of his racing career, and the Tiger 70 was the machine upon which John, then just sixteen years of age, made his road-racing debut at Brands Hatch, Kent, in a 250cc heat on Easter Sunday, 9 April 1950. In the months leading up to this, John Surtees had campaigned the little Triumph in local grass-track events and a solitary scrambles meeting. The Brands Hatch tarmac circuit, one mile (1.6km) in length, also made its debut that same day in April 1950; previously (since pre-war days) the famous Kentish venue had been a grass track. In fact, this 250cc heat was the first race over the new circuit, and it was started by none other than the 1949 500cc world champion, Les Graham. Unlike today's Brands Hatch, the circuit then ran anti-clockwise.

John's baptism on the tarmac went exceedingly well, and the youngster finished an impressive third in the heat when conditions were dry; in the final, however, it was very damp, to say the least. Coming into the final lap John found himself on the heels of another Tiger 70 ridden by Harry Pearce (later to become head of the McLaren Formula 1 car machine shop). In sight of victory, John's inexperience nevertheless got the better of him,

A young John Surtees (just sixteen years of age) on the start line at Brands Hatch, 9 April 1950, with his two-fifty Tiger 70 (number 23). The race winner was Harry Pearce (also on a Tiger 70).

and as he says: 'I thought I could go by him, and I think I did, but the only problem was that I wasn't on my bike!'

During that spring of 1950 the young Surtees rode the Triumph – purchased as a roadster from Harold Daniels' south London dealership – at other meetings, both on tarmac and on grass. In road racing the standard nature of John's bike was exposed, with the engine's bottom end proving a definite weak point. The quicker models, ridden by the likes of Pearce and Percy Tait, sported works-developed Conway and Lilley square aluminium cylinder heads and barrels, and – though John and his father did not know it at the time – these modified engines were usually fitted with Excelsior Manxman con-rods.

In an attempt to make the Surtees Tiger 70 more competitive, John subsequently acquired one of the Conway and Lilley top ends; he also grafted on a Triumph (Turner-designed) sprung hub to the rear end of the machine to provide a degree of rear suspension. The revised machine was entered for Silverstone during the late spring of 1950, and John remembers feeling 'elated' and 'excited' that his modified Tiger 70 was at last ready for action. But sadly, it was not the dream outing he had been looking forward to: rounding the fast Abbey Curve at the Northamptonshire circuit, the con-rod (still a standard production component) broke, locking the engine and throwing the future world champion 'down the road'.

That was to be the end of John Surtees' Triumph racing career: after the Tiger 70 came a Vincent Grey Flash, followed by a succession of machinery including Bob Geeson's REG twin, an NSU Sportsmax, his own private Manx Nortons and finally works Nortons, MV Agustas, and even a single outing on a factory BMW in the 1955 German GP.

As the 1950s unfolded and more competitive machinery became available, the pre-war Tiger singles were soon replaced by the new breed of faster mounts; but as one section of the Triumph single-cylinder racing story came to an end, another was about to begin.

The T15 Terrier

At the beginning of November 1952 a brand new Triumph single was announced just in time

The T15 Terrier and the original T20 Tiger Cub had a plunger frame and also a one-piece crankcase.

for the London Earls Court Show later that month: the T15 Terrier, a 149.3cc (57 × 58.5mm) overhead valve single, with its cylinder inclined forward by some 25 degrees from vertical. It was the first post-war Triumph with unit construction of the engine and gearbox assemblies, and thus pre-dated by several years the twin-cylinder models that eventually followed this route. When it was launched, Edward Turner was asked why he had opted for 150cc, and he had this to say:

> I did so because world economic conditions today are such that the present high rate of production of expensive motorcycles cannot be maintained. And because a modern 150cc ohv engine will provide ample power to propel a rider and pillion passenger at cruising speeds in the region of 45–50mph [65–80kmph] and to reach a 60mph [100kmph] maximum. It is a four-stroke, because the aim is to provide the maximum power output for a given capacity. Further, it was felt that the cost of overhead valves, timing gear and a proper dry-sump lubrication system, in proportion to the cost of the machine as a whole, was well worthwhile; moreover, a well designed four-stroke, because of its positive carburation and automatic ignition advance and retard, provides certain starting. Also a four-stroke is more easily silenced than its two-stroke counterpart.

He could also have said that the other choices – using a bought-in Villiers two-stroke power unit, or designing and building a two-stroke engine from scratch – were never seriously considered.

Edward Turner was enthusiastic about the new model, and had every confidence in it – as is evidenced by his scheme for a trio of new models to be ridden from Land's End to John O'Groats, under official observation, plus some extra miles to bring the total to 1,000 miles (1,600km). The intention was to try to better averages of 30mph (50kmph) and 100mpg (35km per litre). The choice of riders was also quite clever: Edward Turner himself, service manager Alex Masters and works director Bob Fearon – Turner's idea, to prove that motorcycle industry executives were also riders!

The run was an undoubted success. The target speeds were easily exceeded, with figures of 36.68mph (59kmph) and 108.6mpg (38.8kmph), and all three machines and riders had a largely trouble-free journey.

Technical Details

The cylinder barrel of the Terrier was of cast iron, whilst the cylinder head, with its integral rocker boxes, was a die-casting in light alloy. The valves were operated by pushrods enclosed in a separate chromed steel external tube on the offside (right) of the engine. Rockers were of orthodox design, with simple screw and lockout adjustment, and coil valve springs were specified. The valve gear was positively lubricated from the scavenge side of the gear-type oil pump. An aid to cooling around the exhaust valve and port was the exhaust rocker box, which was horizontally finned right up to the inspection-plate joint face.

On the Terrier and early versions of its larger brother the Cub, the crankcase and gearbox shells were formed as a single casting. This was unusual, as other British machines normally had their crankcases in two pieces, split along a centre line. There were plain bearings for both the big end and the timing side main, with a ball race on the other side. Each piston was a three-ring affair, whilst the small end was a phospher-bronze bush. Transmission comprised a four-speed gear cluster, simplex primary chain and a three-plate wet clutch. There was also coil ignition, plunger rear suspension and telescopic front forks.

Contemporary advertising promoted the newcomer as 'A real Triumph – in Miniature!' – and really, that is exactly what it was. The styling was clearly taken from the twins, complete with headlamp nacelle, tank badges and clean handlebar line, and the finish was

1953 T15 Terrier

Engine:	Air-cooled ohv single with vertical cylinder; timing gears, plain big-end and timing side main, ball-race primary side, alloy head, cast-iron barrel; inner and outer coil valve springs, one-piece crankcase, unit construction
Bore:	57mm
Stroke:	58.5mm
Displacement:	149.3cc
Compression ratio:	7:1
Lubrication:	Double-plunger pump, dry sump
Ignition:	Coil with distributor at rear of cylinder barrel
Carburettor:	Amal type 33 2¾in, 120 main jet
Primary drive:	Chain
Final drive:	Chain
Gearbox:	Four-speed
Frame:	All-steel welded tubular construction; single front down-tube
Front suspension:	Telescopic forks
Rear suspension:	Plunger
Front brake:	5.5in drum, SLS
Rear brake:	5.5in (rigid) or 8in (sprung hub) drum, SLS
Tyres:	2.75 x 19 front and rear

General specifications

Wheelbase:	49in (1,245mm)
Ground clearance:	5in (127mm)
Seat height:	28.2in (716mm)
Fuel-tank capacity:	2.62gal (11.9ltr)
Dry weight:	175lb (79.4kg) (185lb/84kg from 1955)
Maximum power:	8.3bhp @ 6,500rpm
Top speed:	64mph (103kmph)

Triumph's amaranth red. As one journalist said, 'Truly, another Triumph baby!'

The 150cc engine size was almost as if Turner did not want the new Terrier to take part in competition events, with the defined classes being 125, 250, 350 and 500cc at the time. Soon, however, 150cc races were being held at several of the smaller British short circuit venues, including Alton Towers (now a theme park). At that and other venues the usual competition was either tuned BSA Bantams or various Villiers-powered specials. The tiny Triumph provided spectators with a welcome variety in noise, at least, from the 'ring-ting' two-strokes. In standard guise the Terrier put out 8.3bhp at 6,500rpm, but when tuned for racing could be considerably improved upon, particularly if dope instead of petrol were allowed, the former allowing a much higher compression ratio.

The Tiger Cub

A year later, in November 1953, the Terrier gained a bigger brother: the Tiger Cub. This model was destined to become a far more popular motorcycle that the Terrier, and to outlive it by a dozen years. It was based very closely upon the smaller-engined bike, but the bore and stroke dimensions were increased to 63 × 64mm, giving a displacement of 199.5cc. The compression ratio remained at 7:1 and the cam timing was not altered, but the power rose to 10bhp at 6,000rpm. Technical changes between the initial Cub and the Terrier were minimal: the Cub had the gearing raised by an additional tooth on the gearbox sprocket, and was fitted with wider section tyres and a different carb – and that was about it. Cosmetically it was finished in a pale shell-blue sheen for the tank and mudguards, with the other parts in black.

Although the Terrier was discontinued in mid-1956, the Tiger Cub (coded T20) survived until the late 1960s, and during its relatively long life it was produced in a wide range of variants. Certain improvements were also introduced over the years, the most important of which are listed below:

1957 Swinging-arm frame, damped front forks, also T20C (Competition) introduced.

1958 Duplex primary chain, deeper chaincase, cast-iron clutch drum, T20C front fork gaiters.

1959 T20C new cylinder barrel, deeper finning, double gearbox seal.

1960 New two-piece crankcases (from engine number 57617), vertically split on centre line. T20 17in wheels, modified cylinder head, larger inlet valve, modified gearing. T20S (Sport) new model – combination of T20 and T20C, with energy transfer ignition, direct lighting, small headlamp and heavy-duty forks (from 350cc twin).

1961 New oil pump, oil feed to skew gears. T20T, a new model purpose-built for trials. Also T20 S/L, much as the outgoing T20S, but with close-ratio gearbox, higher compression piston, hi-lift cam and Amal 376 15/16in Monobloc carburettor; optional rev counter.

Improved oil pump with cast-iron body, T20 S/S and T20 S/H models introduced. The S/H featured a two-piece crankpin, ball-race timing main bearing, pressed-in timing mainshaft, skew and timing separate, increased oil flow, coil ignition. TR20, new trials model with T20 S/H engine changes, plus low-compression piston, energy-transfer ignition, wide-ratio gears. TS20 new scrambles model incorporating T20 S/H engine (including close-ratio gears) but with energy-transfer ignition.

1963 All models contact breakers now in timing cover, clutch-cable access hole in cover, finned rocker-box covers.

1964 All models solid crankpin, aluminium-bronze skew gear for oil-pump drive, reshaped clutch shock-absorber rubbers.

1965 T20 S/H and TR20, new fork sliders.

1966 T20 S/H and TR20, sliding-block oil pump, roller big-end bearing. T20 BSA Bantam cycle parts including frame and front forks (Bantam Cub).

1967 T20 S/C (Super Cub), as 1966 T20 but with full-width brake hubs.

1968 T20 S/C, no changes, production phased out late in year.

1962 Tiger Cub S/H

Engine:	Air-cooled ohv single with vertical cylinder; timing gears, plain big-end, ball timing and primary-side mains, alloy head, cast-iron barrel; coil valve springs, vertically split crankcase, unit construction
Bore:	63mm
Stroke:	64mm
Displacement:	199.5cc
Compression ratio:	9:1
Lubrication:	Double-plunger pump
Ignition:	Coil with distributor at rear of cylinder barrel*
Carburettor:	Amal type 376 15/16in, 140 main jet
Primary drive:	Chain
Final drive:	Chain
Gearbox:	Four-speed
Frame:	All-steel welded tubular construction; single front down-tube;
Front suspension:	Telescopic forks from 350 unit-twin, oil damped with gaiters
Rear suspension:	Swinging arm, twin shock
Front brake:	5.5in drum, SLS
Rear brake:	5.5in drum, SLS
Tyres:	Front 3.00 × 19; rear 3.50 × 18
General specifications	
Wheelbase:	49in (1,245mm)
Ground clearance:	6in (152mm)
Seat height:	30in (762mm)
Fuel-tank capacity:	3gal (13.6ltr)
Dry weight:	230lb (104kg)
Maximum power:	14.5bhp @ 6,500rpm
Top speed:	76mph (122kmph)

*From 1963 model year points in timing case

A Dual-Purpose Bike

Right from the start the Terrier, and even more so the Cub, were popular machines, not just as the clubman's road racer for the lightweight class, but also for off-road sporting events, particularly trials and scrambles. The first of these dirt-bike efforts was when Triumph's 'number one' trials star, Jim Alves, built himself a one-off Terrier feet-up bike. Alves found he actually enjoyed riding it, the little model being 'so much easier to handle than the big twins'. This was really the point where the trend to lightweight trials bikes began. When the Cub came along, Jim Alves transferred to it at once, as the more powerful engine was a decided asset. Similarly in scrambles, the Cub found favour with the likes of works stars Johnny Giles and Roy Peplow; there were even Cub sidecar trials outfits, one being campaigned by road-race star Arthur Wheeler. In 1959 a Cub ridden by Roy Peplow was victorious in the legendary Scottish Six-Day Trial. Other well known off-road Cub riders included Artie Ratcliffe, Roy Sayer, and later Gordon Farley.

Ulsterman Paddy Hoey with his 199cc Tiger Cub race, ca. 1969. Northern Ireland and Scotland were the last bastions of the once-popular 200cc racing class in the British Isles.

As far as the tarmac was concerned the Tiger Cub usually played a supporting role, rather than a starring one. This was mainly due to the fact that it was giving away cubic capacity when raced in the 250cc class, with the larger possible boring exercise giving around 230cc. However, this did not stop many from competing, particularly during the late 1950s and early 1960s, before the era of affordable over-the-counter 250cc racers such as the Greeves

Silverstone and Cotton Telstar that began in 1963. Before that, the British scene comprised either ultra-expensive works machines from the likes of NSU, MV Agusta and Moto Guzzi, or home-brewed specials using a variety of engines, many of which were of pre-war origin such as Excelsior or Rudge.

It was in the 200cc class that the Cub really made an impression. Several riders, including Percy Tait and Fron Purslow, were capable of getting their Cubs on the leader board even at the major circuits. However, as time went by, the 200cc class was dropped from the southern circuits such as Brands Hatch, Crystal Palace and Thruxton, and by the early 1960s had retreated to the lesser circuits, plus Scotland and Ireland. Although perhaps lacking the glamour that the full 250s provided, the 200s did have the advantage of lower costs for the riders.

The Formula Cub

During the mid-1960s, following the big success of the Bantam one-model race series, staged at club events by the BRC (Bantam Racing Club), another model series was launched, the Formula Cub. Organized by the BFRC (British Formula Racing Club), it was very much intended as a cheap way of going racing, and races were staged at Snetterton, Cadwell Park and Lydden Hill. The Cub formula made certain restrictions, these being essentially as follows:

- Engine capacity limited at 200cc
- Engine tuning allowed
- Four speeds
- Standard Cub (or Sports Cub) frame, swinging-arm, wheels
- Steel wheel rims
- Any make of spark plug, tyres or rear suspension units
- Dolphin race fairing allowed
- Non-standard tank, seat and mudguards allowed
- Pump fuel
- Rev counter
- Open exhaust

Although never as popular as the Bantam series, Formula Cub races were nonetheless hotly contested and produced some close racing. I competed in the series during 1968, and my particular bike, on which I won several races in the second half of that year, was essentially a Sports Cub fitted with a two-piece crankcase engine with the distributor to the rear of the

The Walker Cub raced to victory by the author at several circuits, including Snetterton, Cadwell Park and Lydden Hill in Formula Cub races during 1968.

ABOVE: A Cub competitor at Laconia, summer 1958. The Triumph unit singles were widely used in AMA events in the United States during the late 1950s and early 1960s.

From 1963 the Cub engine had the points in the timing cover, rather than in the distributor at the rear of the cylinder barrel, as on earlier engines.

Mark Wake with his 199cc Cub special (1966), waiting to go out on the Regularity Parade, Donington Park, 27 July 1986.

cylinder barrel. It was extremely reliable – certainly it never retired from a race when being ridden by myself. All the engine parts were original Sports Cub bits, plus an Amal Monobloc carb. After having raced motorcycles such as BSA Gold Stars, an AJS 7R, a Greeves Silverstone and various two-fifty Ducatis, I found the Cub to be a brilliant little bike – easy to ride, easy to start and having (for its class) a good performance – it was capable of reaching almost 90mph (145kmph) down the old Norwich Straight at Snetterton – good brakes and superb handling, at least as good at going around corners as the pukka racers I had previously ridden.

Probably the most astonishing performance of all by a single-cylinder Triumph came in 1959, when a 200 Cub ridden by Bill Martin, a Triumph dealer in California, set a new AMA (American Motorcycle Association) two-way speed record of 139.82mph (225kmph) for 200cc motorcycles over the measured mile. Even more incredible was a one-way speed of 149.31mph (240.28kmph). As outlined in Chapter 9, Triumph had a strong representation in the USA for many years, and was certainly by far the most successful British marque across the Atlantic.

BSA Group Developments

During the era of the Terrier and the Cub, Triumph was very much a part of the giant BSA Group, and there is no doubt that the basic engine design of the Terrier/Cub series was utilized for the BSA unit-single range that began with the 249cc BSA C15 two-fifty in 1958. Not only was there a sports version (the SS80), but there were also 343cc (B40) and 440cc (Victor) versions. Later still came the B50 (499cc), and finally, after BSA, the CCM, a development of the Jeff Smith World Championship winning motocross bike. Less well known today is the fact that both the 75cc BSA Beagle and the 50cc Ariel Pixie engine units were based around the original Edward Turner Triumph power units.

In many ways the old saying 'First is best' applied to the Terrier and the Cub, since they offered exactly what the Triumph publicity machine said they did: 'easy and safe to ride, ...and sports performance at very low cost.'

7 The Pre-Unit Bonneville

The legendary Bonneville was launched at the London Earls Court Show in November 1958, and was, without doubt, the most famous of all Triumph twins. From its launch until the end of 1962, it was built in pre-unit guise; thereafter it was redesigned with the engine, gearbox and clutch assemblies housed in a common crankcase, and became known as the unit Bonneville. In this chapter we are purely concerned with the original pre-unit version.

The Bonneville evolved from various factors: the splayed head, twin-carb Tiger 100 offered for the 1957 model year; the twin-carb conversion for the Tiger 110 for 1958 (only offered as a separate kit of parts); the demand from the west and east coast American distributors for ever greater performance; and Johnny Allen's streamlined projectile that on 6 September 1956 sped across the famous Salt Flat at Bonneville, Utah, at 214mph (344kmph) (*see* Chapter 10). As John Nelson was later to recall:

> It was the introduction of the splayed head, twin-carburettor Tiger 100 that created an almost uncontrollable demand for a similar ported 650cc version from both American coasts, and especially from Rod Coates and Pete Coleman, who had been spending many hours welding up and boring out the inlet ports of the 650cc Delta (single-carb alloy) heads to make them suitable for the souped-up Thunderbirds, Tiger 110s and the new TR6s they were now tuning.

As outlined in Chapter 5, the early examples of the Delta cylinder heads had been prone to cracking between the holding down studs and valve seats, so for 1958 the combustion spheres were reduced in size; this also meant reshaped piston crowns, together with smaller diameters for both the inlet and exhaust valves. It is generally agreed that this also restricted performance to some degree, so – purely from a racing viewpoint – the older head design is thus superior.

Another vital revision, and one that was introduced in the Bonneville, was a one-piece crankshaft instead of a three-piece assembly. Up to 1958 the six-fifty Triumph twin-cylinder engine had been equipped with the crankshaft design used ever since the first Speed Twin had appeared in late 1937. This comprised two crank halves attached to each other by bolts, which passed through a central cast flywheel sandwiched between the cheeks of the aforementioned crankshaft halves. Alignment and balancing of the three components was carried out after they had been assembled. However, with ever-greater power output and torque loadings, the original three-piece design was approaching the very limit of its reliability. So, during early 1958, an extensive test programme was undertaken using a crankshaft manufactured from a single forging. This new type, intended for the 1959 range of 650cc engines, was a one-piece forging incorporating both the outer 'halves' and a ground central diameter which accepted the centrally mounted cast-iron flywheel, held in position by a trio of bolts.

John Nelson, in his 1979 book *Bonnie*, commented as follows:

> The *Experimental Instruction Sheet 419*, dated 19 March 1958, listed test-bench results of a T110 engine with splayed port head, twin type 6 (Amal Monobloc) carburettors, and E3134 camshaft at

8.5:1 pistons. A flexibly mounted float chamber had been used, and the best power of the day was 48.80bhp (corrected) on a 1¾in-diameter exhaust pipe system. The engine had been stripped for examination after the test, and passed inspection with flying colours, no fault being found. The remarks column of the instruction sheet reported cryptically that 'Mr Turner expressed satisfaction'. Under the subsequent section headed 'Further Instructions', experimental manager Frank Baker (with Triumph since 1938, and an ace engine builder of racing and record-breaking power units) was detailed to rebuild the engine and install it into the frame of the high speed T110 machine for test at the Motor Industries Research Association (MIRA) high speed test track at Lindley, near Nuneaton. Even then, no one knew that it would turn out to be the Bonnie!

After the MIRA test it was confirmed that factory tester and well-known racer Percy Tait had managed to be electronically timed on the official MIRA strip at 128mph (206kmph). An interesting question is whether the winning Tiger 110 machine ridden by Mike Hailwood and Dan Shorey in the Thruxton 500-mile race at the end of June 1958 used the then still experimental one-piece crankshaft. It certainly made use of the twin-carb splayed cylinder head.

The New Model is Launched

As my friend and fellow author Roy Bacon described in his 1981 book *Triumph Twins and Triples*:

> In August 1958 the Speed Twin and TR5 Trophy were dropped from the range to make way for a unit construction 500, and the following month the 1959 range was announced, with all the models being fitted with the new crankshaft.
>
> At the last moment a new machine was added to the list, destined to become one of the legends of motorcycling: the T120, called the Bonneville to commemorate the speed records set up on the Salt Flats. In its essentials it was the Tiger 110, with the splayed head and twin carburettors without air filters, and the 1959 version was the only one to be built with the headlamp nacelle. It had touring handlebars, and was finished in tangerine and pearl with black cycle parts. As well as the two Amals, it had a higher compression ratio, so produced 46bhp at 6,500rpm. Also from the start it had a normal clutch lift, without the Slickshift device.

There is no doubt that, with the T120 Bonneville, Edward Turner had reached what he considered were reasonable limits for a 360-degree parallel twin with no form of specialized counterbalancing. Other manufacturers (notably Royal Enfield and Norton) built bigger twins, and there were several oversize kits from specialist suppliers boosting displacement of Turner's creation to 750 and even 850cc. Even Triumph eventually produced a seven-fifty version, the T140, during the 1970s (by which time Edward Turner was no longer involved). But none of these possessed the same combination of speed, reliability and smoothness. For example, Norton resorted to their 'Isolastic' frame mounting system in an attempt to beat the vibes!

A comprehensive range of factory high-performance parts was made available for the newcomer. As with the Tiger 100 five-hundred, the Bonneville T120 was viewed as a model worthy of promoting the Triumph name if owners wished to take part in Production-type events or clubman's short circuit racing. It also offered the factory a relatively cheap way of entering 'works' bikes (usually via the dealer network) in prestigious events such as the Thruxton 500 Miler.

The special tuning bits offered for the 1959 Bonneville included racing camshafts, racing cam followers, different diameter exhaust pipes, close-ratio gears, megaphones (including the reversed-cone type), larger (1gal) capacity oil tank (rubber-mounted), racing-type handlebars, lightweight mudguards, competition number plates, and rear set foot controls (including footrests, gear lever and brake pedal).

At that time the original Grand Prix tachometer drive gearbox was still available,

Edward Turner's Contribution to Triumph

In the Turner era, as the late Ivor Davies once remarked, 'A love-hate relationship with road racing was almost official policy at the Triumph works.' This goes a long way to explaining why Triumph racing was largely based on production bikes, rather than works specials of the sort made by companies such as Norton, Gilera, MV Agusta and Honda.

Edward Turner was born in London on 24 January 1901. He was called Edward because he was born just a few hours after the death of Queen Victoria, and so was the first true Edwardian in the family of seven – he had three sisters and three brothers. His father owned a light engineering concern that manufactured a wide range of products for the tradesmen of the day. He was first head-hunted during the late 1920s by Charles Sangster, then boss of the Ariel works. At Ariel, Turner designed the legendary Square Four, and later the first of the famous Red Hunter singles. As revealed in *Ariel, The Complete Story*, he joined Ariel following publicity in the motorcycle press about the design of a 350cc overhead camshaft engine at his South London motorcycle repair business.

During the early 1930s Jack Sangster had succeeded his father and subsequently added Triumph to his portfolio, and he moved Edward Turner to his new acquisition, installing him as managing director and chief designer. In the latter role Turner's first creations for Triumph were the range of Tiger singles (the 250, 350 and 500cc), the first of which made its debut in the middle of 1936. However, as we have seen (*see* Chapter 2), it was the launch of the brand new Speed Twin a year later that was really to cement his reputation. The five-hundred twin was without doubt one of the truly great motorcycle designs of all time, and set the pattern for the next thirty years. A sports version, the Tiger 100 (*see* Chapter 4), made its debut in 1939, on the very eve of World War II.

Turner's main objection to racing was that it sponsored the development of specialized machinery that usually bore no relationship whatsoever to anything the man in the street could purchase from his local dealer, and Turner's policy can be seen clearly in virtually every subsequent involvement in racing by the Triumph marque. Even the racing-only Grand Prix (*see* Chapter 3) was still closely related to the standard-production Speed Twin and Tiger 100. Famously, he commented that 'when true production racing was introduced, Triumph would be interested'. This came later, and as can be seen in this book, was to lead the company to considerable success.

Edward Turner's great gift, apart from creative design, was an ability to manage costs: in other words, his designs for Triumph made money, and this ensured that his time as the company's boss, post-war till the mid-1960s, was Triumph's most successful period. He also had time to design the Daimler SP250 V8-engined sports car.

He visited Japan in 1960, subsequently writing a detailed report on the Japanese motorcycle industry and the threat it posed. Unfortunately, no one responded to his warning, so no creditable challenge was mounted either by the BSA Group (of which Triumph had become a part) or the remainder of the British industry, to Japan's growing dominance.

After designing the 350cc overhead camshaft, twin-cylinder Bandit roadster – listed as part of the 1971 programme, but never mass produced – Edward Turner went into retirement. He died on 15 August 1973.

The Thruxton 500 race of 1959, with Tony Godfrey piloting one of the original 'Tiger 110-type' T120 Bonnevilles produced during the first twelve months of the new model's life. Features included headlamp nacelle, deeper mudguards and a single front down-tube frame.

and could still be utilized by removing the dynamo and using its drive mechanism (from the exhaust camshaft pinion). In addition, and in conjunction with Triumph Service Department's *Technical Information Bulletin No. 2* ('Tib Two'), a number of other high performance components continued to be made, such as a larger carburettor (the standard was 1$\frac{1}{16}$in), carb adaptors, higher compression pistons, even fiercer camshafts and the three-way keyway camshaft pinions (for accurate timing). Tib Two, Triumph Service Department's most popular ever bulletin, listed the various ways in which the performance-oriented owner of either the five-hundred or six-fifty twin could modify and tune his machine – depending, of course, upon his technical ability – to obtain the maximum power output for road racing and other forms of sport, including straight-line sprinting and off-road competition such as TT racing in the States (short track racing over the dirt, rather than Isle of Man racing!).

Even so, in many ways, Triumph's motorcycles and their design had as their number one priority the normal road rider, the off-road scrambles, trials and track racing, before finally road racing.

1959 T120 Bonneville (commencing engine 020076)

Engine:	Air-cooled, ohv, vertical twin, alloy splayed 'Delta' head and cast-iron barrel (eight-stud), one-piece crankshaft, E3134 inlet and E3325 exhaust camshafts
Bore:	71mm
Stroke:	82mm
Displacement:	649cc
Compression ratio:	8.5:1
Lubrication:	Double-plunger pump, dry sump
Ignition:	Magneto
Carburettor:	Two × Amal Monobloc 376 1$\frac{1}{16}$in, with centrally located Amal GP circular float chamber
Primary drive:	Chain
Final drive:	Chain
Gearbox:	Four-speed
Frame:	All-steel tubular construction; single front down-tube; duplex lower rails
Front suspension:	Telescopic fork, oil-damped
Rear suspension:	Swinging arm, twin shocks
Front brake:	8in drum SLS
Rear brake:	7in drum SLS
Tyres:	Front 3.25 × 19; rear 3.50 × 19

General Specifications

Wheelbase:	55.75in (1,416mm)
Ground clearance:	5in (127mm)
Seat height:	30.5in (775mm)
Fuel-tank capacity:	4gal (18ltr)
Dry weight:	404lb (183kg)
Maximum power:	46bhp @ 6,500rpm
Top speed:	122mph (196kmph)

The Evolution of the Bonneville

In retrospect, the Bonneville offered for the 1959 season was really little more than a twin-carb Tiger 110, and the first year's production showed up a small number of weaknesses. One of these concerned instances of flywheel-bolt breakage on the new one-piece crank; this was overcome by increasing the interference fit of the flywheel bore and the corresponding spigot diameter of the crankshaft by 0.0025in. Another problem centred around early pistons, and was cured by increasing the thickness of the piston crown. Yet another was cracking of the front mudguards, and was cured by spot-welding its centre-mounting bridge. Transmission glitches included needing longer screws to secure the outer primary cover to the inner assembly, and an additional gearbox adjuster.

In an attempt to overcome premature wear of the gearbox cam-plate (notably in American dirt-bike events), a modification was made to the case-hardening process; the clutch sprocket centre received similar treatment. A more robust voltage regulator was also introduced, and the internals of the silencers were redesigned to pacify those who complained that the exhaust noise was too high (only applicable to the standard road-going rider).

Improvements for the 1960 Model Year

When the details of the line-up for the 1960 model year were announced in mid-October 1959, the big news for the Bonneville and the other 650s was the introduction of a new frame. Formerly the frame had featured a single front down-tube; the new one had duplex tubes extending all the way from the base of the steering head to the lower rear next to the centre-stand pivot. Compared with that of the former frame, the steering head angle was steeper. Of traditional Triumph brazed-lug construction, the new frame embodied a bolt-on tubular rear sub-frame, which embodied the seat loop.

The front fork had been redesigned to make it more responsive to minor road bumps. To this end, guide tubes were fitted inside the spring coil; also, the volume of oil available for damping was increased. Similar in style to that used on the Trophy models, the new fork sported gaiters. From the 1960 year onwards, the nacelle on the Bonneville was abandoned, though it was retained on the Thunderbird and Tiger 110 models.

Also new for 1960 on all six-fifties was the new, all-steel tank with three-point rubber mountings, located and retained in place with a central rubber-lined strap. In fact these straps were to prove a real headache, fracturing in what service manager John Nelson called 'epidemic proportions'. A quick-release filler cap and chrome-plated parcel grid were fitted as standard equipment.

Another 1960s problem was a carburation glitch caused by the rubber mounting of the centrally fitted remote float chamber; this was traced to high frequency vibration being transmitted to the carburettor mixing chambers, and creating misfiring when the engine was subjected to hard acceleration. It was overcome by fitting a brass shroud around the needle jet, where it protruded into the choke of the jet block, avoiding the rich mixture condition created by aeration of the fuel. The factory's eventual cure for series production (introduced as a standard fitment on the 1961 Bonneville) was to dispense with the rubber-mounted, single remote, centrally mounted float chamber, and simply fit stock Monobloc carbs. However, for racing use, the famous 'clopped off' Monoblocs made their debut. This needed a return to the rubber-mounted (with a metalastic bush) single float chamber.

In their report on the 1960 range in the issue dated 15 October 1959, *The Motor Cycle* said:

> Most potent of all Triumphs, the Bonneville 120 is suitable for club-type racing, and in consequence it is fitted with a quickly detachable headlamp which, incidentally, is chromium plated. To

The 1960 model year T120 Bonneville from the factory catalogue published in October 1959. This introduced the duplex frame, fork gaiters, separate chrome headlamp, and other details.

simplify the wiring harness the lighting switch is mounted beneath the dual-seat nose, and the three cables to the headlamp are connected by a multi-pin plug and socket.

And concerning the fitment of the remote float chamber:

> ...Previously the float chamber that served the two adapted Amal Monobloc carburettors was mounted to the seat tube. In that position, however, sudden closure of the throttle could give rise to a surging effect, which caused richening of the mixture. In the latest arrangement, surge is obviated by suspending the float chamber from a rubber diaphragm attached to a steel-plate cylinder head steady, and the chamber is positioned between the carburettors.

The 649cc twin carburettor, splayed alloy head engine of the 1960 T120 Bonneville.

Including taxes, in October 1959 the price of the Bonnie was £284 13s 6d.

The 1960 model-changes to the frame and other cycle parts meant that much of the existing range of Triumph factory performance extras concerning the running gear was no longer compatible. This meant that components such as redesigned footrests, brake pedals and the like were a problem for those wishing to campaign the latest (1960) Bonneville, and it wasn't until just prior to the 1961 race season that this was rectified. However, one really useful addition was made, namely a new tachometer drive kit. Much neater than the old Grand Prix-derived component, the new one (Pt No. CP 181) comprised a complete timing cover, into which the tachometer drive was integrally built. This featured the gears driven from the exhaust camshaft by means of a slot cut across the face of a new camshaft pinion retaining nut. This enabled the Bonneville to be raced under the existing Production Racing regulations, which said that the dynamo must remain *in situ*.

Included as part of the kit was not only the timing cover assembly, but also the Smiths instrument, drive cable and instrument mounting bracket. In addition a special speedometer was made available for use when the gearbox had been equipped with a set of close-ratio gears. This became necessary because the speedometer drive was taken from the gearbox layshaft, as with close-ratio gears the layshaft rotational speed differed from that of the standard layshaft, affecting the speedo cable drive speed.

The 1960 Bonneville duplex frame, subsequently modified by the addition of a lower tank reinforcing rail for 1961.

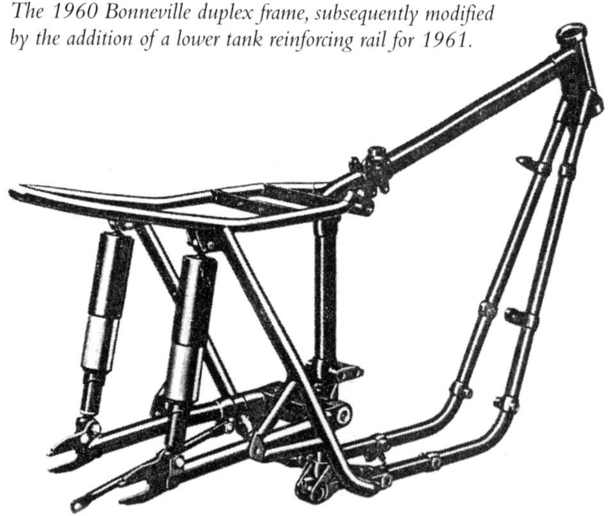

The new (1960) duplex down-tube frame was to suffer a limited number of breakages of the front down-tubes when used in competition, including Production racing. These fractures occurred immediately beneath the steering-head lug, and the problem was addressed for the 1961 model by the addition of a lower tank rail similar to that found on the earlier single down-tube frames from pre-war days.

1961 T120 Bonneville (commencing engine no. D7727)

Engine:	Air-cooled, ohv, vertical twin, alloy splayed 'Delta' head and cast-iron barrel (eight-stud), one-piece crankshaft, E3134 inlet and E3325 exhaust camshafts
Bore:	71mm
Stroke:	82mm
Displacement:	649cc
Compression ratio:	8.5:1
Lubrication:	Double-plunger pump, dry sump
Ignition:	Lucas K2F magneto incorporating auto advance
Carburettor:	Two × Amal Monobloc 1⅟₁₆in, with integral float bowls
Primary drive:	Chain
Final drive:	Chain
Gearbox:	Four-speed
Frame:	Brazed duplex cradle with twin front down-tubes and revised head angle, extra reinforcing lower tank
Front suspension:	Telescopic fork, oil-damped 100lb/in rate springs
Rear suspension:	Swinging arm, twin shocks
Front brake:	8in full-width drum; SLS; fully floating shoes
Rear brake:	7in cast-iron drum integral with forty-three-tooth rear chain sprocket; SLS; fully floating shoes
Tyres:	Front 3.25 × 19; rear 3.50 × 19
General Specifications	
Wheelbase:	56.5in (1,435mm)
Ground clearance:	5in (127mm)
Seat height:	30.5in (775mm)
Fuel-tank capacity:	3gal (13.5ltr)
Dry weight:	404lb (183kg)
Maximum power:	46bhp @ 6,500rpm
Top speed:	122mph (196kmph)

Modifications for the 1961 Model Year

When the annual range of changes was announced at the beginning of October 1960 for the 1961 model year, *The Motor Cycle* was able to tell readers:

> A year ago the six-fifties were given a new duplex frame with a steeper steering head and a strap mounting for the fuel tank. Steering was markedly improved (but still not up to Norton standards!) by the new frame, which was later strengthened by the addition of a tube to triangulate the steering head. In deference to cross-country racers the steepness of the steering head has now been reduced two degrees to give the front fork a better angle of attack on bumps, without detracting from reliability at high speeds.

This showed that the Triumph engineering team was having to compromise between the differing needs of the road racer/high-speed public roads users, and the off-road brigade. *The Motor Cycle* went on to say:

> To cater for the heaviest competition duty, Torrington needle-roller bearings supersede bronze bushes at both ends of the gearbox layshaft and, incidentally, fit in the same diameter holes. Another modification inspired by competition work is the use of gearbox adjusting screws on both sides of the top clamp, instead of on the right-hand side only. The idea is to prevent the box from skewing in the mountings under maximum rear chain pull. To boost top gear flexibility, acceleration and speed, all three models (Bonneville, plus 6T and T110) have had their overall gearing lowered nearly 5 per cent by engine sprockets with one tooth fewer than fitted previously (the number of teeth now being twenty-one).

The front and rear brake shoes were now fully floating, and to suit the Lucas K2F magneto ignition (with auto-advance mechanism), a lower output AC generator stator was fitted.

Also introduced in 1961 were the T120R (Road) and T120C (Competition) models with specialized specifications to suit both west- and east-coast Stateside markets.

Modifications for 1962

For 1962 a wider and heavier central flywheel was specified for the crankshaft; this increased the balance factor from 50 to 71 per cent. The idea behind this was to provide greater flywheel inertia, which gave the competition models much greater grip in American-type short-track TT racing and motocross events. As John Nelson commented:

> This advantage was further consolidated when the existing crankshaft, which had straight-sided balance-weight cheaks, was replaced with a new component on which the cheaks were pear-shaped. This new crankshaft, together with the heavier flywheel, enabled the balance factor to be increased further to 85 per cent; this new pear-shape crankshaft was introduced after engine number D17043. The 'H' section RR56 alloy connecting rods and plain big-end shell-bearing inserts remained unchanged.

Other 1962 changes included the fifth (and final) fuel-tank strap design, and new 'gas tap' taps (one of which became a reserve). The 1962 Bonneville was the first to have this latter facility, but for racing or other high-speed work it was to prove absolutely vital that both taps remained fully open to avoid fuel starvation. Girling 145lb/in rear-suspension shock-absorber springs were now used, a 140mph (225kmph) speedometer, and cosmetically, the dual seat now incorporated a grey top cover section. Electrical equipment changes included a new lighting switch, rectifier and ammeter, and the deletion of the wiring harness QD headlamp plug on safety grounds that it was a potential fire hazard.

At the end of 1962 came the launch of the new-for-1963 unit-construction Bonneville. This was a significantly different motorcycle. But although superior in several respects, somehow it does not create the same level of enthusiasm that the original pre-unit design commands today – or, for that matter, the similar inflated prices that the 1959–62 versions generate in the classic bike marketplace. The powder-blue T120 Bonneville of 1961 seems the most collectable, good examples now approaching the figure of £10,000!

Ned Minihan with his T120 pre-unit, duplex-framed Bonneville during the 1962 Thruxton 500-Miler.

Another 1962 Thruxton picture, this time of the John Stacey machine: Stacey shared it with Norfolk schoolteacher Brian Denehy.

8 Unit Twins

The Triumph Engineering Company Ltd celebrated its twenty-first anniversary in 1957, following its formation in 1936, after Jack Y. Sangster had purchased the Triumph motorcycle division from the old regime. During the intervening years Edward Turner had been the company's design chief as well as its managing director, a situation virtually unheard of in the rest of the British motorcycle industry. But it had paid off, Triumph becoming a kingpin of the motorcycle world, highly profitable and with a huge range of bikes: Turner had done a good job.

The Twenty-One

Turner decided on an unusual celebration: not for him a traditional rejoicing party, but instead a new motorcycle, the Twenty-One, marked the firm's twenty-first birthday. It was also intended as an indication of how important the American market had become to himself and Triumph, for the newcomer was a three-fifty, and therefore in American terms a 21cu in model. It was also the first of the 'C' range of Triumph's twin-cylinder unit-construction family that was ultimately to replace the existing 'B' pre-unit twins. The Twenty-One displaced 348cc, and featured bore and stroke dimensions of 58.2 × 65.5mm respectively.

Although known as a unit-construction layout – meaning that the engine and transmission were made in one unit – the Twenty-One and the subsequent Triumph 'unit' twin that followed were not of the type favoured by either the Italians or later by the Japanese. In these foreign motorcycles the engine, gearbox and primary drive usually shared the same lubricant, and, on the Japanese models at least, the crankcases were split horizontally rather than vertically.

Again, on the Italian and Japanese power units the primary drive was invariably gear driven (often using helical cut gears for quietness). However, the Twenty-One and the other unit Triumph twins used the 'Turner formula' of separate oil supplies, a vertically split crankcase and chain primary drive. In fact the Turner formula was used in the majority of Triumph engines, so the unit Triumph was not really a new design at all, but rather a rehash of the original – which had the effect of providing a more compact motorcycle that weighed less, and probably cost less to produce!

The Twenty-One Engine

This is not to say it was a bad design: in fact, from personal experience, the unit Triumph was every bit as good as the originals, if not better. So the Twenty-One engine followed the Turner way of doing things, with a forged one-piece crankshaft central flywheel retained by a trio of radial bolts, and two separate gear-driven camshafts located in the top of the crankcase to provide short pushrods. The connecting rods and pistons also followed conventional Triumph practice, with split big ends, bolts with location diameters and three piston rings (two compression and one oil scraper). The top end of the engine was equally conventional, with a cast-iron, one-piece barrel and one-piece alloy head held together by eight studs. The pushrods were still located in tubes fore and aft of the cylinder barrel. There were also duplex coil springs, valve seat inserts and screwed-in exhaust-pipe adaptors, plus separate alloy rocker boxes, each of the latter with its own circular inspection cap. In other words, the top half of the unit engine was very much 1937, rather than 1957 technology.

The only new design was the crankcase assembly. The left (nearside) half extended backwards and formed the inner well of the primary chaincase, also taking in the gearbox sprocket area. Access to the sprocket was by way of a detachable circular plate retained by six bolts and featuring an oil seal at its centre. The right (offside) crankcase half was considerably more complex because it also incorporated the gearbox shell. The casing was machined much as before, meaning that it included holes for the camshaft bushings, mounting faces for the oil pump, and bosses for the pressure-relief valve and sump filter. The gearbox section was open on the offside (right) with the nearside (left) wall machined for the sleeve gear bearing, and a needle race located at the rear to support the layshaft. The gearbox part protruded past the casing centre-line, incorporating the rear mounting lug for the entire unit. This featured a filler plug at its top, together with a combined drain and level in the base of the standpipe design, where the pipe was hollow, to provide the correct oil level whilst its removal drained the gearbox.

Crankshaft material was En.16B steel. The axes were 3⅜in apart. Diameters of the big end and main bearings were both 1 7/16in, whilst crankshaft rigidity was aided by an overlap of approximately ¼in between the big end and the main bearings.

The connecting rods were of conventional H-section Triumph pattern, but were steel stampings rather than aluminium, as in the

The first of the unit twins, the Twenty-One (3TA), arrived in 1957. Displacing 348cc (58.25 × 65.5mm), the bike was a tourer, not a racer, but it is still important in the evolution of the Triumph unit twins' racing history.

past, and incorporated split big ends with Vandervell thin-wall micro-babbit shells that not only provided a long service life, but could also be replaced easily and inexpensively. At the upper end of each con-rod the gudgeon pins ran in a wrapped Vandervell bush.

A further wrapped bush was employed for the timing-side main bearing, whilst a positively located ball bearing supported the drive-side shaft. To allow for differential expansion between crankshaft and crankcase, the timing side of the shaft was not located laterally.

Electrical Equipment

A splined extension of the crankshaft left (nearside) end carried the engine sprocket, outboard of which was the rotor of the Lucas RM 13/15 alternator. *The Motor Cycle* described this as a 'compromise unit', comprising as it did an RM15-type rotor and RM13 stator. The result was a generator that was lighter than the RM15, yet which featured a lower cutting-in speed than the RM13. The stator was mounted on a trio of equally spaced pillars projecting horizontally from the inner half of the chaincase. No engine-shaft shock absorber was fitted, and the smoothness of transmission was greatly helped by a vane-type, rubber-block cush drive in the clutch.

At the timing end of the crankshaft a Woodruff key secured the half-time spur pinion, immediately above and rotating on a fixed spindle; and to provide a means of varying the valve timing, the camshaft gears were each provided with three alternative keyways – the shafts, of course, each having a single Woodruff key.

As with the pre-unit Triumph twins, the inlet and exhaust cams were located respectively to the rear and front of the unit. These camshafts were forgings in 3–4 per cent nickel steel, and were case hardened, the integral cams being of precisely the same profile as those found on the pre-unit Speed Twin of the same era. Whereas the exhaust camshaft performed the sole duty of operating the valves via cam followers, pushrods and rockers, the inlet camshaft performed other functions:

- Driving a double-plunger reciprocating oil pump;
- Ignition distributor (positioned at the offside rear of the cylinder barrel), driven by a skew gear machined on the shaft inboard of the timing-side camshaft bearing.

At the extreme end of the shaft was a timed crankcase breather of orthodox Triumph design.

AC Electrical Equipment

The use of AC electrical equipment was not a feature new to Triumph. Previously, in the case of the twins, it had been adapted to existing designs (for example, the Speed Twin), on which the timing case dimensions were not reduced although dynamo and magneto drives were no longer necessary. Beginning with a clean piece of paper when drawing out the new unit engine, the Triumph engineering team, headed by Edward Turner himself, evolved a compact timing case for the Twenty-One and the 350/500 engines that followed. *The Motor Cycle* called it 'heart-shaped', and it measured 8in wide by 6½in deep (20 × 16.5cm). Projecting forward from the base of the timing chest was the conventional Triumph-type plunger oil-pressure indicator button; feed and return pipes from the oil tank were coupled to the rear of the timing chest. The only other external oil pipe was the pressure feed to the rocker boxes.

At first sight the Twenty-One engine appeared to be of all-alloy construction, but this was not the case, as cast iron was used for the cylinder barrel (block) – a finish of metallic silver sheen being the reason for the illusion. An unusual design feature was that the cylinder finning of the barrel was continued right to the barrel's base flange, and in fact the flange itself was finned. Cylinder-head material was of DTD424 light alloy, with integral slots to assist air cooling. As was usual Triumph practice, the valve seats were of austentic iron, whilst the combustion chambers were hemispherical in shape. Silchrome steel was used for the inlet valves, and Jessop G2 steel for the exhaust valves; valve-head diameters were both 1¼in.

As already mentioned, the valve gear was of conventional Triumph (Turner) layout – and thus straightforward. Cam followers were cylindrical, of steel and tipped with Stellite; at the upper end of each follower was a cap to accommodate the base of the Duralumin pushrod, which in turn actuated the rocker. A valve-clearance adjuster with lock nut acted directly on the top of the valve stem. The exposed pushrod cover tubes, recessed at the front and rear of the cylinder barrel, were interposed between the cylinder-base flange and the underside of the cylinder head; at the upper end of each pushrod tube was a washer of silicone rubber – at that time a relatively new material – this being resistant to heat and oil.

Again very much a standard Triumph feature, separate rocker boxes were specified, and therefore recessed-head Phillips screws were employed to secure them to the cylinder head.

The Gearbox Assembly

The gearbox assembly was located in a compartment in the offside (timing-side) crankcase. There was no communicating passage to the engine's internal components, so gear lubrication was entirely divorced from that of the engine. The layshaft was located to the rear of the mainshaft, and since the centre's measurement was only $1\frac{13}{16}$in, the arrangement was very compact. The cam plate was mounted horizontally in a similar fashion to the unit singles, the T15 Terrier and T20 Cub (*see* Chapter 6). Pegs formed on the bosses of the gear-selector forks were arranged to operate in profiled tracks of the cam plate.

A design feature to ease maintenance was that, after removing the clutch, the complete gear cluster assembly could be withdrawn from the housing without disturbing the adjustment of the gear change or selector mechanism. In addition, the big ends could also be replaced without disturbing the gears. The overall ratios were 5.31, 6.30, 9.32 and 13:1.

Primary drive was via a non-adjustable, non-tensioned, $\frac{3}{8}$in duplex roller chain. Interestingly Triumph sources claimed that no adjustment was necessary, citing a factory test in which the chain slack was increased by no more than $\frac{1}{16}$in in the first 1,000miles (1,600km), after which a further 17,000 miles (27,350km) were completed without any measurable extension.

Clutch and Clutch Adjustment

Cast iron was, as *The Motor Cycle* described in their 28 February 1957 issue, 'the rather unexpected choice' of material for the combined clutch drum and dual sprocket. Triumph claimed, 'An advantage of the design is that the grooves in which the four driven plates are located are internal, and thus not liable to spread.' The body casing was thickened locally to allow for the internal grooves. A thrust rod passed through the axis of the gearbox in the conventional manner, and was actuated by a worm mechanism at the right-hand end.

Adjustment of the clutch was by means of a screw-in thrust button secured by a lock nut in the centre of the pressure plate. A slotted inspection cap in the outer half of the primary chaincase made adjustment a relatively simple matter. The clutch cable emerged from the upper face of the crankcase, with the cable neatly encased within a moulded rubber, waterproof cover enclosing the distributor top and HT leads.

In the Triumph tradition the gear pedal operation of up for up, and down for down, was retained; a pointer and quadrant on the upper surface of the gearbox inner-end plate provided a means by which the road rider could visually check which gear was engaged.

Removing the Engine and Gearbox

The Triumph engineering team advised that for extensive work (including race preparation and tuning) on the engine and gearbox assembly, these should be removed from the frame. Removal is actually quite simple and straightforward, because the unit 350 and 500 has virtually a three-point mounting. Single through-bolts locate the lugs at the rear of the gearbox and below the crankcase, whilst at the front of the engine it is necessary only to slacken the three bolts that secure the crankcase to the engine plates, and to remove the forward mounting bolt. In addition, the steady bars to the cylinder head must be detached, plus such component parts as the carb or carbs, cables and exhaust.

External Appearance

A composite frame was employed. In appearance it resembled that of the Terrier/Cub, with a similar dropped tank rail swept upward at the front to run parallel with the front down-tube. Unlike the small unit-singles, however, the Twenty-One and the other 350/500 middleweight twins featured a substantial steering-head lug with double sockets into which the frame tubes were brazed; for tank rail, front down-tube and saddle-tube members the material was 1⅜in outside diameter, twelve-gauge steel tubing.

On the front down-tube was a brazed lug to locate the power-unit forward mounting, and the lower end of the tube was plugged. Fourteen-guage duplex tubes of ⅞in outside diameter were welded to the front down-tube member to form an engine cradle, whilst the rear ends of the cradle tubes were brazed into sockets in a large H-section malleable-iron bridge section at the base of the saddle tube.

An unusual construction feature was employed at this point. The bridge section had ears that projected backwards to carry the pivots of the centre stand. Forgings brazed to the lower ends of the subframe embodied taper mountings for the footrest hangers. Each lug was angled to lie alongside the forward extension of the bridge section, to which it was attached by two set-screws; one of these also served to locate the footrest hanger on its tapered boss. The assembly was both neat and practical, dispensing as it did with the need for a long footrest mounting bolt passing from one side of the motorcycle to the other with attendant distance-pieces and other associated problems.

The subframe was manufactured in tubing of 1in diameter, fifteen gauge, to which the uppers were attached to a loop of ⅞in, fourteen-gauge tubing that formed a base for the seat.

Conventional Triumph design practice was seen in the layout of the swinging arm, the malleable support for the pivot bearings being brazed to the frame's saddle tube. Plain bushes were employed for the pivot. The swinging arm's movement was controlled by Girling suspension units that were adjustable to suit various loads and conditions.

Although the front fork design generally followed the type fitted to the larger twins, there were differences. Besides its size and weight, there were internal modifications in the hydraulic damping system. Instead of the knock-out wheel spindle normally fitted, the fork ends featured split spindle eyes and removable caps. As was usual Triumph practice, a screw-down type steering damper was fitted. It is interested to note that this basic fork was used for both the other C unit 350/500 twins as well as the 200 Cub sporting models.

An unusual feature of the Twenty-One (coded 3TA) was the use of 17in rims and tyres – this when 19in or 18in were the norm. At the beginning of the twenty-first century, 17in is considered the ideal in sports and racing motorcycles, but back in 1957 it was most unusual. Brakes were of 7in diameter, the front being of the full-width type. Although adequate for the meagre 18.5bhp (at 6,500rpm) of the Twenty-One, on the higher performance unit models such as the T100A, Tiger 100SS and Tiger 90, the poor braking performance was to prove the design's weakest point.

The newly introduced unit-construction Triumph three-fifty twin proved a good seller (at that time British riders were able to ride machines above 250cc as novices; this changed at the beginning of the 1960s to 250cc and under). But the Twenty-One was very much a tourer, rather than a sportster, and it was the first production Triumph to feature extensive body panelling – the rear end was referred to as the 'bath-tub'. It was left to the introduction of a five-hundred version before any serious consideration was given to using the new unit design for sporting purposes.

The Unit Speed Twin, the 5TA

In the 23 October 1958 issue, *The Motor Cycle* presented the 1959 Triumph models, including a new unit 500, saying:

> Pioneer of the modern fashion in parallel twins, the Speed Twin, Triumph's illustrious five-hundred roadster, holds a secure place in the affections of enthusiasts the world over. The name lives on for 1959, but the latest Speed Twin (coded 5TA) is a machine in the modern idiom.

For now, not only was there the traditional pre-unit 498cc, but a new 490cc version with short stroke 69 × 65.5mm bore and stroke dimensions (in fact sharing the same stroke as the Twenty One three-fifty).

Although the Twenty One employed forged steel connecting rods, those on the Speed Twin were, like its predecessor, of H-section con-rods of RR56 light alloy, with steel big-end caps; the big-end bearings of both the 350 and 500 unit engine were of the thin-wall steel-backed variety with micro-bobbit lining.

Both engines had the same gearbox internals, but a twenty-tooth sprocket gave overall gear ratios of 11.56, 8.35, 5.62 and 4.8:1. Each model was equipped with an Amal Monobloc carburettor; that of the Speed Twin was $\frac{7}{8}$in, compared with $\frac{25}{32}$in of the smaller-engined model.

One of the very few other differences between the 5TA and 3TA unit was the use of a larger 3.50-section rear tyre, in place of the 3.25 of the three-fifty.

Those who wanted a performance five-hundred Triumph twin could still purchase the latest 498cc pre-unit Tiger 100, now with a one-piece forged crankshaft (like the 1959 650s).

The T100A

With the sales success of both the Twenty One and the Speed-Twin unit-construction models, the obvious step was to produce a sports version of the larger model. As John Nelson explains:

> It was therefore logical that, since the earlier pre-unit 5T Speed Twin had given way to the new unit-construction 5TA Speed Twin, its original pre-unit stablemate, the Tiger 100, should, in 1960, give way to its natural successor the new T100A.

The first sports unit-construction Triumph twin was the T100A five-hundred of 1960, very similar in outline to the Twenty-One but now boasting 32bhp (raised to 34bhp for 1961). The period headlamp peak is non-standard.

The T100A was described in the 1960 sales catalogue as 'something really new in the way of quick 500s' – whereas fellow author Steve Wilson called the newcomer 'a poor substitute' (for the outgoing pre-unit Tiger 100). Yes, the T100A was only a modestly tuned 5TA Speed Twin, but it was a full 50lb (22kg) lighter than the bike it effectively replaced.

The 1960 T100A

Engine:	Air-cooled ohv vertical twin, alloy head and cast-iron barrel, 360-degree one-piece crankshaft, plain big ends, vertically split crankcases; unit construction
Bore:	69mm
Stroke:	65.5mm
Displacement:	490cc
Compression ratio:	9:1
Lubrication:	Double-plunger pump, dry sump
Ignition:	Energy transfer
Carburettor:	Amal Monobloc 376 1in
Primary drive:	Duplex chain
Final drive:	Chain
Gearbox:	Four-speed
Frame:	Brazed and lugged tubular loop-type with single front down-tube; duplex lower rails
Front suspension:	Telescopic forks, oil-damped
Rear suspension:	Swinging arm, twin shocks
Front brake:	7in full-width drum, SLS
Rear brake:	7in drum, SLS
Tyres:	Front 3.25 × 17; rear 3.50 × 17

General Specifications

Wheelbase:	52.75in (1,340mm)
Ground clearance:	5in (127mm)
Seat height:	28.5in (72.4mm)
Fuel-tank capacity:	3.5gal (16ltr)
Dry weight:	350lb (159kg)
Maximum power:	32bhp @ 7,000rpm
Top speed:	94mph (151kmph)

Engine Specification

As regards cycle parts, it was identical to the 3TA/5TA, but the engine of the T100A introduced E3325 sports-type camshafts (coded E4022 and E4033), which continued to employ the original ¾in radius cam followers/tappets) introduced on the 3TA Twenty-One. No change was made to the one-piece forged steel crankshafts or to the radial bolted-on central cast-iron flywheel.

Unlike its pre-unit Tiger predecessors, the T100A did not use polished versions of the 5TA Speed Twin H-section con-rods, and no change was made to the lubrication system. The alloy cylinder head originally introduced for the 5TA was used without alteration for the T100A, complete with cast-iron valve guides and 5TA valves and springs; the major departure (besides the aforementioned cams) was the introduction of 9:1 compression pistons with the cast-iron cylinder barrel and steel-capped aluminium alloy push rods to suit the new sports camshafts.

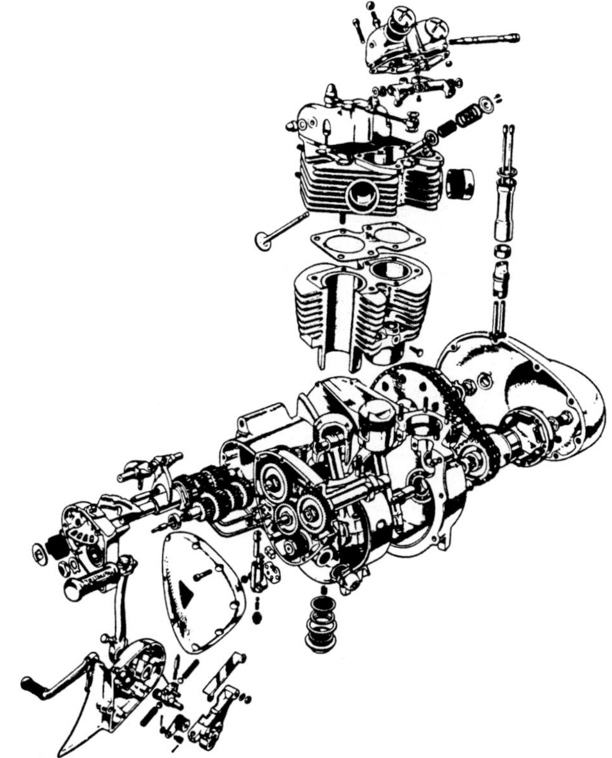

Unit-construction T100A engine, ca. *1960.*

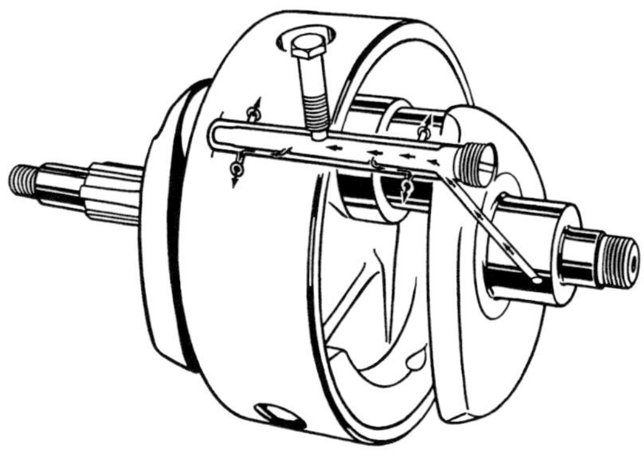

Unit 350/500 one-piece forged crankshaft with bolt-on flywheel and sludge trap.

The single carburettor alloy inlet manifold employed for the 3TA/5TA models was also used on the T100A, and for 1960 alone the ⅞in Amal 375/35 Monobloc carb was standardized on both the 5TA and T100A models with a 160 main jet (and air filter). The RM12 AC alternator used on the 3TA/5TA, with a rectifier to supply the combined 6-volt DC coil ignition and lighting circuit, was replaced on the T100A by the recently introduced Lucas RM13/15 energy transfer ignition system. In this, a six-pole magnetic rotor was peg-located to the engine drive sprocket to ensure a 'timed' generator pulse, thus creating a maximum electrical energy pulse when the distributor contacted the breaker points to fire up the engine. The battery charging and lighting circuit were separate and independent from the ignition system.

During 1961 the T100A continued largely unchanged except for a change to E3134 cams for both inlet and exhaust. Also full coil ignition was adopted from engine number H22430. 1961 models (T100A, 5TA and 3TA) introduced fully floating brake shoes, which in theory, at least, were supposed to improve braking performance.

The Tiger 100SS

For the 1962 model year Triumph introduced the much improved Tiger 100SS (Sports Specification) model, the origins of which can be traced to the works' TR5A six days' trial machines used by factory riders during 1961. Although this was a specialized 'competition' machine, it nonetheless pointed the way forward for future Triumph sports bike development. The T100SS was the first true sports unit

Ken Buckmaster with the 1962 Tiger 100SS he shared with Arthur Jackson, on which the pair finished eighth overall in the 1963 Barcelona 24 Hours; the British team also won the over 250cc class, around the tortuous Montjuich Park Street circuit.

1962 Tiger 100SS

Engine:	Air-cooled ohv vertical twin, alloy head and cast-iron barrel, 360-degree one-piece crankshaft, plain big ends, vertically split crankcases; unit construction
Bore:	69mm
Stroke:	65.5mm
Displacement:	490cc
Compression ratio:	9:1
Lubrication:	Double-plunger pump, dry sump
Ignition:	Coil with distributor at rear of cylinder barrel *
Carburettor:	Amal Monobloc 376 1in
Primary drive:	Duplex chain
Final drive:	Chain
Gearbox:	Four-speed
Frame:	Brazed and lugged tubular loop-type with single front down-tube; duplex lower rails
Front suspension:	Telescopic forks, oil-damped
Rear suspension:	Swinging arm, twin shocks
Front brake:	7in full-width drum, SLS
Rear brake:	7in drum, SLS
Tyres:	Front 3.25 × 19; rear 3.50 × 18

General Specifications

Wheelbase:	53.5in (1,359mm)
Ground clearance:	7.5in (190mm)
Seat height:	30in (762mm)
Fuel-tank capacity:	3.5gal (16ltr)
Dry weight:	336lb (152kg)
Maximum power:	34bhp @ 7,000rpm
Top speed:	98mph (158kmph)

* From 1963 model year, points in timing case

construction twin-cylinder Triumph, and the news of this new production model was first published in September 1961, when Triumph released details of their 1962 model range. The T100SS replaced the Tiger 100A, and this was no mere changing of prefixes: instead it saw considerable changes to both the engine and styling.

To start with, the bathtub rear enclosure was replaced by a much abbreviated version, cut off along a line running from the rear of the gearbox to the top rear suspension unit mounting. The headlamp nacelle was discarded in favour of a separate chrome-plated, Lucas-made headlamp with a chrome-plated shell, mounted on headlamp brackets. Because of this change, the ignition and light switch were moved to a position just aft of the engine unit and below the dual seat on the nearside (left) panel. The forks themselves acquired gaiters, and the wheel sizes went up to 19in front and 18in rear; sports mudguards were fitted on both wheels.

Although the engine specification remained unchanged from that of the 1961 T100A (34bhp at 7,000rpm), the electrics and exhaust were revised. The new Lucas RM19AC generator was fitted, feeding the battery via a full wave rectifier and ammeter, the output controlled by a PRS8 switch. The ignition part of this switch also provided an emergency start facility in the event of a flat battery, its normal function being to supply battery current to the ignition coil, which was triggered via the contact breaker within the distributor unit.

The exhaust was a two-into-one system obviously developed from the works' TR5A 'competition model', down-swept and joining a single silencer on the offside (right) of the bike. An Amal 1in Monobloc carb was fitted.

The T100SS was a particularly attractive motorcycle. The 1962 production batch example was finished in two-tone metallic 'Kingfisher Blue' and 'Silver', with a light grey covering to the top of the dual seat, and the whole effect was extremely pleasing. And even with the increase in wheel diameters, it was still a compact bike with smooth lines.

Improved Performance

In standard guise the Tiger 100SS would reach 100mph (160kmph) in favourable conditions, and with the addition of fiercer cams, high compression pistons, a port job, larger carburettor and dual exhausts with open megaphone (or simply straight-through pipes), it could reach between 100–115mph (160–185kmph). For example, several leading club riders of the day (including Cyril Jones) built just such machines for British short-circuit racing. For this, all the bodywork and lighting equipment was discarded, then a single racing seat was fitted, also alloy rims (18in on both wheels), lighter mudguards, clip-on handlebars and rear-set foot controls.

Obviously, these tuned unit five-hundred Triumphs couldn't match the 'up-market' Norton Manx or Matchless G50 singles, but they were a fraction of the cost to build and maintain – and there was a certain buzz to be had from having the quickest Triumph racer at any one meeting. Unlike the six-fifty engine, the five-hundred unit motor was rarely seen in a Norton chassis, for no other reason than it would then be much more bulky and the weight advantage would be sacrificed.

Another racing modification at this time on the five hundred – and also on many three-fifties being raced – was one that had been pioneered in American dirt-bike events. This involved strengthening the standard-issue 'swan-neck' steering-head lug, so that it formed a brace to the frame's upper rail and to the stressed fuel tank. This bolt-on component was placed under the tank, effectively triangulating the frame's upper section. This modification was not applied by the factory until 1965, and it can be retrofitted to any of the pre-1965 C-series unit twins (the 350 and 500cc).

Changes for 1963 and the Tiger 90

For 1963 Triumph introduced what was essentially a smaller-engined T100SS, the Tiger 90 (at the Paris Show in October 1962). Similarly styled and tuned, it raised the 3TA Twenty One's modest 18.5bhp to a much more convincing 27bhp at 7,500rpm. (This also meant that for the first time a Triumph twin officially exceeded 7,000rpm, thus breaking Turner's unwritten law of 'Never go more than seven'.)

Running on 9:1 pistons and using a new cylinder head (only interchangeable with the Twenty One's components as a completed assembly), the Tiger 90 also had higher overall gearing (a seventeen-tooth gearbox and forty-six-tooth rear wheel), larger inlet valves, and the same camshafts as the T100SS. This resulted in a much improved performance, *The Motor Cycle* reporting a maximum speed of over 90mph (145kmph). However, compared to the touring spec, Twenty One, the newcomer had a distinctly narrow power band (my personal experience can vouch for this!) of between 4,500 to the 7,200rpm recommended limit – totally different, in fact, from the machine's bigger brother, the T100SS. Some Tiger 90s suffered from quite serious vibration, enough to split fuel tanks! (Though this is strange, as mine was smooth.)

Electrical Changes

For the 1963 model year Triumph decided at last to reposition the distributor (situated at the rear of the cylinder barrel) on the T100SS, as well as on the new Tiger 90. The new set-up consisted of twin Lucas 4CA contact breakers mounted to the rear of a plate in a newly conceived timing cover, and driven by the exhaust camshaft. For points models, the latter was now tapered to accommodate the auto-advance unit, whilst the inlet cam no longer carried the distributor skew gear. The ignition coils for the new twin contact-breaker system were carried on an extension of the head steady bracket – where they were subjected to the effects of vibration. This, combined with the fact that the two sets of points (being on the same plate) could not be timed individually, meant that the timing had to be compensated for by varying the points gap! Of course this was not an ideal solution even for a road bike, let alone a motorcycle that was to be used in competition. As Steve Wilson says in his *British Motor Cycles Since 1950*: 'The answer to the contact-breaker problem would not come from 1968 on with the 6CA and later 10CA points, which had neither set of points mounted directly on the metal plate, so that each cylinder could be timed independently.'

The two separate condensers were also moved elsewhere, so there was then more room for manoeuvre behind the points cover, which in previous years (1963–1967) had a tendency to short out on the condenser terminals. Luckily, for classic racers, the later systems can be substituted for the earlier components – the condensers mounted with the coils, an additional spacer placed beneath the pillar bolts, and the later, deeper points cover fitted; or even better, an aftermarket electronic ignition system can be purchased and fitted, for example a Boyer Bransden or Lucas Rita.

Improved Cylinder-Head Design

Another change for the 1963 model year on the T100SS was an improved cylinder-head design, allowing the use of a thinner and more flexible copper head-gasket, whilst for all the C-range of unit twins, the rocker-box caps now featured a knurled edge and were 'locked' by a sprung steel strip. Previously, owners had had to make their own attempts at preventing the rocker caps working their way loose and disappearing, a nuisance ever since the original pre-war Speed Twin and Tiger 100 models – and even this new design was not to prove a 100 per cent cure!

The clutch's shock absorber was changed from a four-vane to a three-vane type, with the clutch components modified to suit (including springs, cups and a three-hole pressure plate). The rear sprocket went to a forty-six-tooth component, and the front wheel size was reduced to 18in.

Changes for 1964

The changes introduced in 1964 included a revised pushrod sealing arrangement on both the 350 and 500cc models; a redesigned clutch-operating mechanism on all 350cc, 500cc and 650cc models to facilitate easier removal; and a completely redesigned front fork, again, not only on the 350/500 twins, but also on the 650s. Triumph claimed that this gave 'progressive damping, resulting in improved suspension and road-holding characteristics'. But in fact, early versions of this new fork were widely criticized as being 'far too harshly sprung' (Steve Wilson), and this led to a revision for 1965, although a final solution did not come until the 1968 model year. The Tiger 90's cylinder head was also modified to accept smaller-diameter 1¼in exhaust header pipes.

Visually – and mentioned here mainly as a way of identification for standard specification machines for production-type racing events – the two Tigers lost their panelling, and reverted to separate exhaust pipes/silencers. Also, for the first time on the home market, both the Tiger 90 and T100SS were offered for sale with matching rev counter and speedometer, the drive for the former coming from the nearside (left) end of the exhaust camshaft. However, its press-in slotted drive thimble was to prove wear-prone in service.

1965: Chassis Changes

1965 was notable mainly for chassis changes. The frame now adopted the top rail-bracing strut referred to earlier, and which was pioneered in competition across the Atlantic. Measures were taken to improve the over-stiff front forks. The upper stiffening strut in the C-range unit twins was bolted on (as it had been by the Americans), to prevent the stressed fuel tank from fracturing. The tank itself was changed to a 3½ gal (16ltr) assembly, and insulated from the frame rail at its four fixing locations by rubber buffers.

The front forks had been criticized for their harshness, and in response to this, longer, lower-rate springs were adopted (though these were not altogether successful); the fork tubes (stanchions) were also increased in length, together with matching components such as inner damping sleeves and bottom fork sliders. This did provide some improvement, but not enough, giving an additional 1in of travel.

In an attempt to improve oil-tightness, the leak-prone oil indicator button was axed, and replaced by a blind domed cap. The centrally located crankshaft flywheel's three bolts dispensed with their washers, and instead were secured by Loctite. Also on the flywheel there was now a milled slot, so that by removing a threaded plug machined in the nearside (left) crankcase behind the barrels, a service tool could be inserted and TDC (Top Dead Centre) found, to assist accurate timing of the engine in conjunction with a timing disc.

Updates for 1966

For 1966, the engines for the 350 and 500 unit twins were largely unchanged except for the introduction of a new heat-treated intermediate wheel, complete with bronze bush, from which the pinion teeth had been cut and subsequently heat-treated. In addition the cylinder head now boasted Hidural inlet and exhaust valve guides, and increased valve-loading inner springs were specified. Transmission updates included a crankcase protector against the possibility of a broken final drive chain, and a more durable primary chain tensioner blade.

A new, larger, 6pt (3.4ltr) oil tank was introduced for the Tiger 100SS (replacing the old 5pt/2.8ltr assembly). Also, the additional frame-stiffening strut previously specified for competition use and given to the 1965 Tiger 90/100SS models with the new 3.5gal (16ltr) tank, was now integrated into the actual frame design. This was important from a racing viewpoint, as it finally meant that the steering-head area was less prone to flexing under extremes of use.

Another important modification for racing use was the introduction of a separate 'bolt-on' rear wheel sprocket. This meant that not only did the racer have the choice of alternate size (teeth) sprockets, but he no longer had to buy a complete brake drum and sprocket as before. The standard bolt-on sprocket retained the

A 1966 Tiger 100SS; by now it had not only received points in the timing cover (from the 1963 model year), but it had also lost its rear enclosure (1964). For 1966 it had received 18in wheels, 12-volt electrics and frame changes.

forty-six teeth from the original combined drum/sprocket.

Also in 1966 a 12-volt electrical system was installed on the coil ignition-equipped models utilizing the 120-degree 4CA contact breakers and auto-advance mechanism originally introduced in 1963. Early models used a pair of Lucas MK29E 6-volt batteries in series, until Lucas made the purpose-built PUZ5A 12-volt battery. In addition, some early 12-volt models suffered from pre-ignition glitches, but this was cured by their replacement by a 160-degree dwell auto-advance cam assembly (Pt No. 54419254). No other changes were made to the rotor, stator or rectifer, the 12-volt system now being controlled by a newly introduced 12-volt zenor diode.

Important Changes for 1967

In 1967 the sports/racing-oriented twin-carb T100T was introduced, and a host of other important changes were made, which effectively were to place the five-hundred Triumph sports twin right back on top of the pile when it came to Production-type racing. Previously it was left to owners to do the work, and also for Production racing they had been limited by the single carburettor on the Tiger 100SS (which continued to be offered in single-carb form).

The T100T Daytona

On the T100T (to become the Daytona, after the factory's race success at Daytona in 1966 and 1967) and the American market T100R, the engine specification comprised twin Amal Monobloc $1\frac{1}{8}$in carburettors, racing form E3134 inlet and exhaust camshafts, together with $1\frac{1}{8}$in radius cam followers. The exhaust camshaft now included an internally machined rev-counter drive slit. Another change was the use of larger $1\frac{17}{32}$in inlet valves, in place of the single-carb model's $1\frac{7}{16}$ components. The exhaust valve size remained at $1\frac{5}{16}$in, but they were now manufactured from a new, more heat-resistant material. The twin-carb cylinder head was also modified to provide a bigger combustion sphere, to allow the fitment of the larger inlet valves and their respective seats.

1967 T100T Daytona

Engine:	Air-cooled ohv vertical twin, alloy head and cast-iron barrel, 360-degree one-piece crankshaft, plain big ends, vertically split crankcases; unit construction
Bore:	69mm
Stroke:	65.5mm
Displacement:	490cc
Compression ratio:	9:1
Lubrication:	Double-plunger pump, dry sump
Ignition:	Coil/battery with points in timing case
Carburettor:	2 × Amal Monobloc 376 $1\frac{1}{8}$in
Primary drive:	Duplex chain
Final drive:	Chain
Gearbox:	Four-speed
Frame:	Brazed and lugged tubular loop-type with single front down-tube; duplex lower rails
Front suspension:	Telescopic forks, oil-damped
Rear suspension:	Swinging arm, twin shocks
Front brake:	8in full-width drum, SLS
Rear brake:	7in drum, SLS
Tyres:	Front 3.25 × 18; rear 3.50 × 18
General Specifications	
Wheelbase:	53.5in (1,359mm)
Ground clearance:	7.5in (190mm)
Seat height:	30in (762mm)
Fuel-tank capacity:	3.6gal (16.4ltr)
Dry weight:	337lb (153kg)
Maximum power:	39bhp @ 7,400rpm
Top speed:	108mph (174kmph)

To improve the engine's lubrication, the oil pump scavenge plunger diameter was increased from a nominal 0.437in to 0.487in.

Other details included the fact that the new combustion spheres allowed the twin-carburettor T100T and T100R machines to be equipped with 9.75:1 compression Hepolite pistons, whilst on all unit 350/500 models the

The T100R Daytona 500 twin carb (Amal Concentric Mk1's) engine, cut away to show the working parts. The T100R was introduced for the 1967 model year.

Mick Chatterton with his 500 T100T Daytona during the Production TT in the Isle of Man in 1969, entered by Monty & Ward. Note the 2LS front brake and Avon fairing.

1966 models featured UNF gearbox mainshaft threads.

In response to its more serious approach to providing a true sports machine that could be successfully raced, the Triumph engineering team (which by now included the experienced Doug Hele) introduced revisions for both the frame and swinging arm. With his considerable racing experience (having worked at Norton during the late 1950s and early 1960s on Manx development), Hele understood that additional engine power and speed is of no use unless the rider can exploit this additional performance.

A feature of the new-for-1967 frame was the use of a fully triangulated steering-head lug, which featured an integral top rail and bracing tank rail, and brought about a revised fork stem angle of 65 degrees instead of 62 degrees to the horizontal. The rear frame section now featured 'out-board', triangular, swinging-arm, pivot-bracing plates, whilst the more rigid swinging arm was also wider allowing the fitment of a wider-section rear tyre.

The effect of these changes was to provide a chassis that could more than cope with the additional power provided by the twin-carb motor.

Improvements for 1968

The only weak point remaining concerned the front forks, and these were dealt with the following year. In 1968 greatly improved forks were introduced, featuring 'shutter valves', UNF threads, sintered iron fork bushes – soon axed in favour of the original sintered bronze component from engine number H57470 – and extruded bottom outer sliders. The traditional Triumph manually operated steering damper (passing through the steering head) was deleted. In any case, by now, racing Triumphs were beginning to use the new aftermarket hydraulic steering dampers (pioneered by Girling) that were reaching the market.

The engine for the 1968 model year received small but still important changes. The rocker boxes, although visually the same, were now cast in thicker material, whilst the cylinder barrel was secured at its base by twelve-point fixing nuts. Another change was made as a consequence of the increasing theft of Triumph engines for use in other machines: the crankcase assembly (also on the six-fifties) now incorporated a raised section (on the nearside), to accommodate the new factory-applied engine number inscription. The forged one-piece steel crankshaft (still with bolt-on flywheel), incorporating the revised 38° BTC (Before Top Centre) slot, now carried heavier duty connecting rods on the twin-carburettor models, also manufactured from RR56 alloy and equipped with Vandervell VP3 big-end liners.

A switch was made for the 1968 model year to the new Amal Type 900 concentric carburettors. These featured the float bowl, which could be accessed through the bottom, rather than the side, as on the outgoing Monobloc instrument.

The gearbox was unchanged except for the top gear: this now incorporated a bronze bush that extended into the increased bore, chaincase cover-plate oil seal (to prevent the ingress of foreign particles, and thus reduce wear). The primary drive cover was now equipped with an inspection cover (to allow the use of accurate strobe ignition timing).

The T100T and T100R model received a new, 8in-diameter SLS front brake: this was badly needed, as the old 7in drum was now totally inadequate. Of course, in open-class racing it had long been the norm to swop this ineffectual device with one from another make and model, but for production racing, where only factory-fitted or approved parts were allowed, this had been a major problem.

The 1969 Model Year

The new T100T and T100R twin-carb models certainly revitalized Triumph's fortunes in the five-hundred class in both sales and racing, and for the 1969 season, the development team introduced a significant number of changes to both the power unit and chassis.

For the engine, nitrided, heat-treated, racing lift E3134 inlet camshafts were introduced on both twin- and single-carb models, with nitrided racing E3134 exhaust cams used for the twin-carb engines, and E3325 sports cams for the single-carb T100SS and C versions. Cam followers were 1⅛in radius on the twin-carburettor engines and ¾in on single-carb units. A new timing cover incorporated an oil-pressure indicator switch (now with UNF threads).

A new (but still cast-iron) cylinder barrel of increased wall thickness also made its debut, with the crankcase assembly being modified to accommodate a new one-piece forged crankshaft. This was supported by a nearside (left) roller bearing, and a ball race on the offside (right); this became known as the 'ball and roller' type.

Changes to the lubrication system were also made for 1969. The oil-pump output to the crankshaft assembly was made directly from the timing-cover labyrinth, into the new crankshaft's extended shaft via a timing-cover oil seal. The new crankcase (nearside half) was, as John Nelson pointed out, 'at last' machined to accept the new left-hand threaded rev counter drive gearbox adaptor – finally solving the problem of the assembly coming loose. Again an important change, not just for the road rider, but the racer too. The new crankshaft retained the earlier 'bolt-on', cast-iron flywheel incorporating the 38° BTC finder slot, which was now a new forging. A third version of stronger con-rods was specified for the twin-carb bikes.

The primary chaincase was given a detachable rotor cover (with the Triumph logo), and from engine number H65011 an ignition pointer was incorporated, to be employed in conjunction with a scribed line on the rotor, for strobe timing.

The SLS 8in front brake from 1968 had still not fully proved the answer, and for 1969 an 8in two leading shoe (2LS) affair with fully floating shoes was introduced on the T100T and T100R twin-carb models. The single-carb bikes received a 2LS 7in assembly of similar design. The brake plate incorporated an external twin-cam linkage and a chromed wire-mesh air scoop. The width of the front forks' stanchion centres was increased from 6½in to 6¾in to allow the fitment of a wider section tyre, together with an appropriately longer front wheel spindle.

Another 1969 model year change was a new, fully encapsulated Lucas RM21 strator, feeding Siba-type 32,000 ignition coils, triggered by Lucas 6CA contact-breaker points in the timing cover. A separate 2CP capacitor pack was situated beneath the forward fuel-tank mountings. UK and some export models were equipped with Lucas-type MA12 ignition coils.

Following on from Triumph's success at the Daytona 200 in 1966 and 1967, Percy Tait campaigned this works five-hundred Triumph in European races. A highlight was finishing runner-up behind MV star Giacomo Agostini at the 1969 500cc Belgian Grand Prix.

The End for the 500 Twin

As the 1960s became the 1970s, there were significant changes to the marketing policies of Triumph's main rivals the Japanese, and to racing itself, and this meant that the five-hundred twin, and even more so the smaller three-fifty, were suddenly to become obsolete. First there had been the Yamaha TD2/TR2 twin-cylinder two-stroke, which had arrived in time for the 1969 season: all other open-class racers (except the works MV Agustas) were therefore no longer competitive, so even at the smallest club affair, the 350- and 500-unit Triumphs had had their day. In the Production class, which the Triumph T100T Daytona had dominated following its introduction for the 1967 season, things were much the same from 1970 onwards, with a new breed of high performance Japanese production 500cc bikes, such as the Kawasaki Mach 3 triple, the Suzuki T500 twin, and finally the Honda CB500 four. Besides, from early 1970 the Triumph race department was fully occupied with the race programme for the 750 triple (*see* Chapter 13), and all the twins, including the Bonneville 650, were abandoned in favour of that.

The Unit Bonneville

In 1963 the revamped T120 Bonneville was introduced, and it was virtually a new motorcycle, as John Nelson, Triumph's former service manager, was later to recall: 'In 1963, the Bonnie virtually started again.' It still displaced 649cc, and shared the same 71 × 82mm bore and stroke dimensions, but otherwise it was really a new motorcycle. The series began with engine number DU101.

1910 Triumph publicity illustration for the original Triumph Motors company, at that time owned by two Germans, Siegfried Bettmann and Mauritz Schulte, and based in Coventry.

Introduced for the 1939 season, the Tiger 100 was the performance version of the five-hundred Speed Twin that had been launched a few months earlier in 1938. This is the 1939 model of the Tiger, complete with special detachable-end megaphone silencers for racing use.

Following Ernie Lyons' spectacular victory in the 1946 Senior Manx Grand Prix, Triumph built replicas of the winning machine, called appropriately the Grand Prix, for sale to private owners.

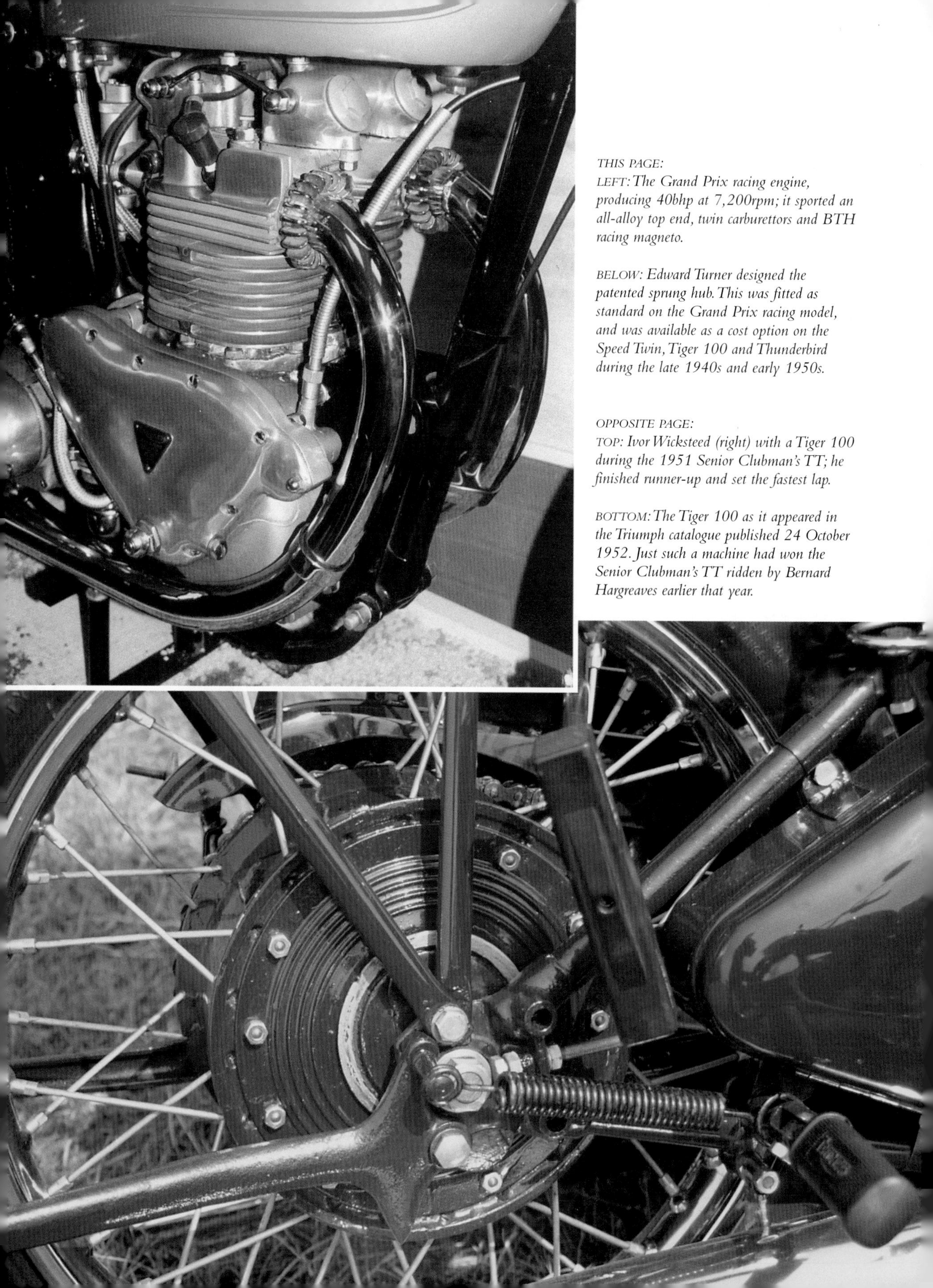

THIS PAGE:

LEFT: *The Grand Prix racing engine, producing 40bhp at 7,200rpm; it sported an all-alloy top end, twin carburettors and BTH racing magneto.*

BELOW: *Edward Turner designed the patented sprung hub. This was fitted as standard on the Grand Prix racing model, and was available as a cost option on the Speed Twin, Tiger 100 and Thunderbird during the late 1940s and early 1950s.*

OPPOSITE PAGE:

TOP: *Ivor Wicksteed (right) with a Tiger 100 during the 1951 Senior Clubman's TT; he finished runner-up and set the fastest lap.*

BOTTOM: *The Tiger 100 as it appeared in the Triumph catalogue published 24 October 1952. Just such a machine had won the Senior Clubman's TT ridden by Bernard Hargreaves earlier that year.*

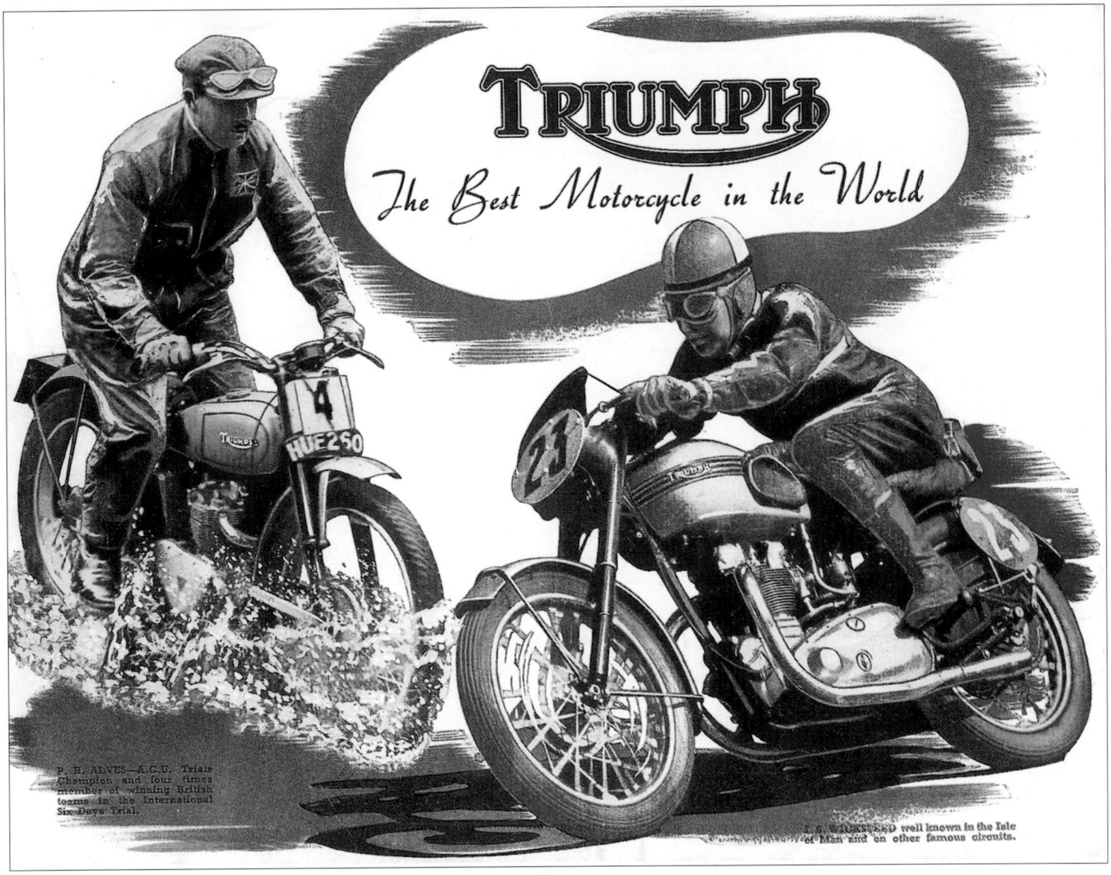

TRIUMPH
The Best Motorcycle in the World
4
HUE 260
23
P. H. ALVES—A.C.U. Trials Champion and four times member of winning British teams in the International Six Days Trial.
well known in the Isle of Man and on other famous circuits.

TRIUMPH TIGER 100

500 c.c.

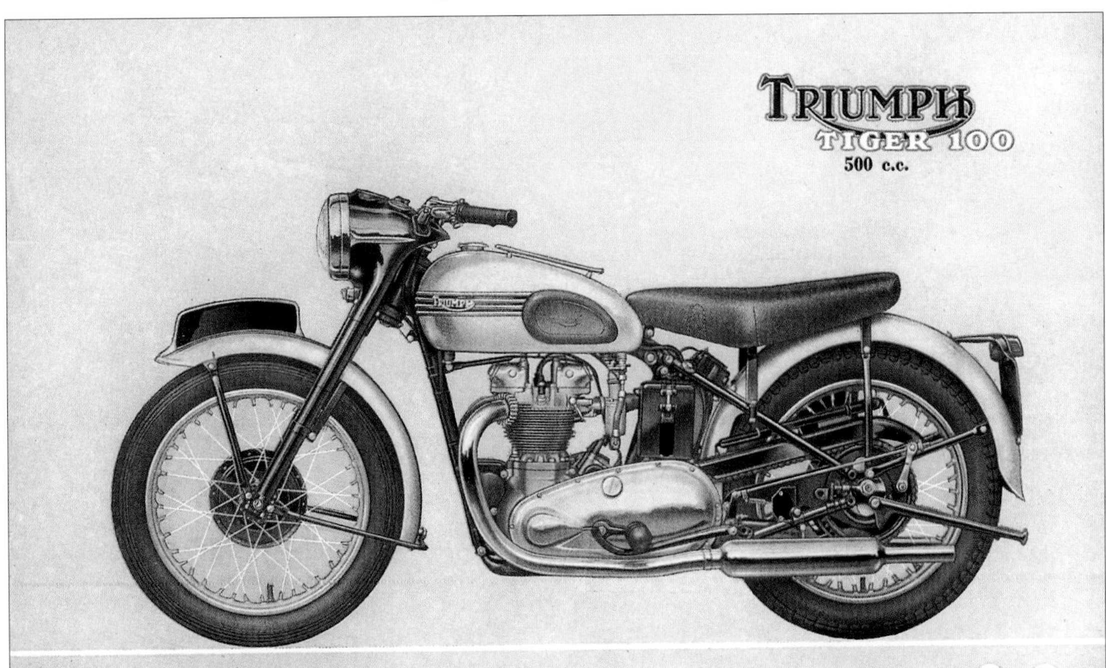

The Triumph Tiger 100 is the supreme mount for the sportsman. Very fast, tractable and reasonable in weight, it provides a performance which will satisfy the most exacting requirements. All alloy engine with die-cast head and barrel and unique close-pitch finning. Superbly finished in silver sheen and black, with many parts highly polished.

Patent Nos. 475860, 474963, 482024

The legendary American Triumph rider of the 1940s and 1950s Ed Kretz Jnr, photographed by the author in March 2002. His father, Ed Kretz Snr, won the first Daytona 200 (in 1937).

BELOW: Ed Fisher's 1951 Tiger 100, De Land, Florida, 1 March 2002; very much 'as raced' during the period.

BOTTOM: The original T120 Bonneville as it appeared in 1959. For this year only it was very much a twin-carburettor version of the T110, rather than the purpose-built model of later years.

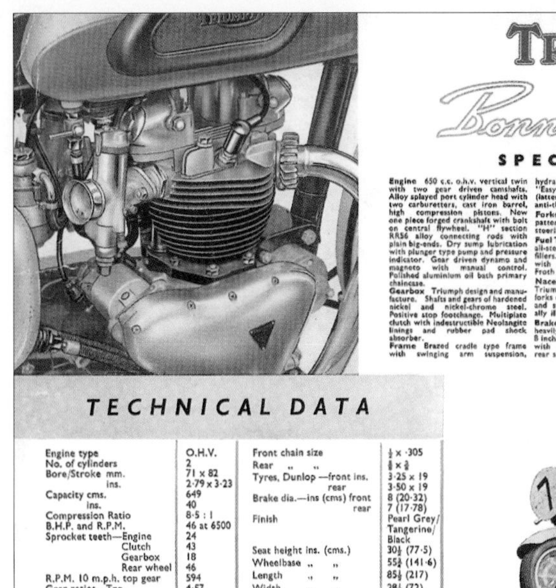

TRIUMPH

Bonneville 120

SPECIFICATION

Engine 650 c.c. o.h.v. vertical twin with two gear driven camshafts. Alloy splayed port cylinder head with two carburetters, cast iron barrel, high compression pistons. New one piece forged crankshaft with bolt on central flywheel. "H" section RR56 alloy connecting rods with plain big-ends. Dry sump lubrication with plunger type pump and pressure indicator. Gear driven dynamo and magneto with manual control. Polished aluminium oil bath primary chaincase.

Gearbox Triumph design and manufacture. Shafts and gears of hardened nickel and nickel-chrome steel. Positive stop footchange. Multiplate clutch with indestructible Neolangite linings and rubber pad shock absorber.

Frame Brazed cradle type frame with swinging arm suspension, hydraulically damped and adjustable. "Easylift" centre and prop stands (latter optional extra). Provision for anti-theft lock to steering head.

Forks Triumph design telescopic pattern with hydraulic damping and steering damper.

Fuel Tanks Handsome large capacity all-steel welded tanks. Quick release fillers. Oil tank in "one-piece" unit with battery and tool container. Froth tower on oil tank.

Nacelle (Patent No. 647670) Triumph design integral with top of forks enclosing headlamp instruments and switchgear. Instruments internally illuminated.

Brakes Front: Full width hub, heavily finned, incorporating efficient 8 inch brake. Rear: 7 inch diameter with cast-iron drum integral with rear sprocket.

Wheels & Mudguards Triumph design wheels with plated spokes and rims. Fully valanced rear guard and side lifting handles.

Lighting Equipment Lucas 6 volt 60 watt dynamo with ball bearing armature. 12 a.h. battery, powerful headlamp with combined reflector, front lens assembly, "pre-focus" bulb and adjustable rim. Wide angle rear/stop light with reflector.

Speedometer Smiths 120 m.p.h. (220 Km.p.h.) chronometric type with r.p.m. scale, internal illumination and trip recorder.

Handlebar Comfortable shape with quick action twistgrip and adjustable friction control. Integral horn push. Ball ended clutch and brake levers with cable adjusters.

Twinseat Triumph design, Latex foam cushion covered in black waterproof "Vynide".

Tools Kit of good quality tools and tyre inflator.

TECHNICAL DATA

Engine type	O.H.V.	Front chain size	½ x ·305
No. of cylinders	2	Rear ,, ,,	⅝ x ⅜
Bore/Stroke mm.	71 x 82	Tyres, Dunlop —front ins.	3·25 x 19
ins.	2·79 x 3·23	rear	3·50 x 19
Capacity cms.	649	Brake dia.—ins (cms) front	8 (20·32)
ins.	40	rear	7 (17·78)
Compression Ratio	8·5 : 1	Finish	Pearl Grey/ Tangerine/ Black
B.H.P. and R.P.M.	46 at 6500		
Sprocket teeth—Engine	24		
Clutch	43	Seat height ins. (cms.)	30½ (77·5)
Gearbox	18	Wheelbase ,, ,,	55¾ (141·6)
Rear wheel	46	Length ,, ,,	85½ (217)
R.P.M. 10 m.p.h. top gear	594	Width ,, ,,	28½ (72)
Gear ratios—Top	4·57	Clearance ,, ,,	5 (12·7)
Third	5·45	Weight—lbs. (kilos)	404 (181·8)
Second	7·75	Petrol—galls (litres)	4 (18)
First	11·2	Oil—pints ,,	5 (2·8)
Carburetters (2)	Amal 376/204		

1959 Bonneville brochure, showing the twin-carb engine, specifications, and Mike Hailwood winning the Thruxton 500 race the previous year.

BMCRC (British Motor Cycle Racing Club) Trophy Day Meeting, Saturday 17 August 1963. The illustration shows a pre-unit T120 Bonneville.

Patent Nos. 475860, 469635, 684685

With the highest performance available today from a standard fully equipped production motorcycle, the Triumph Bonneville 120 is intended primarily for the experienced rider. The two-carburetter engine with splayed port light alloy head, although tremendously powerful, is smooth and tractable at low speeds. The duplex frame provides handling of the highest order.

The 1961 Triumph model year catalogue showing the T120 Bonneville of that year, with the famous sky-blue tank top and silver mudguards with a sky-blue stripe, gold-lined. The lower petrol tank, oil tank and battery box were also in silver.

ABOVE: On 5 September 1962 at Bonneville Salt Flats, Utah, Bill Johnson set a new outright world motorcycle speed record at 224.57mph (361.33kmph) with this, a 649cc Triumph-engined streamliner.

RIGHT: The programme cover for the Mallory Park Derby Cup Meeting, 23 May 1965. The photograph shows one of the new T120 Bonneville unit-construction models, with optional hi-level exhaust system.

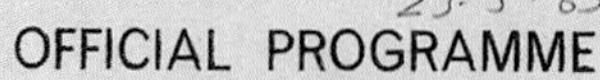

23-5-65

OFFICIAL PROGRAMME

MALLORY PARK

motor cycle road racing

DERBY CUP MEETING

ORGANISED BY
EAST MIDLAND CENTRE A.C.U.
FOR MALLORY PARK CIRCUIT LTD.

23 MAY 1965

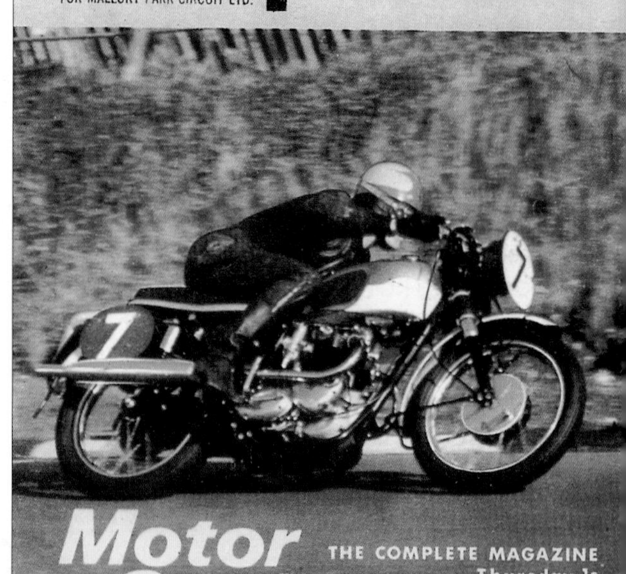

ABOVE: The author (right) at Cadwell Park in May 1969 with his rider Derek Ward and the Walker 199cc Formula Cub racer.

ABOVE RIGHT: The late Leslie Boustead with a very special Triton. Specification includes Grand Prix five-hundred engine, Manx Norton frame, Roadholder forks, 7R rear hub and 2LS front brake.

BELOW: In the early 1970s the 740cc Triumph Trident ruled supreme in both the newly introduced Formula 750 and Production classes. Besides the works models, many owners constructed their own Trident racers, this being a typical example, seen at the Classic Racing Club's Cadwell Park meeting in October 2002.

Jack Lilley Motorcycles of Shepperton, Middlesex, were one of the first organizations in the world to actively race the new Bloor Triumphs when they appeared during the early 1990s. This is their Saxon-framed 900 triple with Mez porting, PFM brakes and Motad exhaust, dating from the middle of the decade.

ABOVE: Stuart Noon with Ron Mays' 350 Triumph Tiger 90 Twin at the eleventh milestone in the Manx Grand Prix in the early 1990s. Probably the quickest 350 Triumph ever in the island, with a fastest lap at just over 87mph.

LEFT: Jack Lilley Racing-sponsored rider Francis Williamson cresting the famous Mountain at Cadwell Park on the team's T595 triple; ca. 1998.

1963 T120 Bonneville (commencing engine number DU101)

Engine:	Air-cooled ohv vertical twin, alloy splayed head and cast-iron barrel (nine-stud), one-piece crankshaft
Bore:	71mm
Stroke:	82mm
Displacement:	649cc
Compression ratio:	8.5:1
Lubrication:	Double-plunger pump, dry sump
Ignition:	Coil/battery with twin contact-breaker assembly mounted on timing cover
Carburettor:	2 × Amal Monobloc 376 1¹⁄₁₆in, 240 main jets
Primary drive:	Duplex chain
Final drive:	Chain
Gearbox:	Four-speed
Frame:	Brazed cradle, incorporating a new, single, large-diameter front down-tube; duplex lower rails
Front suspension:	Telescopic forks, oil-damped
Rear suspension:	Swinging arm, oil-damped
Front brake:	8in full drum, SLS, fully floating shoes
Rear brake:	7in drum, SLS with integral chain sprockets, fully floating shoes
Tyres:	Front 3.25 × 19; rear 3.50 × 18

General Specifications

Wheelbase:	55in (1,397mm)
Ground clearance:	5in (127mm)
Seat height:	30.5in (775mm)
Fuel-tank capacity:	4.8gal (22ltr)
Dry weight:	363lb (165kg)
Maximum power:	46bhp @ 6,500rpm
Top speed:	122mph (196kmph)

There is no doubting that from a racing viewpoint, the 1963 Bonneville was inferior to the outgoing pre-unit 1962 model, except in terms of handling; it also had a lower dry weight, by some 30lb (13.6kg). Like the 350/500cc unit twins, the new six-fifty design's gearbox (using the original cluster) was in the offside (right) crankcase half, and accessible without disturbing the engine.

Many of the internal parts of the actual engine were the same as in the pre-unit. However, the cylinder head was new, with increased finning area (the fins extended to the side of the rocker boxes); also with the new head casting, the opportunity had been taken to place the fixing bolts at a wider spacing, and to incorporate a ninth one between the cylinders. All this was aimed at curing, once and for all, the problems associated with cylinder head cracking and gas sealing that had afflicted the old pre-unit engine. The new splayed twin-carb head had its manifold not in alloy, as before, but of steel screw-in adaptors.

A particular problem of the new unit 650 was that access for tappet clearance was not good, and a 'cranked' feeler gauge was required. Another nuisance was that the new 'ninth' stud required a socket to remove it, and it was difficult to access with the exhaust rocker covers still in place. Yet another glitch – shared with the 350/500 unit twins of the same era – was the lack of individual timing adjustment for each cylinder, thanks to the timing cover located points, of the same 4CA type as used for the smaller twins. (The problems for this system have already been covered earlier in this chapter.) Coil ignition replaced the magneto of the pre-unit six-fifties.

When launched, the valve sizes of the unit Bonneville were the same as the outgoing pre-unit model, though the new valve springs were shorter. Also different was a hollow dowel fitted in the joint faces between the head and barrel (the latter still in cast iron), for oil feed to the tappets. On the six-fifties the camshafts ran in Oilite bushes, unlike the C-range 350/500 models that ran directly in the crankcases.

In the bottom end, the new crankshaft (Pt No. E4643) was still one piece, but was now lighter, with a less substantial flywheel and an 85 per cent balance factor. However, because it shared its essential dimensions with the old pre-unit one-piece crank, with appropriate balancing it could be retro-fitted into the pre-unit crankcases. The unit engine also used the same polished aluminium connecting rods. The new crankshaft did, however, feature an extended offside (right) and ground surface journal, which replaced the original oil-control bush in the timing cover, for the shaft mated up with a new (and very effective) timing-side oil seal in the timing cover. This was a good move, as it made sure of a constant flow of lubricating oil under pressure to the big ends. The crankshaft timing gear was also changed, due to variations in the timing-side shaft clamping, with a revision to the intermediate cam gear wheel. On the crankcase itself, the oil-pressure indicator button moved round to the front, while the oil pump's scavenge plunger was now on the left, as with the C range.

A new ⅜in duplex primary chain (twenty-nine teeth drive sprocket) replaced the pre-unit's ½ × 5/16in single chain. There was also a new multi-plate clutch assembly in a new (fifty-eight teeth) cast-iron clutch housing, with Langite cork friction linings, but incorporating an additional driven plate. A trio of heavy-duty clutch springs and a three-vane clutch shock-absorber unit incorporating a bronze-faced clutch thrust washer (to eliminate clutch rattle) provided a longer clutch life; this was operated by a new three-ball clutch-operating mechanism in the gearbox outer cover.

A return was made to the traditional, single front down-tube frame – this down-tube being in a thicker, 1⅝in diameter, twelve-gauge tubing. But the most significant (and useful) change came at the rear, where the brazed-in forged lug carrying the swinging-arm pivot, which was new, had its ends secured to the rear engine-mounting plates, and these in their turn were bolted to struts on the rear subframe. As Steve Wilson remarked:

> There was a definite, noticeable improvement in rigidity on the previous unbraced 'torsion bar' arrangement, though until the introduction of the O-ring the new set-up was still prone to rapid wear, particularly on the inner faces of the end plates that controlled swinging-arm float, and this could then lead to renewed poor handling.

Other Specification Details

An integral forty-six- (instead of forty-three) teeth final-drive sprocket and cast-iron brake drum was used as before at the rear, with 18in instead of 19in wheel rims and tyres. Six-volt electrics were still employed, whilst a 2:1 rev-counter instrument was not supplied as standard, but the drive facility was provided by means of an externally mounted crankcase union adaptor and direct cable drive available from the exhaust camshaft when needed. As for the camshafts themselves, E3134 inlet and E3325 exhaust profile were specified. There were 8.5:1 pistons, but of course like the cams, valve springs and exhaust, these were usually changed when used in open-class events, or as Production racing rules allowed.

The factory listed several official high performance components. These included 8.5:1 (or 11.2:1) compression pistons with the crowns machined to accept larger-diameter inlet and exhaust valves, the latter in Nimonic material (both were 3/32in larger than standard); double-lipped roller main bearings; full racing camshafts; larger Amal type 389 Monobloc carburettors; close-ratio gears; heavy-duty racing clutch springs; a rev-counter kit; and racing handlebars. Several of these components were largely aimed at American competition.

The 1964 T120 Bonneville

The 1964 T120 Bonneville began with engine number DU5825. Another problem experienced on the early unit Bonnevilles was the persistent failure of the drive-side main bearings, even though by 1964, three-spot (greater clearance) bearings were being used. Otherwise it was very much a case of the model evolving over the next few years – although the limited-production Thruxton Bonneville (*see* box) was offered to a select few for the sole purpose of allowing Triumph to win the annual 500-Miler Production event (held during

The Thruxton Bonneville

A surprise introduction at the Earls Court Show in November 1964 was the Thruxton Bonneville. This was made available only on the home market, and then only in sufficiently large numbers for it to meet the FIM requirements for Production machine racing. A development of the series-production T120 Bonneville, the Thruxton was Triumph's key to winning the prestigious 500 Miler endurance race (*see* Chapter 11); as well as at Thruxton, this was also staged at Castle Combe in 1965 and at Brands Hatch from 1966 to 1968.

The most successful of all Thruxton Bonnevilles was the Lawton and Wilson machine, prepared by Syd Lawton; it continued Lawton's successful record by winning first time out, at the Castle Combe 500 Miler in 1965. This bike incorporated several non-standard components that, according to the organizers' regulations, were permitted to be altered. The main differences consisted of E4220 cams; larger radius followers with a 3in (76mm) front radius instead of ¾in (19mm); pressure-side lubrication of the exhaust cams; and very careful assembly and testing.

The cams were not a new development: they provided a lot of overlap, and valve drop at TDC (top dead centre) had to be measured. Compared with the more common E3134, these gave 200 through to the inlet instead of 130, and 175 to the exhaust instead of 120, a large increase at a significant time. Valve springs were stock T120/6T components, and fairly light. Since crankcase splash favoured the inlet cam, and its valves did not have the oil scorched off their stems, only the exhaust side was pressure-fed. The bleed was taken from the big-end supply.

At that time the Triumph frame had a 62 degree drawing-board angle (which was effectively 63 degrees with the wheels on the ground). Also the trail gave a weight distribution that was further back than the Norton 650SS that Syd Lawton had worked on before he switched to Triumphs.

At this point it should be mentioned that Doug Hele, who was now Triumph chief engineer, had convinced the Lawton and Wilson team to make the switch. Hele also considered that the smoothness and general lack of vibration had not come from any change to the standard T120 balance factor, but was rather, as he put it, 'largely due to the short balance pipe jointing the exhaust pipes near the ports'; and he went on to say that 'a short exhaust pipe designed with the silencer also helps matters'. Syd Lawton always worked on the basis of 'not straying far from the makers' specification for a long-distance bike. I tune for reliability rather than speed, and play safe all along the line.'

In preparing the 1965 Thruxton 500 Miler machine, Lawton made various changes: he lowered the compression ratio from 8.8 to 8.5:1, in case either rider missed a gear; this was achieved by using a 62 instead of a 48 thou thick, solid copper head gasket. He enlarged the valve pockets in the piston (to prevent a valve hitting the piston if the engine was over-revved). He softened the rubber battery mounting, and used rubber insulation for the rectifier. He fitted a spare battery, with snap connectors in case of failure. He also found that the installed length of the standard outer valve spring was vital: the inlets had to be 1$\frac{3}{16}$in + $\frac{1}{32}$, and the exhausts 1⅛ + $\frac{1}{32}$ minus nothing, disregarding the $\frac{1}{16}$ that couldn't be measured in the cup. Valve clearance was 13 thou cold.

The Thruxton Bonneville was offered in limited numbers during the mid-1960s, to allow Triumph to consolidate their 'works-backed' effort. This resulted in several years of Production racing successes in both the Thruxton 500-Miler and the Production TT between 1964 and 1969, before the arrival of the new 750 Trident Triple. This bike has a 4LS front brake and large Isle of Man tank.

(continued overleaf)

The Thruxton Bonneville *(continued)*

He reduced the main jets from 320 to 270, and stipulated a rev limit of 7,200. Lodge RL49 plugs were gapped at the usual factory-recommended 18 thou. Another change concerned the exhaust system, which was raised on the offside (right) to provide additional ground clearance. Rubber bushes were added to the top fixings of the silencer steadies. The front forks were fitted with SAE10 oil in place of SAE50.

Attention was given to the free running of the wheel bearings, and any unnecessary grease was removed. Regarding the brake linings, Lawton commented: 'I am very happy with Ferodo, and used green AM4 in the front, and red AM3 in the rear.' In fact, all that the Lawton-prepared Thruxton Bonneville machines needed during their first year of life were oil changes and contact-breaker adjustment. The only hiccup was a tendency to miss second gear occasionally; certainly the old Triumph bogey found in the original pre-unit Bonneville, and even in the first of the unit models, of 'wriggling and snaking', had finally been cured. In April 1966, *Motor Cycling* tester Bruce Main-Smith carried out a racer test of the Lawton bike, and in the newspaper issue dated 30 April, his only criticism was that: 'It was only just possible to keep in the power band even with the close ratios'; and that he found that 'the brakes faded a little, but this initial fade did not get any worse'. As for its handling, Bruce Main-Smith said:

> Any bike that will top the ton on Maggots (the test was conducted at Silverstone) will become 'interesting' if the steering is at all suspect. The Bonneville passed this test. There was no twitching at the back, head nodding at the front, pitching or line-wandering. I'd be prepared to press this Triumph over any circuit in Britain.

And from a man who had once sworn he would 'never race a 650 Triumph again', this was praise indeed. In fact he ended the Silverstone Test with this to say: 'No apologies are offered for eulogizing the Triumph's handling – because they've got it right at last!'

As already explained, this was largely due to the arrival of Doug Hele, a development engineer of great experience.

For the classic racer and the collector today, the main problem concerning the Thruxton Bonneville is whether the example you have, or are proposing to acquire, is a genuine example, or a Thruxtonized standard example.

The Ken Buckmaster/ George Collis 650 Thruxton Bonneville during the 1967 24-Hour race at Zandvoort, Holland. The team was eventually forced to retire with a broken throttle cable.

ABOVE: The Thruxton Bonneville dominated the large-capacity Production class from its introduction in 1964 until the arrival of a new breed of seven-fifties that appeared at the end of the decade, such as the Norton Commando, the Honda CB750, and of course Triumph's own T150 Trident triple.

RIGHT: 1967 shot of a Thruxton Bonneville during that year's 500 Mile race at Brands Hatch.

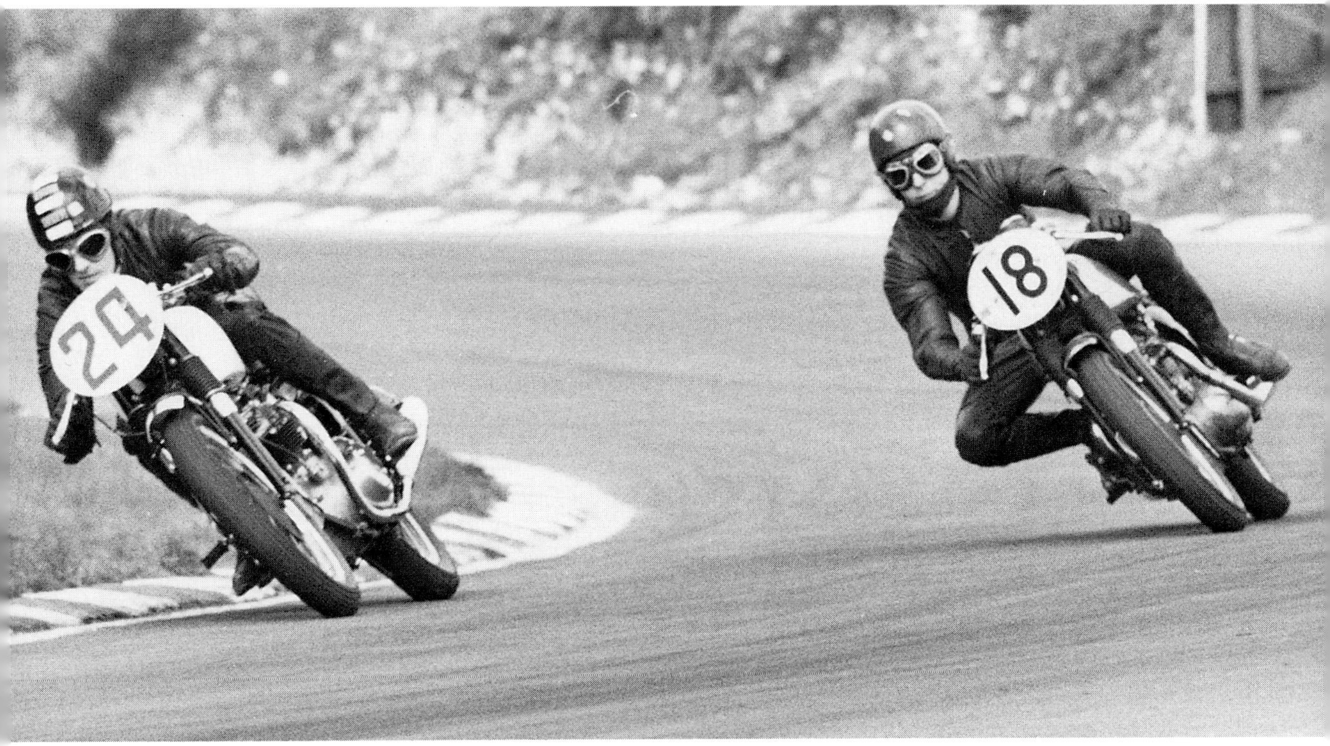

Easter 1968, and the Boyer of Bromley team of Pete Butler (24) with his T120 Bonneville and Dave Nixon (18) and his T100T Daytona on local ground at Brands Hatch. The pair won many races, dominating their respective classes.

this era at either Thruxton, Castle Combe or Brands Hatch). It was therefore not really a series-production model generally available to the general public via the dealer network.

T120 Construction Changes Year by Year

Many of the construction changes year by year have already been charted in the C series unit 350/500 history related earlier in this chapter, as they also apply to the smaller-engined machines. But a number of important improvements were made, and these are listed below, by year:

1964 beginning engine number DU5825
- Amal 1⅛in Monobloc carbs
- Inlet valve $1\frac{19}{32}$in
- Exhaust valve $1\frac{7}{16}$in
- Three-spot main bearings
- Revised crankshaft to improve oil-pump scavenging
- New sump filter and drain plug
- Revised gearbox sprocket/high gear, larger splines
- Improved clutch shock-absorber rubbers
- Double-lipped fork oil seals

1965 beginning engine number DU13375
- Crankshaft now incorporated with new TDC location slot facility
- New engine sprocket
- New timing pinion
- New oil-pressure relief valve
- Minor gearbox changes
- Minor frame changes
- Increased (1in) fork travel
- Aluminium exhaust-pipe adaptors

1966 beginning engine number DU24875
- New Red Spot inner and outer valve springs
- Reintroduction of steel exhaust-pipe adaptors (from DU39464)
- 9:1 compression pistons
- New, narrower flywheel of reduced weight (2½lb/1kg)
- Heavier duty, single-lipped roller bearing on drive side
- Modified oil supply
- 1⅛in radius (high performance) 'R'-type cam followers (tappets) for inlet camshaft, and 1⅛in radius oil-fed tappets into the new exhaust
- New straight-walled and -flanged pushrod tubes, with silicon-rubber washer
- New large-diameter clutch-adjusting screw
- New frame with new head lug casting and revised steering-head angle (65 degrees to 62 degrees) to improve high-speed handling
- New 6pt (3.4ltr) oil tank
- New 8in full-width front brake hub
- New 7in cast-iron rear brake drum
- New (46T) bolt-on rear sprocket (but not on QD wheel)
- Twelve-volt electrics with Zenor diode control
- New rev counter and drive (2:1)

1967 beginning engine number DU44394
- Copper-plated E3134-profile camshaft specified for exhaust, but continuing with (oil-fed) ¾in radius cam follower
- Amal concentric carburettors type 930 (30mm), from engine number DU59320
- New 9:1 Hepolite pistons
- New heavy-duty increased cross-section RR56 polished aluminium con-rods with plain big-end shell bearing inserts
- New oil pump
- New 160 degree dwell auto-advance unit, from engine number DU51771
- New Lucas encapsulated stator, from engine number DU58565
- 19in instead of 18in front wheel

1968 beginning engine number DU66246
- Green spot outer valve springs
- Timed tappet (cam followers incorporate machined flats, allowing oil under pressure to be fed to camshaft lobes at a predetermined interval prior to initial cam lift)

- Rocker arms left undrilled, from engine number DU79965 (giving advantage of additional strength to the rocker arms)
- Hepolite 9:1 pistons with reinforced crown
- Crankshaft modified to incorporate three different conditions of TDC/38° notches in first 1,800 machines, culminating in reinstatement to the rear of the cylinder barrel from DU74052
- Cylinder barrel modified to provide adequate spanner clearance for servicing base nuts
- New Lucas 6CA contact breakers (allowing individual setting)
- New deeper timing cover to accommodate new CB assembly
- Changes to gearbox, including extended-length gearbox mainshaft (to allow UNF threads at both ends)
- Permanent fixed pointer indicating 38° BTC (ignition fully advanced) on primary cover, from engine number DU83021
- New frame and swinging arm
- New front fork with 'shuttle valve' controlled oil-damping system
- New full-width 8in finned cast-iron front brake hub with 2LS brake plate and air scoop
- New Lucas 6CA contact breakers (now independently positioned and fully adjustable); external twin condensers

1969 beginning engine number DU85904

- UNF threads adopted throughout engine unit
- Increased feed capacity for oil pump (larger-diameter feed plunger into new oil-pump body)
- New heavier flywheel
- New connecting rods (with tightening torque changed from 28lb/ft to 22lb/ft)
- New Hepolite pistons with thicker crown and shorter gudgeon pin
- Nitrided surface treatment for camshafts, from engine number DU87105 (finally eliminated cam-lobe wear problems)
- Cam wheels with revised timing marks from JD 25965
- Change to left-hand rev-counter gearbox thread (eliminating slackening/fracturing of drives)
- Revised gearbox components, including new 'shaved gears'; mid-season modified cam plate and lengthened selector forks (from DU88630); finally from engine number CC15546, gearbox-shaft running diameter and gear-pinion diameter changes (potentially a major problem if mixed with previous components)
- Statically balanced clutch housing (from engine number DU88383)
- Front-fork stanchion-tube centres increased from 6½ to 6¾in. Other minor fork modifications
- New swinging arm in heavier gauge material

From 1970 Onwards

As with the smaller unit twins, the end of the 1960s heralded a change in the fortunes of the Bonneville, both in the showroom and the race circuit. A new crop of seven-fifties were to emerge, including Triumph's own three-cylinder Trident (*see* Chapter 13). So after 1969 the Bonneville suddenly lost its competitiveness, a situation that happened almost overnight.

In the British industry, the two top bikes in 1970/71 were the Triumph/BSA triple and the Norton Commando. However, as the 1970s advanced, the foreign opposition grew even stronger: from Japan came the Honda CB750, the Kawasaki Mach 3 500 and Z1 900, and the Suzuki GT750; from Italy came the Ducati 750V-twin, the Moto Guzzi V7 V-twin series, and the Laverda SF750 series of vertical twins; and from Germany the BMW R75/5. All in all this presented a bleak picture for the Triumph Bonneville. Then, of course, there were the politics that were responsible for first the BSA Group's ultimate financial collapse, then NVT (Norton Villiers Triumph) and finally the Meriden Works Co-operative.

The 500 unit Triumph has proved a popular choice in classic racing events from the late 1970s onwards. This is Neil Blackburn with his Seeley-framed T100T Daytona at Oliver's Mount, Scarborough, 9 May 1982.

BELOW: This beautifully constructed machine is a replica of the works 500 Daytona racers, seen here at Snetterton CRMC meeting in September 1985; the rider was Rob Prior.

ABOVE: Richard Thirkell (organizer of the well-known Lansdowne Cup classic race series) with a borrowed 500 unit Triumph at Snetterton in September 2001. The machine typifies the race-prepared Triumphs that are widely used today.

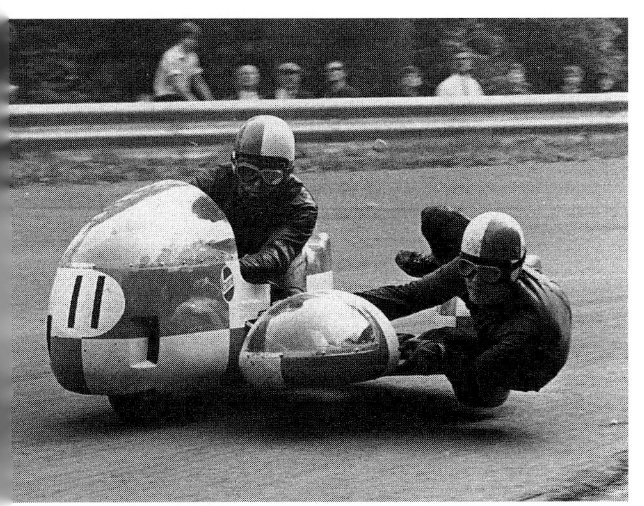

Sidecar racing was another sector of motorcycle racing in which the unit six-fifty Triumph enjoyed considerable success over many seasons. Here, John Crick puts his outfit through its paces at the Cadwell Park international meeting on 10 September 1970.

A popular modern racing modification for the unit Bonneville has been belt primary drive; this example has a Devimead QPD conversion.

Three racing Triumphs from the 1960s and 1970s at the National Motorcycle Museum, Birmingham, during the mid-1980s. Nearest the camera is a 1965 Thruxton Bonneville; the other two are Tridents. The fourth machine (almost totally obscured) is the famous four-times TT-winning 'Slippery Sam' triple.

Yet through all this dissension somehow the Bonneville survived, even being re-hashed as a seven-fifty, the T140V (five-speed); though by then its day as a serious racing motorcycle was over. Nevertheless, with the birth of the classic scene at the end of the 1970s, the Bonneville, and all the other Triumphs that had been campaigned in yesteryear, were given a new lease of life at classic (and vintage) racing events. There was also the popular BOTT (Battle of the Twins), although in this latter class – equally popular on both sides of the Atlantic – the Triumph twin was soon outpaced by the offerings from Harley Davidson and Ducati, in particular. So it was in classic and vintage events that the twin-cylinder Triumph family could still be raced to a competitive level.

A 1970 six-fifty T120 Bonneville pictured at the CRMC's (Classic Racing Motorcycle Club) Donington Park meeting, 29 September 1985.

Triumph Vertical Twin-Cylinder Evolution

1909	616cc side-valve, using imported Berley engine, with 360-degree crank.
1913	August: 600cc side-valve twin announced with own engine and 180-degree crank.
1933	Two prototypes of new Vale Page-designed vertical twin, coded 6/1. Limited production until 1935. Ohv, one-piece cylinder barrel and separate heads. 646cc (70 × 84mm), 25bhp @ 4,000rpm; 360-degree crank; gear primary drive and semi-unit gearbox.
1937	July: Speed Twin launched. Designed by Edward Turner: 498.76cc (63 × 80mm), iron head and cylinder barrel; vertically split crankcases; built-up 360-degree crank; full skirt pistons; Tiger 90 single-cylinder cycle parts.
1938	Enters series production as 5T with six-stud barrel; Lucas magdyno electrics; girder forks; rigid frame.
1939	Eight-stud barrel. New Tiger 100 performance model launched with high-compression slipper pistons; optional bronze/alloy cylinder head available at extra cost.
1940–45	Production of civilian motorcycles halted due to war. Special all-alloy engine for AAPP generator for use by RAF ground maintenance staff.
1946	5T Speed Twins and Tiger 100 models – based on pre-war models, but with engines modified to run on low-grade (pool) petrol; also telescopic front and 19in front wheel. Speedo drive now from rear wheel instead of front, as previously. Smaller 3T with 349cc (55 × 73.4mm) iron head and barrel introduced.
1947–48	Optional Turner-designed sprung rear hub available. Tank-top instruments. Speedo drive from gearbox when sprung hub specified.
1949	Headlamp nacelle introduced. Tank-top instrument layout axed; parcel grid offered as option. Oil-pressure button on timing chest; speedo drive from gearbox standardized. TR5 Trophy on-off road model introduced.
1950	Gearbox redesign, Mark 2 version of Turner-designed sprung hub. Larger 6T (650cc) Thunderbird introduced, with 649cc (71 × 82mm) iron head and cylinder barrel.
1951	T100 and TR5 – new head and barrel in aluminium; racing kit for T100 (twin carburettors, open exhausts, remote float chamber, larger oil tank and revised controls). All models equipped with new front brake with cast-iron drum. Parcel grid standardized. 3T dropped.
1953	5T Speed Twin fitted alternator in place of magneto. New T100C model race kit for T100; dropped at end of year.
1954	High-performance version of 6T Thunderbird, the T110 (Tiger 110), introduced with 8in front brake and swinging-arm frame. T100 now with swinging arm and 8in front brake as T110.
1955	All models now have swinging-arm frame; introduction of larger main bearings and shell-type big ends. T100 and TR5 model with high-compression ratios.
1956	T110 model given light alloy head. Ventilated front brake. TR6 on-off road model introduced.
1957	5T, 6T and TR5 given full-width front brake hubs. T100 twin inlet port head. TR6 8in front brake. First unit-construction model introduced, the 3TA Twenty-one, with distributor ignition and fully enclosed (bathtub) rear enclosure; deeply valenced front mudguard. 349cc (58.25 × 65.5mm) alloy head, iron cylinder barrel; 17in wheels.
1958	All 500 and 650 models given 'slickshift' gearboxes. T100 and T110 given 8in full-width front brake, and the T110 a twin-splayed inlet port head. 5T and TR5 models dropped mid-year.
1959	5TA Speed Twin unit-construction model introduced, based on 3TA. All 500 and 650 models acquire new crankshaft. T100 (pre-unit engine) discontinued in June. New, high-performance T120 Bonneville 650cc with twin carbs introduced.
1960	T100A, high-performance version of 5TA, introduced using same cycle parts, including deeply valenced front mudguard and bathtub rear enclosure. 650cc models given new frame and front forks. 6T and T110 have same styling as 3TA, 5TA and T100A. TR6 discontinued mid-year.
1961	All unit models given modified steering-head angle and floating brake shoes. T100A has high-lift camshaft; model discontinued in August, as is T110. TR6 re-introduced as single carb T120. All 650 models given modified frame with lower tank and floating brake shoes. 6T now with alloy cylinder head and 8in front brake.

(continued overleaf)

Triumph Vertical Twin-Cylinder Evolution *(continued)*

1962 T100SS introduced as replacement for T100A, with half-bathtub rear enclosure and sports-type front mudguard, new camshafts, and siamezed exhaust system. T120 heavier crankshaft flywheels, balance factor changed. 3TA and 5TA given new clutch operations; also siamesed exhaust systems.

1963 5TA and 3TA modified with twin (separate) exhausts, three-vane clutch, improved rectifier. T90 sports model introduced – as T100SS, but with smaller 350 engine size. Points in timing cover, with T100SS given same modification. New unit-construction 650 range (T120, TR6 and 6T) with new nine-bolt heads. 6T given partial rear enclosure.

1964 5TA/3TA given partial rear enclosure as per 6T; points in timing cover. All 650 twins feature new front forks. 6T only 12-volt electrics; T120 only, induction balance pipe.

1965 5TA/3TA new front forks. T90/T100SS new forks. All 650 models receive new forks and modified rear brake.

1966 5TA/3TA frame modifications, partial rear enclosure deleted, 18in wheels; 12-volt electrics. T100T twin carb model introduced mid-year. 3TA, 5TA and 6T models discontinued mid-year.

1967 T90 and T100SS new frame, as T100T. T100T 8in front brake.

1968 T90 and T100T, modified front forks, separate points. T100SS fitted with T100T head, modified forks, separate points. TR6 and T120 modified front brake and forks, separate points. T90 discontinued in October.

1969 All models, modified silencers, exposed rear suspension springs, exhaust balance pipes. T100SS 7in 2LS front brake. T120 twin wind-tone horns, air filters.

1970 All models – minor changes to carb mountings, ignition coils, engine breather and suspension units. Complete range replaced end of year.

1971 New range of 650 models with new frame containing engine oil; new front forks with exposed stanchions; conical brake hubs.

T100R, as T100T but updated spec including rubber-mounted indicators, new switches and indicators. T100C street scrambler version of T100R, but only one carb.

1972 Mid-year five-speed gearbox on T120 (model V). Later in year, 750 T140V 744cc (76 × 82mm): five-speed, ten-stud head, new crankcases, triplex primary drive.

1973 TR5T Adventurer trail bike introduced.

T140V 10in disc front brake replaced original drum. TR7RV street scrambler version of T140V T100R. Some examples built with disc front brake. Late 1973: all models except T120 discontinued.

1974 Workers' sit-in at Meriden works; few bikes produced.

1975 T120 discontinued. Left-hand gear-change mid-year onwards.

1976 T140V and TR7RV 750cc five-speed.

1977 Silver Jubilee Bonneville produced, basically T140V but with special blue, silver and chrome finish.

1978 Halogen headlamp, new cylinder head, Amal Mark 2 Concentric carburettors.

1979 Electronic ignition. Also some machines with case alloy wheels and 2-into-1 exhaust.

1980 Electric starter available as an option.

Late in year, 750 Tiger Trail produced.

1981 Budget-priced 650 (named the Thunderbird), 649cc (76 × 71.5mm) engine; essentially a 750 engine with the stroke reduced. Coded TR65, a trail version was also offered.

1982 New eight-valve version of 750, the TSS built in limited numbers.

1983 Thunderbird engine displacement reduced to 599cc, by reducing stroke to 66mm. Also offered with twin carburettors as the Daytona 600. Mid-year, Meriden finally closes.

1985–92 T140 750 Bonneville built under licence (from new owner of the Triumph name, John Bloor) using a mixture of British and Italian components by Les Harris of the Racing Spares Company in Devon. When Bloor relaunched the Triumph brand name with brand new three- and four-cylinder models in the early 1990s, Bonneville production ended.

9 The American Scene

Unlikely though it may seem, a young lawyer's holiday in Hawaii during the 1930s was the unlikely beginning to a vast sales network of Triumph dealers during the post-war years, up to the end of the 1960s. That young lawyer was William E. 'Bill' Johnson, and the other contributory factor to this story was a six-hundred Ariel Square Four motorcycle. As Don Brown, senior marketing manager and sales executive with the Johnson Motor Company for nearly ten years, was later to remark: 'Bill wasn't a motorcyclist *per se*, but he had a fierce love of machinery, and he was always in awe of people who could design things that looked good, and worked too.'

Bill Johnson was certainly taken by the designs of the Ariel, and on his return to Los Angeles, where he had his law practice, he promptly ordered an example himself. This led him to write to the bike's designer, Edward Turner, who by then had joined Triumph Engineering Ltd in Coventry; Turner replied, and the two men became friends via their correspondence. This kindling of interest resulted in Bill Johnson taking his hobby a stage further and buying out the local dealer, British & American Motors, for a reported $1,800,000. Initially this purchase was not, as one might have imagined, for its import trade, but rather to ensure a good supply of spares, since British & American were agents not just for Triumph, but also for Ariel and Calthorpe.

Business Booms for Johnson Motor Incorporated

Johnson was increasingly influenced by Edward Turner, becoming more and more involved in the motorcycle business, and practising less and less as a lawyer. But his qualities were later to stand him in good stead, and he was able to show that not only was he a shrewd businessman, but that he was also exceptionally good at promoting this business. Finally he opted to embrace the motorcycling business full time, and at this juncture he changed the company's name to Johnson Motor Inc., and moved the operation to what Don Brown describes as 'a rather fancy facility' in Pasadena. Business boomed, and the Johnson enterprise grew and grew.

Soon he had acquired direct sales' rights for Triumph in Southern California, and so moved his entire operation to Los Angeles. But this was only the start: what really clinched his success was the combination of Turner's support, his own drive – and the arrival in 1939 of the new Speed Twin on the west coast of America. In the 'sunshine state', as California was known, this machine above all other imported models was an instant hit and a big seller. And racing this new machine was, as far as Johnson was concerned, the best way of increasing sales, and thus market shares, even more. But it was also racing that stirred up the first differences between the two men, Edward Turner warning Bill Johnson that 'racing was a road to bankruptcy'. However, in the words of Don Brown again:

> The Americans were mavericks, and E.T. (Edward Turner) got a taste of what was to develop into a life-long contest when the Johnson organization began to win constantly in the American-style dirt-track TT racing in California.

From this time onwards there is no doubting that Bill Johnson became increasingly absorbed with the glamour and excitement of racing. He soon hired the great Ed Kretz Snr as one of his mechanics: Kretz Snr was already a legend in racing (including winning the first ever Daytona 200 in 1937) with the Indian marque. Then in the summer of 1939 Johnson sold not just Triumph, but also Ariel and Indian.

The war necessarily seriously inhibited development of the business on both sides of the Atlantic. For the period 1940–45, Johnson Motors was a defence subcontractor – although even then, racing wasn't entirely forgotten, with Bruce ('Boo-boo') Pearson dominating the racing scene with a Tiger 100 in Southern California during the period 1939–41.

Edward Turner's 'personal' message to American enthusiasts in 1940, whilst Europe was at war.

Turner Goes to America

When the conflict was over, Edward Turner went to America, and he and Bill Johnson became even closer than they had been before, a friendship due in no small part to their mutual respect. In the words of Don Brown again: 'The two men had a lot in common, and respected each other for what the other didn't have.' Johnson was a qualified lawyer, a Stanford University graduate, and well connected with society. Turner, on the other hand, had been a merchant seaman and in his spare time an engineering student. Through his own ability and natural skill as a designer, he had created bikes such as the Ariel Square Four and the Triumph Speed Twin.

Before he left America to come home, Turner offered his friend the Triumph distribution rights for the entire United States. The year was 1946 and, full of enthusiasm, Bill Johnson relocated his operation to Colorado and Vernon Streets in Pasadena, California: by the time this facility was completely renovated, both inside and out, it was most definitely the most modern motorcycle business in America. As Don Brown said: 'It looked a great deal more like a current-day Cadillac dealership than it did a motorcycle operation.'

The Triumph Corporation is Founded

Bill Johnson saw racing as his main source of publicity; there was always something of a standoff between the two men on this subject. Racing at this time in the United States meant mainly dirt track, rather than road racing, with the annual Daytona Beach races starting off the season in early spring, to catch the Florida sunshine.

By 1950 with Turner as its chief executive, Triumph was back to full production and the general feeling was that Johnson should put more effort into increasing sales and less on racing. Also, because there was such a vast mileage between east and west, California was effectively cut off from the bulk of the population, who lived in the eastern states, particularly up in the north around New York and Washington DC.

Bill Johnson, president of Johnson Motor Inc. (Triumph distributors for the USA) and Edward Turner (right), managing director of Triumph Engineering Co. Limited, photographed outside the Triumph factory at Meriden, near Coventry, on 5 July 1948.

Rod Coates after winning the 100-mile Amateur race at Daytona Beach, in March 1950. The bike is a Triumph Grand Prix five-hundred twin. Coates also worked for Triumph as a service manager, and later as race chief in the United States.

So Turner recruited the services of the Market Research Corporation of America, whose president, Percival White, was also a keen motorcyclist. White's organization came to the conclusion that there was a vast potential market for Triumph bikes, but it needed two importers, one in the west (which it already had, in the shape of Johnson Motors) and one in the east – and it was here that a new company was needed. So the British company decided to found such a company, calling it the Triumph Corporation. It had its base in Baltimore, Maryland, and as its president they recruited an ex-patriate Englishman, Coventry-born Denis McCormack.

McCormack worked hard, and rapidly recruited a team of men and women who were to serve both him and the Triumph Corporation well over the succeeding years. These included Earl Miller (accountant), John Wright (legal affairs), Jack Mercer (sales), Phillis Fransler (office manager) and Rod Coates; Coates had won the Amateur 100 Miler at Daytona Beach in spring 1950 on a Triumph Grand Prix, and was appointed service manager. He was also to play a vital role developing the Triumph United States race programme right into the 1970s. He was already widely respected: *The Motorcyclist* in their February 1951 issue commented: 'Coates – one of the most popular men in the eastern motorcycle world – knows his stuff, as mechanic, builder of racing mounts, tuner and also as engineer.'

So at the start of the 1950s decade there were two distinct Triumph distributors, Bill Johnson having sportingly accepted that the outlay needed to set up an effective eastern dealer network was more than he had means for. And so Johnson Motors and the Triumph

Daytona Beach 1952: Richard Brase (116) Triumph Tiger 100, and Scot Rogers (92) with his Manx Norton, taking on fuel before the race; they were both early retirements.

BELOW: Much of American motorcycle sport during the 1950s and 1960s was on the dirt rather than tarmac. This is a pre-unit 650 taking part in a desert race.

Corporation began a two-pronged attack on the American market, one that was to prove hugely successful over the next two decades. It was not easy going, however, as Harley-Davidson did everything to stop Triumph – even banning their entire dealer network from selling the 'foreign product'!

The Value of Competition Success

Competition success was a significant influence in Triumph's American success, and in this, Bill Johnson's enthusiasm played a vital role. It was Johnson who signed up Bud Ekins in 1955 – and Bud promptly won first time out on a five-hundred Trophy in the Catalina Grand Prix. Not only this, but Hazen Bair (Terrier) and Don Hawley (Tiger Cub) won their classes, too. That same year Sal Scirpo, riding another Trophy

(sponsored by the Triumph Corporation), won the legendary Jack Pine Enduro, and Ed Kretz Jnr won the TT National Championship title at Peoria, Illinois, on a six-fifty Tiger 110.

From then on it was almost continuous sporting success for the British company through their American distributors. They became leaders in the field of record breaking (*see* Chapter 10), a precedent that began in 1955 with Johnny Allen's streamliner designed by 'Stormy' Maugham, and one that continued well into the 1960s with another streamliner, this time constructed by Joe Dudek.

Edward Turner and certain other British factory staff were in the habit of visiting the United States on a yearly basis. Don Brown had just joined Johnson Motors, and at twenty-six years of age was already a former editor of *Cycle* magazine (where he had first met Johnson). The following is Don Brown's account of his first meeting with Edward Turner in January 1957, after recently joining Johnson Motors:

> My first meeting with Edward Turner was in January 1957. Johnson Motors held its dealer meetings in January, not because it made sense, but because the one race Turner immensely enjoyed was the Big Bear Run, the biggest event in the world in terms of the number of entrants – up to 1,200 before it was discontinued. The Big Bear was held in January, and its start was located about ninety miles north of Los Angeles. Bill Johnson and E.T. always made a weekend of it, and the whole affair was a stimulus to E.T. because an English bike was bound to win, whether or not it was a Triumph. After all, Turner considered himself a representative of the Crown!

The 1960s: Increasing Commercial Success

During the 1960s, Johnson Motors and the Triumph Corporation continued to support an active racing programme. As Ivor Davies, the Triumph factory's former publicity chief, said in his book *It's a Triumph* (first published in 1980):

> The two companies converted these victories into ever-increasing commercial success until the shadow of the Rising Sun [the Japanese] loomed over the horizon. The Japanese increased the overall size of the market enormously, and introduced motorcycling to a vast number of entirely new customers. That they were able to do this comparatively quickly was in no small measure due to the considerable pool of skilled personnel and dealers created by Triumph over the previous twenty-five years. Many senior people and dealers moved into the Japanese camp. But the invasion was not all bad for Triumph and the other British importers, since Japanese products at this time were confined to the lightweight end of the market, and British importers prospered when the new customers created by the Japanese wanted something bigger and more exciting to ride.
>
> But this situation couldn't last, and the introduction of big capacity models from Japan was not long delayed. This, combined with the increasing industrial and financial problems of the British industry in the late sixties and early seventies, led to the run-down of that superb organization in America, which had been created from virtually nothing by the combined genius and hard work of Edward Turner, Jack Sangster, Bill Johnson, Denis McCormack and their dedicated staff on both sides of the Atlantic.

Finally, and still on the subject of the American Triumph distribution, it should be remembered that by the time its crisis occurred, the very men who had done so much to create it – on both sides of the Atlantic – were coming to the end of their working lives.

America's Greatest Race: The Daytona 200

For almost seventy years the Daytona 200 has been America's greatest motorcycle race. First staged in 1937, until the end of the 1960s it was dominated by home-produced Indians and Harley-Davidsons or British machinery, notably Norton and Triumph. (There was no race between 1942 and 1946, due to World War II.)

Triumph's year-by-year results are given elsewhere (*see* page 120), but as with the other 'foreign' marques, up to the introduction of the new ruling for the 1970 race, the American machines were allowed to use 750cc side-valve engines, whereas the Europeans were restricted to 500cc twins or singles. AMA Class 'C' rules also called for production-based motorcycles – no factory specials, such as the MV Agusta or Gilera four-cylinder bikes, were allowed.

Since the dawn of the internal combustion engine, Daytona Beach had been a magnet for world speed record attempts; the Briton Sir Malcolm Campbell (father of Donald) was the last man to set the 'world's fastest' on the beach, in his car Bluebird in 1935. The France family was the driving force in establishing the beach as a racing venue. The original course south of Daytona town was 3.2 miles (5km) long, with a flat-out blast down the beach, a 180-degree corner on sand, then full throttle again along a narrow, undulating tarmac road that ran parallel to the beach behind the sand dunes, and back to the beach via another 180-degree turn. The first Daytona 200 took place on 24 January 1937 in front of some 15,000 spectators; on this occasion, from a field of ninety-eight riders, the winner was Ed Kretz on a seven-fifty, 42-degree, side-valve V-twin Indian.

The nearest that Triumph came to winning the 200 Miler on the old beach circuit was in 1953, when Hugh McAfee finished runner-up on his Tiger 100, behind the Harley-Davidson 750 of Paul Goldsmith. The last race at this venue was in 1960; subsequently all races were held at the purpose-built inland International Speedway.

The Daytona International Speedway

This complex was available for use by almost all branches of motorized sporting events – from motorcycles to sports cars, Formula junior stock cars, and even moto cross! The facilities when it opened at the beginning of the 1960s were second to none: there was covered pit accommodation, and a large area for maintenance work, and many of the leading trade sponsors, such as plugs, fuel and tyre companies, had permanent sites and equipment installations. There were five basic circuits. The outer banked course was 2.5 miles (4km) in length; others that took in artificial bends and straights across the infield varied from 1.63 miles (2.6km), 1.66 (2.7km), 3.1 (5km) and 3.81 (6km) – plus a number of variations, one

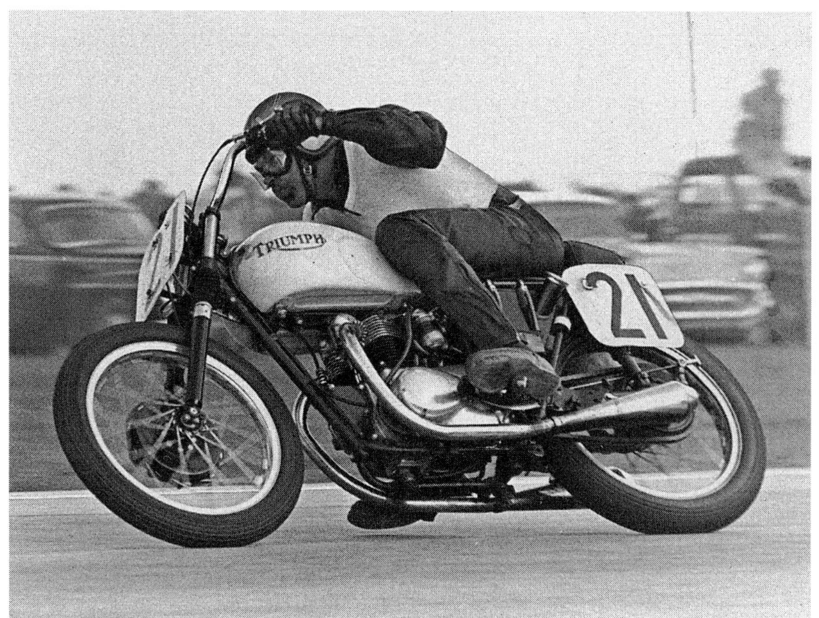

Second finisher in the 1961 Daytona 200 (now on the newly completed Daytona Speedway inland circuit complex), Don Burnett and his 500 unit Triumph; he finished 41sec behind winner Roger Reiman (750 Harley-Davidson V-twin). The following year the same combination of rider and bike was victorious.

of which was used by the AMA for the 1961 200 Miler.

Headlines for the 1961 '200' (the twentieth) included 'Daytona on Tarmac' and 'American Championship: a New Circuit', in recognition of the fact that this famous race would be using the new inland Speedway complex for the first time. Sixty-seven riders started. Race victory went to a 22-year-old Harley-Davidson works rider, Roger Reiman, but a Triumph finished runner-up, with rider Don Burnett; his race-kitted T100A unit-construction model putting in an excellent performance. Similar machines finished sixth and twelfth.

A Triumph Victory at Last

In 1962, the twenty-first running of the Daytona 200 provided what many observers considered to be one of the most exciting contests the race had ever experienced. In the early stages the great Carrol Resweber led, but after twenty-one laps his Harley-Davidson engine completely blew up. Another all-time Daytona favourite, Joe Leonard (also Harley mounted) then took the lead, but he too was soon forced into retirement. From then on there were only two men who had a chance of winning – Dick Mann riding a Matchless G50 single, and the previous year's runner-up, Triumph-mounted Don Burnett. Mann's bike appeared quicker, but then Mann stalled his engine after refuelling. The finish margin between the winning Burnett Triumph, and Mann's Matchless in second place, was a mere 10ft (3m): after 200 miles (320km), this was the closest finish ever seen in the event.

The following year, 1963, Larry Williamson brought his Triumph home runner-up behind the winner Ralph White (HD). In a repeat performance in 1964, Triumph rider Gary Nixon finish second to Roger Reiman (HD), whilst in 1965 George Montgomery and Nixon finished third and fourth respectively. Then came two back-to-back victories: Buddy Elmore in 1966, and Gary Nixon in 1967, when Elmore also finished runner-up. In fact this was Triumph's best '200' ever, with no fewer than six of the top ten on five-hundred Triumph unit twins.

Although a Triumph never won the Daytona 200 again, it certainly wasn't for want of trying. In 1968 Elmore came home in sixth place and Jim Odom in seventh, behind two Harley-Davidsons, two Yamahas and a Suzuki. In 1969

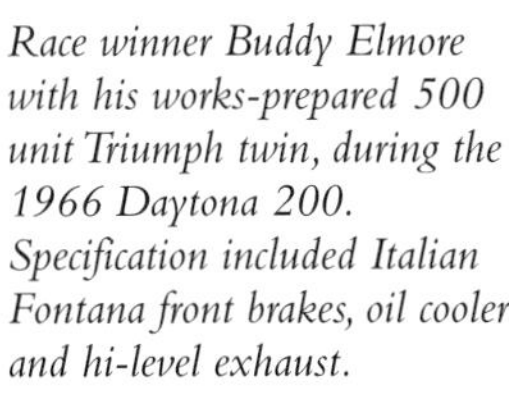

Race winner Buddy Elmore with his works-prepared 500 unit Triumph twin, during the 1966 Daytona 200. Specification included Italian Fontana front brakes, oil cooler and hi-level exhaust.

Buddy Elmore taking the winner's flag at the end of the 1966 Daytona 200. The bike is a works-built, five-hundred twin-carb model with unit-construction engine.

BELOW LEFT: The Triumph pit area during the 1967 Daytona 200 practice period.

BELOW: The engine from one of the 1967 Daytona machines, showing twin Amal GP carbs, central 'matchbox' float chamber, oil cooler, oil-tank, electrics, and the hydraulic steering damper.

the highest Triumph finisher was Gary Nixon in ninth. (This was the last year of the old 750 side-valve, 500 overhead-valve rule.) Then in both 1970 and 1971, Triumph came very close to winning; however, with the new Formula 750 class, the competition was considerable, and the stakes high. Triumph had their new 750 Trident triple, and with the BSA Rocket 3 (also prepared in the Triumph race shop at Meriden), the British bikes led for most of both races. In 1970 Trident-mounted Paul Smart looked to be posing a considerable challenge, as did Mike Hailwood on a Rocket 3; however, both failed to finish. The same thing happened (though without Hailwood) the following year.

So in 1970 that crafty campaigner Dick Mann won, riding a works Honda CB750 (the only one of several to finish!), from Gene Romero and Don Castro on Tridents. In 1971 and with revised bikes (*see* Chapter 13), Triumph and BSA mounted a huge effort – and this paid off, with the British triples taking the top three places: 1st Dick Mann (BSA Rocket 3); 2nd Gene Romero (Triumph Trident); and 3rd Don Emde (BSA Rocket 3). But 1971 was also the year that the BSA Group hit the financial rocks, so from then on the fabulous triples faded from the scene in – a sad ending for the top British marque in postwar American racing.

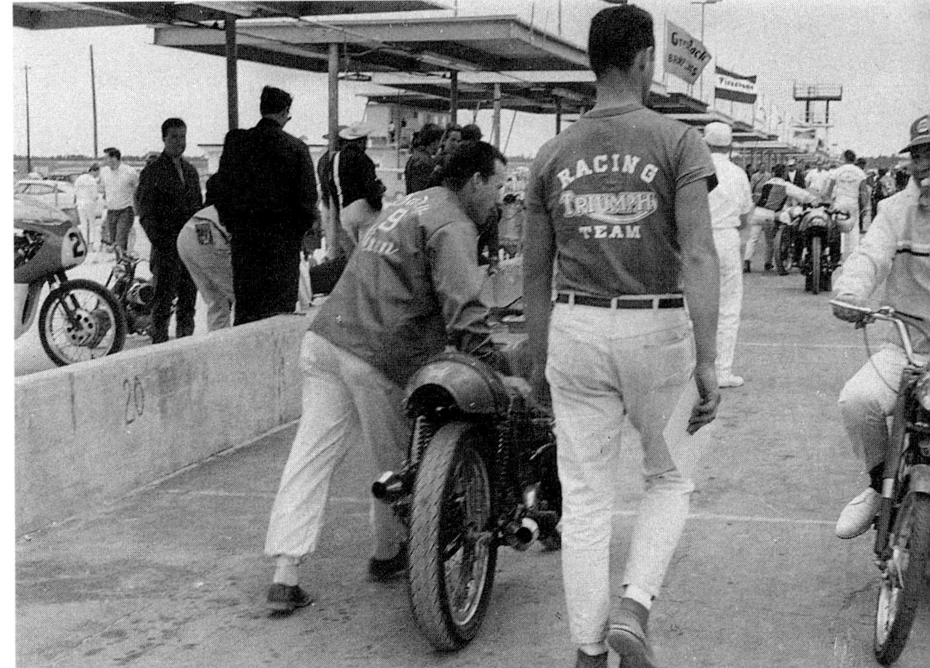

Gary Nixon's machine being wheeled to the start line for the 1967 Daytona 200.

BELOW: Dick Hammer with another of the 500 Triumphs at Daytona in 1967, on the infield section of the Florida course.

Triumph team-mates Gary Nixon (9) and Dick Hammer (16) enter the infield roads from the banked oval section of Daytona International Speedway: the 200-mile Experts race on 19 March 1967.

BELOW LEFT: *Nixon waving to supporters after his Daytona victory.*

BELOW: *A happy Gary Nixon following victory in the 1967 Daytona 200, on his works five-hundred Triumph.*

Triumph's Achievements in American Motor Sport

Triumph achieved a huge array of victories in all branches of motorcyle sport in the United States between the late 1930s and the early 1970s: TT racing (basically similar to European Speedway), desert racing, road racing, scrambling (motocross), drag racing, record breaking – the list is vast, as were the successes gained by countless riders and tuners. In fact, it would

ABOVE: Gary Nixon almost raced the 500cc Triumph in the one and only Canadian World Championship GP at Mosport in 1967. However, Triumph Corporation kept him back in the States to avoid the possibility of injury, which might have prevented him winning the AMA national title. Here are some of the other Triumph personalities that year – including team boss Rod Coates (far left) and Ron Grant (with cap) who actually raced the bike instead of Nixon.

The 1967 and 1968 AMA Grand Champion, Triumph star Gary Nixon.

need an entire book to chart everything that Triumph achieved in American motor cycle sport. These victories also helped Triumph sell a lot of bikes in the United States, thus proving that Bill Johnson was right, and Edward Turner wrong.

There was also the annual Match Race Series between Great Britain and the United States, in which once again Triumph were the pioneers, with the 1971 team being exclusively mounted on either the Triumph or the BSA three-cylinder 750s (*see* Chapter 13). But eventually all good things must come to an end, and so it was with Triumph. Though even here, Triumph had the last laugh, since it was reborn at the beginning of the 1990s thanks to the foresight of John Bloor – *see* Chapter 14.

Triumph's Daytona 200 Race Results

Year	Place	Rider	Year	Place	Rider
1940	17th	H. Lemery	1961	2nd	Don Burnett
1947	8th	Herbert Grooves		6th	Richard Clark
1948	6th	Phil Cancilla		12th	Roy Durham
1950	20th	Ed Kretz Snr	1962	1st	Don Burnett
1951	3rd	Tex Luse	1963	2nd	Larry Williamson
	4th	Don Bishop		14th	Jess Thomas
	6th	Ed Kretz Snr	1964	2nd	Gary Nixon
	9th	Richard Heinzmann	1965	3rd	George Montgomery
1952	3rd	Jimmy Phillips		4th	Gary Nixon
	8th	Robert Fisher		6th	Buddy Elmore
	13th	Walt Fulton Snr		16th	John Hamby
1953	2nd	Hugh McAfee		19th	Robert Sholly
	6th	Al Shaffer		20th	Doug Showler
	11th	Bob Boutwell	1966	1st	Buddy Elmore
	12th	Kelly Myers		6th	Robert Sholly
	15th	George Heck		9th	Gary Nixon
1954	6th	Al Shaffer		12th	Elmer Morra
	7th	Mike Dottley	1967	1st	Gary Nixon
	9th	James Hale		2nd	Buddy Elmore
	12th	Richard McDougall		7th	Dick Hammer
	13th	Johnnie Munoz		8th	Gene Romero
	15th	Dick Beaty		9th	Larry Palmgren
	17th	Jack Davin		10th	Eddie Mulder
1955	4th	Mike Dottley		12th	George Mongomery
	6th	Walt Fulton Snr	1968	6th	Buddy Elmore
	12th	Richard Clark		7th	Jim Odom
	13th	Ed Kretz Jnr		13th	Terrance Knoff
	15th	George Heck		16th	Doug Showler
	18th	Gene Smith		19th	Gary Nixon
1956	11th	J. Sherman Cooper	1969	9th	Gary Nixon
	20th	Richard Moore		15th	Dusty Coppage
1957	4th	Mike Dottley	1970	2nd	Gene Romero
	16th	Richard Clark		3rd	Don Castro
	19th	Al Shaffer		8th	Buddy Elmore
1958	8th	George Heck		17th	Leonard Fortune
	17th	Lloyd Mann	1971	2nd	Gene Romero
	18th	Darold Mathews		7th	Jess Thomas
	20th	Al Fisher		8th	Tom Rockwood
1959	6th	Richard Clark		16th	Don Castro
	12th	George Heck	1972	6th	Eddie Mulder
	17th	Ed Stafford	1973	4th	Dick Mann
				14th	Gary Scott

10 Record Breaking

Maximum velocity has been a target for speed-minded people since the dawn of the internal combustion engine: in the air, on land and on water the quest for yet higher figures has been never-ending, and motorcycling has been no exception. At first when speeds were slower the venue was not so important, and just a straight piece of tarmac, or even a hard-packed sandy beach sufficed. But as speeds increased, it became harder to find venues that were suitable, until finally it came down to just one area that was considered entirely suitable for land speed attempts: the Bonneville Salt Flats, Utah.

The Bonneville Salt Flats

Bonneville is now known throughout the motorcycle (and car) world, and its name is synonymous with record breaking. Basically it is a completely flat bed of rock-hard salt on the Nevada-Utah border, a seemingly endless horizon of salt 'pavement' absolutely devoid of vegetation.

Millions of years ago the entire western area of North America from California to the Rocky Mountains lay at the bottom of carboniferous seas. However, the shrinking and shifting of the planet during the Miocene period raised the land from below the ocean to an altitude many thousands of feet above it. During this process the limestone beds of this sea floor were thrown upward and pushed together, until the area of land that was Western America consisted of a chaotic mix of mountains and valleys. But within a very short period after the mountains were thrust upwards, the forces of erosion began their process of wear and tear, which ultimately resulted in a landscape of weather-worn crags, with some mountains high and mighty, and others little more than hillocks.

However, in the area that was finally to emerge as the state of Utah, a different situation was created, namely a basin with no outlet. Towards the end of the Ice Age, some 100,000 years ago when the Utah climate was wet and cold, small glaciers flowed down from the highest peaks, forming a huge lake. This was Lake Bonneville, and although the lake is now virtually non-existent, the salt basin still bears its name. Lake Bonneville once covered an area measuring 100 × 200 miles (160 × 320km); today the Bonneville Salt Flats are 15 miles (24km) long and 8 miles (13km) wide. To fully appreciate the vast expanse of the original lake, one has to realize that both Wendover and Salt Lake City, 100 miles (160km) apart on opposite shores, rest upon its base, and that the lake water at one time reached a full 1,000ft (300m) above the present site of both these towns!

What process brought about today's situation? Briefly, the giant lake was reduced to a glistening bed of salt by one simple process – evaporation. More water evaporated than flowed in, and the water became more and more saline until it turned into the crust that it is today. Contrary to popular belief, the Bonneville Salt Flats are not dry all the year round, in fact during the winter months the surface is usually covered with a few inches of water, caused by heavy rainfall. Consequently the most suitable time of year for record breakers is in late August or early September, when the salt flats are at their driest.

It was after World War II that Bonneville became the world's centre for the record-

The rocket-like six-fifty Thunderbird-powered machine that set average speeds of 193.72mph (311.7kmph) for the kilometre and 192.308mph (309.424kmph) at Bonneville Salt Flat, Utah, on 5 October 1955. Left to right: Jack Wilson (mechanic), 'Stormy' Maugham (designer of the streamlined shell), Wilbur Cedar (Johnson Motors), Bill Johnson (president, Johnson Motors), John Bough (Lucas) and the rider Johnny Allen.

breaking fraternity. This was for two reasons: the political upheavals caused by the conflict made a European venue difficult to resolve; and with speeds becoming ever faster, it was getting harder to find a suitable venue within European borders. Early personalities to grace Bonneville during the immediate post-war era included the legendary British speedster Noel Pope (Brough Superior) and the American Rollie Free (Vincent). By the end of 1954, the major American national records were held by riders competing for Harley Davidson, Indian and Vincent.

Meanwhile the absolute world motorcycle speed record had been upped to 185mph (297kmph) by New Zealander Russell Wright riding yet another Vincent at Swannanoa, New Zealand, on 2 July 1955. This followed the German Wilhelm Herz, who had reached 180.17mph (290kmph) with a 498cc supercharged NSU twin some four years earlier, on the Munich-Ingoldstadt autobahn.

Records and Record Holders

Now at last Bonneville was to come into its own. Less than a month after Wright's record, a 22-year-old Texan, Johnny Allen, achieved 193.72mph (311.7kmph) using a 649cc Triumph Thunderbird-engined cigar-like streamliner. But unfortunately for both Allen and Triumph, his run was not recognized by the sport's international governing body, the FIM. However, the name Bonneville finally made it into the FIM's record books, when on the 4 August 1956, Herz and NSU journeyed to the venue and set a new world record of 210.64mph (338.9kmph).

Johnny Allen Tries Again

After Herz and the NSU team had departed for the return journey home to Germany, Johnny Allen staged another attempt to wrest the crown. As before, his machine was a 14ft (4.2m) long streamliner, powered by a cast-iron six-fifty Triumph engine; it had been constructed by 'Stormy' Maugham, an American Airlines pilot. The engine was essentially a stock Thunderbird unit, built by American tuning wizard Jack Wilson, a Triumph dealer from Dallas, with years of experience in making Triumph engines into missiles. The whole effect was sponsored by Pasadena, California Western distributor Bill Johnson. There is no doubt that Johnny did go quicker than the Germans, averaging 214mph (344kmph) two-way; and the Germans were not very happy at having seen their speed bettered. The FIM, however, took a whole six months to refuse to recognize the Allen speed, due to some technicality concerning the absence of an official FIM timekeeper.

Johnny Allen getting ready for an attempt on the outright World Motorcycle Speed Record in September 1956.

BELOW: *At Bonneville Salt Flats on Thursday 6 September 1956, a streamlined, unsupercharged six-fifty Triumph broke the World Motorcycle Speed Record with a mean average speed for one mile of 214.4mph (344.97kmph).*

BELOW RIGHT: *Triumph advertisement after Johnny Allen had smashed the world record in September 1956.*

This whole decision had more to do with politics than facts, and also led to considerable animosity between the Triumph factory and the FIM, which dragged on for some time.

Bill Johnson Gains the Record

Triumph finally got their revenge, but had to wait another six years until 1962, when another streamliner, this one built by Joe Dudek and driven by Bill Johnson (not the same man as the Triumph distributor) streaked across the Bonneville Salt Flats to set an average two-way speed of 224.57mph (361.4kmph), this time using one of the T120 Bonneville engines. And as Ivor Davies recalled in his book *Triumph, The Complete Story* (published by The Crowood Press): 'This time the record was recognized by the FIM, and we were good friends again!'

IN 1965 LOOK FOR MORE TRIUMPH SUCCESSES

LIKE THESE:

GOLD MEDALS FOR 350, 500 & 650cc MODELS IN THE INTERNATIONAL SIX DAYS' TRIAL 1964
and a MANUFACTURERS' TEAM AWARD

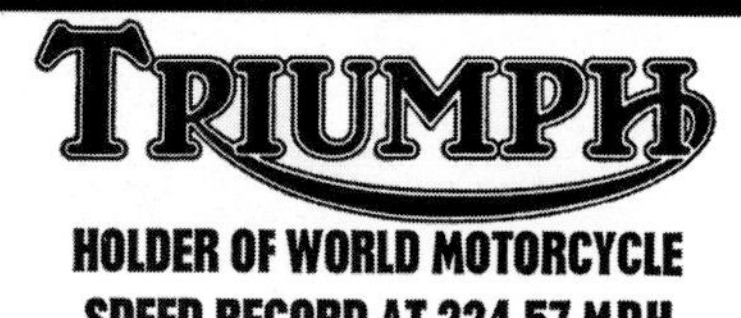

HOLDER OF WORLD MOTORCYCLE SPEED RECORD AT 224.57 MPH

TRIUMPH ENGINEERING COMPANY LTD., COVENTRY

ABOVE: Six years later, on 5 September 1962, Bill Johnson upped the speed record to 224.57mph (361.33kmph); for several years later Triumph used this success in their advertising. This time the streamlining was designed by Joe Dudek.

Bob Leppan's Record

Next on the scene was Bob Leppan, a Detroit Triumph dealer who blasted across the salt flats in August 1966 to set a new speed record of 245.66mph (395.26kmph). To achieve this, Leppan used a twin-engine device displacing 1,300cc (two 650cc engines), named Gyronaut X-1 (this was because originally it was intended to use a gyroscope to aid stability; in practice this was never used). The engines of Leppan's streamliner ran on alcohol, rather than petrol.

In 1970, Bob Leppan made a second attempt on the speed record, then held by Cal Rayborn (Harley-Davidson) at 265.5mph (427.19kmph). But unfortunately the front suspension of Gyronaut (now powered by a pair of Trident three-cylinder engines, giving a total displacement of 1,500cc) collapsed at 270mph (434kmph). Leppan was very seriously injured, and although he eventually made a good recovery, his and Gyronaut's days as a record breaker were over – and with it the era of the Triumph-engined 'cigar'.

Both Johnny Allen and Bill Johnson brought their streamliners to Britain at various times to be displayed on the company's stand at the London Earls Court Show. Many years later, in the mid-1980s, Ivor Davies discovered that

Bob Leppan's record-breaking Triumph on display in 1966.

Johnny Allen's streamliner was still in Jack Wilson's workshop, and organized its purchase by the National Motorcycle Museum, Birmingham. Here it remained on display in one of the halls for many years, until it was destroyed by the disastrous fire that gutted most of the building in September 2003.

Sprinting and Drag Racing

Sprinting – or 'drag racing', as it is referred to in the United States – is yet another branch of motorcycle sport where Triumph ruled for many years. The whole concept is to do with straight-line acceleration, whereby riders would test themselves and their machine against either

This double-engined 1,300cc Triumph-powered Parasite was the Daytona drag-bike winner for 1959, ridden by Tom Grazias and built by John Melnizuk (left, behind board). It achieved 80.71mph (129.86kmph) from a standing start, and its estimated top speed was 150mph (241kmph).

BELOW: *Ilford Speed Shop owner Stan Rodwell with his pre-unit Triumph twin sprinter: NSA (National Sprint Association) 14 October 1961.*

George Buck with his much-modified Triumph hill-climb special, at the Westmorland Sprint Hillclimb on 17 July 1964.

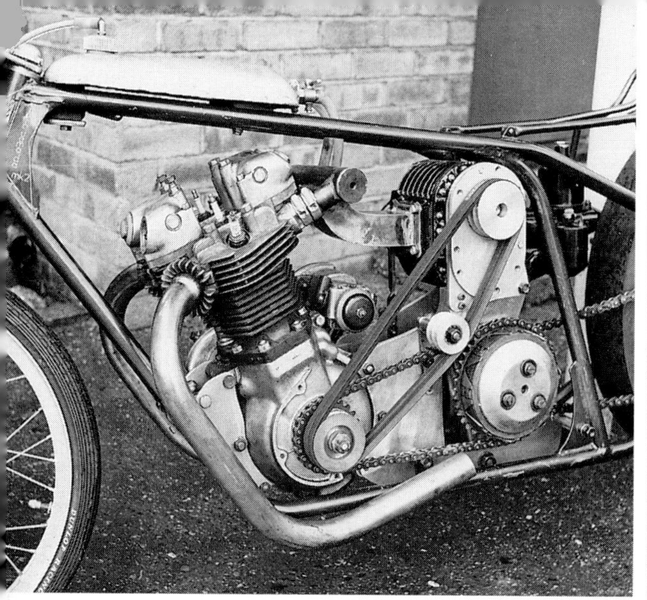

Phil Manzano's supercharged sprinter, March 1967.

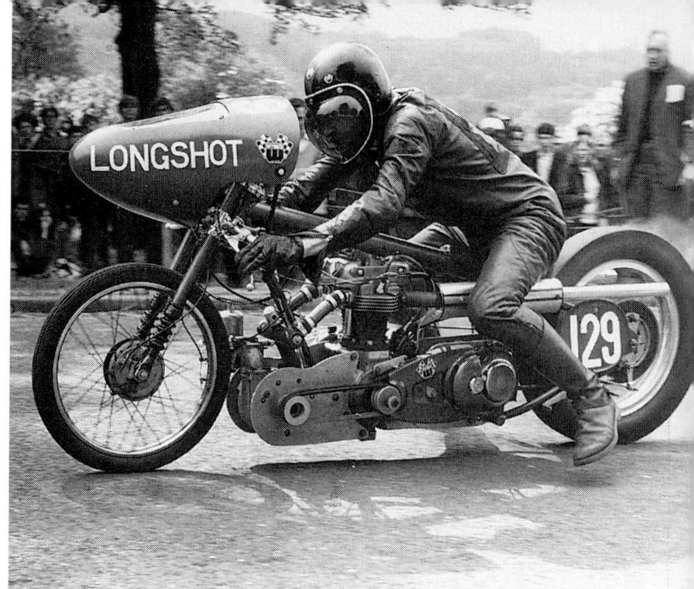

Peter Furness with his 652cc Longshot with reversed heads: Esholt Park, 4 July 1970.

BELOW: At the Brighton Speed Trials, 16 September 1971: Reg May with his 348cc Triumph (a unit-construction Tiger 90, suitably tuned).

the clock, in the early days, or against another rider, to set the fastest time/speed. Also, as compared with other motorcycle sport disciplines, the rules allowed much more freedom in what was allowed. For example one, two or even three engines could be employed, with or without supercharging, and the same went for fuels, tyres and wheel sizes. And there is no doubt that developments in America led to similar developments in Europe; with the Americans of the 1950s and 1960s making Triumph *the* engine for straight-line drag racing.

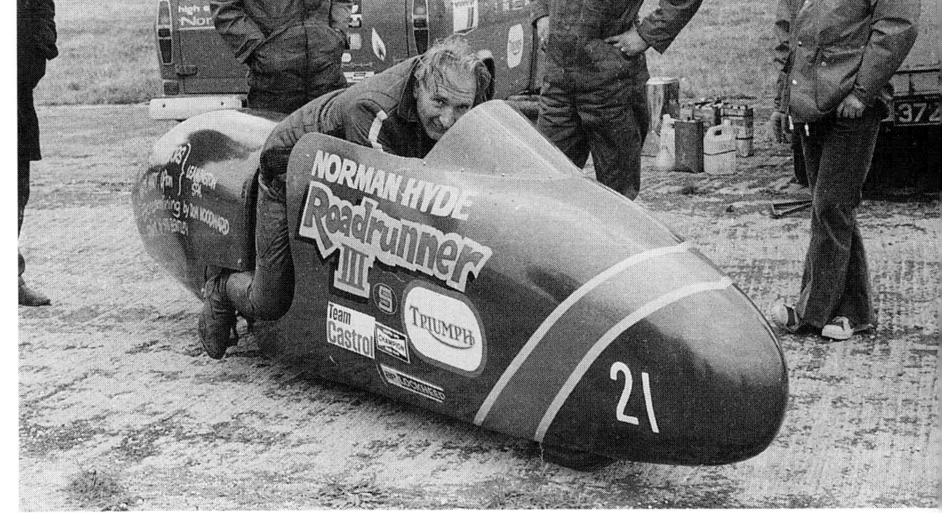

Fairford, Gloucestershire, in 1972: Fred 'Oily' Wells in Norman Hyde's streamlined 831cc Trident-engined dragster.

BELOW: Dennis Allen's Triumph-engined Ram-Rod sprinter at the London Custom Car Show in February 1972.

The first double-engined Triumphs appeared in the United States mainly as pre-unit six-fifties that had begun life as Thunderbirds, Tiger 110s or Bonnevilles. Even without enlarging the displacement, this gave 1,300cc, and with supercharging, ratios could be as high as 14:1. Usually the engines were mounted in tandem (one behind the other), but not exclusively so, as side-by-side twin-engined Triumphs (with superchargers) have also been built successfully.

With all this activity, times dropped dramatically from the end of the 1950s until the mid-1970s. Many of the fastest bikes were Triumph-powered, and this was in all the various classes, so virtually every capacity of twin-cylinder Triumph engine was ultimately employed. So when the new seven-fifty three-cylinder Trident made its debut towards the end of the 1960s, it was perhaps inevitable that this, too, should be campaigned by the straight-line boys.

Just studying the array of photographs on sprint and drag-racing bikes in this chapter gives the reader a good overall view of the variety and ingenuity of the various creations; though of course this is only a sample of the vast numbers that were built.

TOP: Norman Hyde with another version of his 831 Trident three-cylinder sprint iron.

ABOVE: Supercharged Trident sprinter.

Alastair Laurie with one of several incarnations of his record-breaking lightweight 998cc Triumph, easing off the Ramsey Sprint: ca. *early 1980s.*

11 The Thruxton 500 Miler

Many of Triumph's greatest racing successes in its latter years, when it was part of the BSA Group (it had joined in 1951), came in the field of long-distance endurance racing; this included such famous events as the Spanish 24 Horas, the French Bol d'Or, and the British Thruxton 9-Hour/500 Miler.

The First Thruxton: 1955

The Thruxton marathon was first held in 1955 at the airfield circuit near Andover in Hampshire, on Saturday 25 June. The rules stated that only two riders for each machine were allowed, and the winning team would be the one that had completed the most laps on the ninth hour. No one rider was allowed to continue for more than two hours at a stretch. Originally the event's organizers – the Ashton Combine – had envisaged a twenty-four-, or twelve-hour race, part of which was to have been run in darkness. However, they finally decided that for their first venture, at any rate, nine hours would suffice.

As it turned out, this was long enough, because the real problem was not mechanical failure or rider fatigue, so much as tyre wear. The surface at Thruxton in those days was coarse, so that tyre abrasion on corners was considerable. Front tyres suffered more than rear ones, and some of the faster riders were finding that canvas was showing before even half the distance had been completed! This situation soon caused a state of near panic, as very few teams had come prepared with spare tyres or, better still, spare wheels and tyres. Countless emergency calls were relayed over the public address system, helpers and spectators lent tyres from their road-going motorcycles, whilst mechanics were sent hurrying off to scour nearby Andover.

A Tiger 110 ridden by Frank Perris and J.E. Williams led the 1955 Thruxton 9-Hour for well over half the distance; then first Perris crashed, and finally Williams was forced to pit with engine trouble; *The Motor Cycle* race report said: 'It sounded like plug trouble, but investigation revealed a slipped ignition timing. The pinion was tight on the armature shaft, and as they had no puller they were forced to retire. Bad luck at so late a stage.' The overall victory therefore went instead to Eddie Dow and Eddie Crooks riding the very same 499cc BSA Gold Star that the former had taken to victory in the Senior Clubman's TT a few weeks before.

Third overall was a Tiger 100 ridden by H. L. Williams and G.W. Shekell, who completed 217 laps, averaging 66.48mph (106.96kmph), against the Dow/Crook BSA's 221 laps and 67.71mph (108.94kmph); 750cc class winners G.J. Hughes and S.W. Stevens riding a 649cc Tiger 110 finished sixth overall, completing 206 laps at 63.11mph (101.54kmph).

The 1956 Thruxton 9-Hour

Of the sixty teams whose entries had been accepted, fifty-eight came to the line for the start at noon. The Triumph entries for the 1956 9-Hour were as follows:

500cc Class
J.W. Dickenson and Bill Tyack
E.A. Spooner and R. Hurlstone
A. Ashley and B.A. Bennett
H. Russell and M. Wassell

750cc Class
F.C. Gray and A. Burgazzi
P. Tait and K. Bryen
J.A. Winfield and K.G. Buckmaster
H.L. Williams and G.W. Shekell
J.E. Francis and D.H. Leckie
G.J. Hughes and S.W. Stevens
J.V. Hatcher and J.H. Allington

By far the biggest number of entries was in the 350 and 500cc classes, where BSA Gold Stars easily outnumbered everyone else. This was explained by the fact that the Clubman's TT series, held annually at that time, had by then become a Gold Star benefit. Overall the first six places went to the BSA singles, a mixture of 350 and 500cc engine sizes – in fact the winners, K.W. James and I.I. Lloyd, rode one of the smaller models, completing 236 laps, 651 miles (1,047km) at an average speed of 72.3mph (116kmph). The 750cc class winners (Perry Tait and Keith Bryen riding a Tiger 110) completed twenty-two laps at an average speed of 68.01mph (109kmph).

Only two Triumphs retired, both through crashes. This was in stark contrast to no fewer than eighteen BSAs that failed to complete the race.

The 1957 Thruxton

'Heat, rain – and fatigue' was *The Motor Cycle*'s headline in their report of the 1957 event. The race was a three-way contest for honors between BSA, Royal Enfield and Triumph, and during the nine hours there were many retirements, and some extremes of weather for the contestants to endure. At the end, the winner was the 348cc BSA Gold Star ridden by Fred Webber and Rex Avery, covering 217 laps, a distance of 598.92 miles (960km), at an average speed of 74.79mph (120kmph). Second was the 649cc Triumph Tiger 110 of Geoff Hughes and Sydney Stevens, completing 215 laps – 593.4miles (954.8km) – at an average speed of 74.10mph (119.23kmph).

Most significant amongst the failures was the fast bike, the 692cc Royal Enfield Super Meteor entered by Southampton dealer Syd Lawton and ridden by Derek Powell and Brian Newman: it eventually finish third due to fuel tank problems. Perhaps the most unfortunate was the Gold Star bike of Ken James and Ed Minihan, who were in the lead with only a few laps to go when the crankpin seized. By far the most retirements were suffered by BSA machinery with fourteen, as compared to the Triumphs, of which just four retired: two were disqualified, another had big-end trouble, and the fourth suffered a split oil tank and subsequently crashed.

Thruxton 1958: Triumph Succeed at Last

For the 1958 event the Thruxton marathon was reorganized and became the '500 Miler' race for the first time. There was a total of sixty-one teams, and the race was divided into three classes: multi-cylinder, single-cylinder and 350cc. There were twenty-six entries for the multi-cylinder category, of which nine were Triumphs. They were as follows:

S.M.B. Hailwood and D. Shorey (Tiger 110)
G.J. Hughes and S.W. Stevens (Tiger 110)
I. Walton and R. Cowles (Tiger 110)
K. Buckmaster and P. Male (Tiger 100)
M.G. Bourne and M. Uphill (Tiger 110)
J. Oliver and D. Dunnicliffe (Tiger 100)
A. Burton and C.R. Erskine (Tiger 110)
E. Minihan and J.L. Payne (Tiger 110)
D. Peacock and P.H. Tait (Tiger 110)

According to *The Motor Cycle* race report: 'From just about every viewpoint, the 1958 event (now organized by Southampton club) set new levels of vitality and interest in British marathon racing.' It was followed with far more interest from both spectators and manufacturers – and significantly, because for the first time a multi-cylinder machine won, namely the Triumph Tiger 110 six-fifty of Hailwood and Shorey. They completed 220 laps in 7hr 35min, with an average speed of exactly 66mph (106kmph). A speed comparison with previous years was not valid, because the 1958 event was over a new 2.275-mile (3.66km) circuit, used for the first time that year. *The Motor Cycle* race report described the initial action in the following way:

> The start at 11.25am was ragged. McIntyre (riding a Royal Enfield) shot into the lead, but a few riders were left hacking at their kick starters, and some suffered long delays. Soon McIntyre, Percy Tait (sharing one of John Surtees' Triumph T110s with D. Peacock) and Hailwood were streaking away from the field, and it was easy to distinguish the experts from the less experienced competitors. Some riders were pulling standard road gearing, but those with more racing know-how were geared down by about 10 per cent. Some changed up while the engine was still climbing the power curve, but the experts took the revs up to peak power in each gear.

There is no doubt that Mike Hailwood and Dan Shorey made a formidable pairing. But as *The Motor Cycle* went on to say:

> It is certainly arguable that Saturday's race was won in the pits – also that it was won on reliability. The Hailwood-Shorey Triumph made four stops for fuel and change of rider, and Stan Hailwood, Mike's father, controlled those stops to a split second: petrol and oil went into the respective tanks simultaneously; at the same time brake adjustments were made, and the fresh rider pulled the model back on compression. On average he was away within 25sec of his partners pulling in.

For the first time, none of the first six finishers overall was mounted on a BSA Gold Star, and all were twins: Triumph first and fifth (Tait/Peacock); Royal Enfield second and third; Norton sixth; and the first foreign entry, a 595cc BMW R69, came home fourth. But the real duel for the lead was fought out between the Tiger 110 of Hailwood/Shorey and the McIntyre/Powell Royal Enfield Super Meteor, with only a lap separating the two machines at the end. *The Motor Cycle* ended its report by saying:

> It was when Powell handed back to McIntyre at 2.45pm that the seal was set on their defeat, for it was then that the tank was changed and the Triumph usurped the lead. In his second and third stints McIntyre rode at his brilliant best and often pulled back 3s to 4s a lap from Hailwood. Powell, too, did his utmost. But their efforts were unavailing against the trouble-free Triumph pair, and Stan Hailwood's masterly organization.

Of the nine Triumphs that started, two retired: the Bourne/Uphill machine with clutch trouble, and the Minihan/Payne Tiger 110 with a broken piston. It is also important to recall that the winning Tiger 110 was in effect a Bonneville, as it sported the twin-carb head; and the combination of the Tiger 110 and twin carbs was marketed as the T120 Bonneville from the 1959 model year. In Triumph's case, therefore, racing really did improve the breed.

1959: The Bonneville Makes its Debut

The new T120 Bonneville (*see* Chapter 7) made its debut for the 1959 model year – and nearly scored a victory in that year's Thruxton marathon. The initial leaders were Bob McIntyre and Eric Hinton riding Syd Lawton's Royal Enfield Constellation, but their bid for victory came to an end after the Enfield's primary chaincase shed its oil and the chain broke; they managed to repair it, but McIntyre then spilled at the Anchor Corner chichane, and this finally did signal the team's retirement. The lead then went to the T120 Bonneville of Tony Godfrey and John Holder, but seven minutes spent at their pit at the 350-mile (560km) stage to fix a loose dynamo cost them the race. Nevertheless, it was evident that in the Bonneville, Triumph had a formidable machine.

The 1959 Thruxton 500 Miler belonged to John Lewis and Bruce Daniels, who for nearly seven and a half hours piloted their MLG-entered BMW R69 flat twin around the Hampshire circuit with hardly a whisper emanating from its exhausts. Requiring no alteration other than refuelling, the German machine averaged 66.88mph (107.61kmph), to finish as clean as when it began. NSU made it two German wins, with victory in the newly introduced 250cc category.

Thruxton 1960: An Increasingly Prestigious Event

The foreign challenge was curbed the following year when all four classes – general (overall), multi-cylinder (over 500cc), senior (350–500cc) and lightweight (250cc) – were all won by British bikes, though none of them a Triumph. There were eleven Triumph entries:

500cc Senior Class
W. Scott and R. May, 490 Speed Twin 5TA (unit)

Multi-Cylinder Class
C. Rowe and R.S. Mayhew
D. Shorey and J.L. Payne
C. Hubbard and B. Denehy
R. Minto and J. Simmonds
J.R. Holder and P. Webb
D.T. Powell and R.A. Ingram
H. Rayner and R.A. Ingram
R. Fay and F.P. Heath
P.H. Tait and H.R. Anderson
Note: All multi-class machines were T120 Bonnevilles.

Although they missed victory, Triumphs still managed to impress, finishing second, third and fourth overall – D. Shorey/J.L. Payne; J.R. Holder/P. Webb; R. Minto/J. Simmonds. The Triumphs that retired were as follows: D.T. Powell/R.A. Ingram (withdrew over an oil contract dispute); P.H. Tait/H.R. Anderson (suffered a broken primary chain); W. Scott/R. May (crashed); C. Rowe/R.S. Mayhew (suffered an inoperative clutch).

By now the event was becoming ever more important, and was a closely fought contest with thinly disguised works or works-supported entries through the leading dealers in the land. The performances the machines delivered were highly publicised by the press, and by the manufacturers via advertisements and/or brochures. A win at Thruxton was by now a major sales weapon, and would become even more important in future years as the 1960s progressed.

Dan Shorey (who had won the race on a Tiger 110 with Mike Hailwood in 1958) is seen here during the 1960 Thruxton 500 Miler, with one of the new duplex-frame T120 Bonnevilles.

1961: Two Long-Distance Events

In 1961 two rival long-distance events were held in Great Britain during the same year, the first time this had ever happened: the Thruxton Marathon was joined by the 1,000 Kilometres, organized by the BMCRC (British Motor Cycle Racing Club) at Silverstone.

In a virtually mirror finish of the 1960 Thruxton event, the new 1,000 Kilometres was won by the MLG-entered BMW R69S, with Bonnevilles taking the next three places – Percy Tait/Bill Smith, Ginger Payne/Dan Shorey and Roy Ingram/Louis Carr. *The Motor Cycle* dated 25 May 1961 had this to say:

> The Bonnevilles were a full 10mph [16km] faster than the BMWs, but they needed more than fast lappery to win. The Shepherd/Simmons Triumph came in after fifty laps with smoke pouring from the clutch housing, and Brian Denehy's primary chain broke, mangling the inner and outer chaincases.

But Thruxton was still the main prize for both riders and manufacturers. There were twelve Triumph entries in the Multi-Cylinder Class

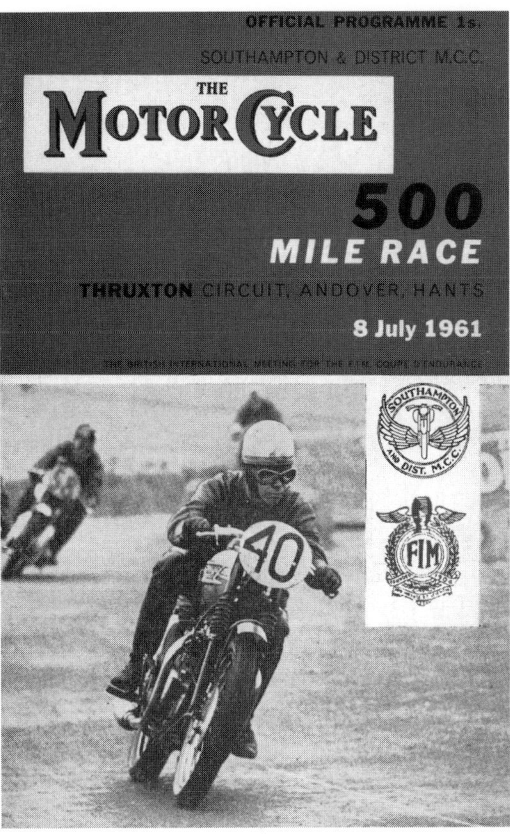

Programme cover for the 1961 Thruxton 500 Mile Race (showing Dan Shorey with his Bonneville from the previous year).

The 1961 T120 Bonneville that was ridden in the 1962 Thruxton marathon by Jack Simonium of Nairobi, Kenya.

and two in the 500cc Senior Class – and a surprise was in store for the MLG team, whose two BMW flat twins retired. The Bonneville of Tony Godfrey and John Holder went on to score a popular victory, completing 200 laps in 7hr 26min 18.8sec, at an average speed of 67.29 (108.27kmph). Incidentally, this team had been entered by former TT winner Alec Bennett of Southampton.

Besides victory overall, Godfrey and Holder also took the Multi-Cylinder Class, ahead of Percy Tait/Ray Fay (Bonneville), Fred Neville/Alan Rutherford (AJS 650 CSR), C. Erskine/A. Burton (Bonneville), Alan Dugdale/J. Buxton (Bonneville) and Jim Baughn/J. Russell (Bonneville). Triumph retirements were Colin Jones/Brian Burgess (engine seizure/crash), Dan Shorey/Ginger Payne (valve gear trouble) and Ron Langston/Tommy Robb (broken valve spring).

Interestingly, stars abounded at the 1961 Thruxton event: these included Bob McIntrye, Alastair King, John Hartle, Phil Read, Sammy Miller, Cecil Sandford and former World Speedway Champion Tommy Price – but they did not figure in the results to any significant degree. For example, the Syd Lawton-entered Royal Enfield Constellation proved so troublesome that Lawton was persuaded to switch to Norton the following year. In fact this decision to switch from Enfield – whose bikes Lawton had supported from almost the first Thruxton marathon – to Norton (the new 650SS) was the beginning of a combination that ruled for the next three years, together with riders Phil Read and Brian Setchell.

Minor Placings for Triumph in 1962

The 1962 Silverstone 1,000 Kilometres was run for the most part in persistent rain and high winds, giving the teams and riders truly tricky conditions. Read and Setchell won on the Norton, but Bonnevilles took the next two places with Ed Minihan/Chris Conn and Brian Denehy/John Stacey, and in the 500cc class J. Tanswell and W. Scott were third on one of the new unit T100A models. Triumph didn't have any greater success at Thruxton a few weeks later, either, their best places being a fourth in the Senior (500cc) Class (P. Carrona/D. Dicker) and fifth in the Multi-Cylinder Class (B. Denehy/J. Stacey).

Another problem faced by competitors at Thruxton during the early 1960s was the condition of the track surface, which by now was

Tony Godfrey during the 1962 race, in which he was partnered by Martin Holder.

Drama in the pits at a 500 Miler, with the cylinder barrel being changed on a T100SS unit five-hundred.

beginning to deteriorate badly. One has to remember that the Hampshire course was still only an old wartime airfield with straw bales to mark the circuit, not a purpose-built venue, as it is today. *The Motor Cycle* in its 28 June 1962 issue summed up the Thruxton 500 Miler perfectly:

> Skill and pluck, excitement, panic and frustration: you find them all at Thruxton's annual marathon. If you relish the full, rich flavour of race enthusiasm – with top stars, rabbits and all grades between dicing for the sheer love of it – you can't afford to miss it.

1963: A Personal View

The second of the Read/Setchell Norton victories at Thruxton was in 1963. I rode there on my Triumph T100SS to spectate, and had the pleasure of watching the victory of a sister T100SS, piloted with considerable skill by Bill Scott and Brian Davis to success in the 500cc Class, ahead of the Geoff Dodkin-entered Velocette Venom of Tom Phillips and Tom Thorp. Behind Read and Setchell came the Bonneville of Syd Mizen and John Holder, and another Bonneville third. Then came an AJS650CSR, followed by the Tiger of Davis and Scott. Incidentally, their machine was finished in white (tank, panels and mudguards), so was easy to follow as it circled the Hampshire track.

Even though, as I write, this event was forty years ago, I can still remember the day vividly, the ride there and back from my home in Stoke Ferry, Norfolk, and then the race itself. It was a lovely sunny day, and the class victory of the T100SS made it seem even better. A few weeks later I left RAF Marham, where I was stationed at the time, for a posting to Aden (now South Yemen). How I longed to be back in the lush greenery of England!

1964: The Last Thruxton Marathon

The following year, 1964, was the tenth Thruxton marathon, and it was also the last for a number of years. It was perhaps fitting that the Syd

Lawton-prepared Norton 650SS should score its third and final victory there. *Motorcycling* in its issue dated 27 June 1964 takes up the story:

> After a desperate seven-hour struggle on Saturday, the Southampton Club's international Thruxton 500-Mile, Production-machine road race was won in an atmosphere of high drama by Brian Setchell and stand-in co-rider Derek Woodman, to give the third successive victory to entrant Syd Lawton's Norton 650SS.

But hard on the winners' heels, a bare half-lap of the bumpy aerodrome circuit astern, Triumph works tester Percy Tait jockeyed one of the new unit Bonnevilles into a well-earned second place, to bring more honor to entrant Syd Lawton (of Southampton dealer Lawton & Wilson Ltd) and co-rider Fred Swift. Nevertheless it was a close thing, as the Norton had in fact gone into the pits to take on fuel, and was declared the winner without the chequered flag being waved! So another lap and the Triumph would have won. Triumph retirements were as follows:

Bonneville:	W. Purnell/D. Cooper – big end
Bonneville:	C. Lodge/E. Webb – gearbox
Tiger 100SS:	D. Chapman/R. Prowting – engine seizure
Bonneville:	J. Kidson/B. Main-Smith – faulty steering
Bonneville:	D. Snow/E. Pitt accident – damage
Tiger 100SS:	B. Davis/W. Scott – ignition

Castle Combe for 1965

In 1965 a Syd Lawton-prepared machine won the 500-Mile Production machine race for the fourth time in succession, but in this year the race was held at Castle Combe rather than at Thruxton, the latter having been closed for racing because of the by now dangerous track surface. The Lawton Bonneville was ridden by Dave Degens (co-winner of the Barcelona 24-Hour race a week before on a Dresda Triton) and Barry Lawton (Syd's son). They had a trouble-free ride, winning by ten laps at 79.16mph (127.37kmph), completing 272 laps in 6hr 18min 58.2sec. But the race, held in a mixture of sunshine and showers, did not have such a happy ending for another Bonneville ridden by Chris Conn and Percy Tait, and also entered by Lawton & Wilson: they led for five hours until an hour before the finish, when a broken primary chain put them out.

I was able to watch this race, as I had just returned from my tour of duty in Aden. My road-going mount was now a Doug Southwell-built, 649cc pre-unit Triumph engine and gearbox, mounted in a wideline Featherbed Norton chassis. Triumph retirements in this race were as follows:

Bonneville:	R. Watmore/J. Hedger - crash
Tiger 100SS:	D. Nixon/R. Knight – engine seizure
T20S Sports Cub:	R. May/C. Thompsett – big-end failure
Bonneville:	D. Chapman/R. Avery – dropped valve
Bonneville:	P. Butler/P. Carrana – broken con-rod
Bonneville:	M. Spalding/P. Fraser – hole in piston
Bonneville:	E. Davies/G. Hunter – broken swinging arm
Bonneville:	P. Tait/C. Conn – broken primary chain

This high level of retirements can be partly explained by the fact that each year the race was growing in importance, and thus, too, in its competitive nature – and by the fact that more teams were using Triumph machinery. Also there did not seem to be a particular weakness, rather a mixture of ailments. Remember these were essentially series-production machines being pushed to the very limit of their endurance.

Triumph's own 'will to win' was also shown by the introduction of the specialized, limited production Thruxton Bonneville (*see* box right).

1966: Triumphs Dominate the Brands Hatch 500-Miler

At the end of June 1966 Triumph machines took the first four of the first five places. The 500 Miler had now transferred to Brands Hatch in Kent, and this year spectators were treated to the closest finish ever, with only 10sec separating the winner and the runner-up at the end of 189 laps. The winner was Dave Degens (for the second year running), partnered by Rex Butcher on the Lawton & Wilson Bonneville; they beat the Bonneville of Percy Tait and Phil Read on a machine entered by Geoff Duke under the Scuderia Duke banner.

This meant that entrant Syd Lawton was in the unique position of being a winner for the fifth time of this by now internationally recognized test of machine durability.

1966 Brands Hatch 500-Mile Race – Overall Result

1st	D. Degens/R. Butcher (649cc Triumph Bonneville)
2nd	P. Tait/P. Read (649cc Triumph Bonneville)
3rd	G.A. Jenkins/D. Dixon (647cc Norton 650SS)
4th	D. Chapman/R. Avery (649cc Triumph Bonneville)
5th	P.J. Dunphy/R. Pickrell (649cc Triumph Bonneville)
6th	T.F. Phillips/D.L. Croxford (499cc Velocette)

It is also worth mentioning that Triumph did almost as well in the 500cc class, the result being as follows:

1st	T.F. Phillips/D. Croxford (499cc Velocette)
2nd	R. Knight/M. Love (490cc Triumph)
3rd	I. Duffell/W. Bowsher (477cc Norton)
4th	B. Bennett/J. Oliver (490cc Triumph)
5th	R. Guy/G. Green (490cc Triumph)
6th	J. Stephenson/E. Bushell (499cc Velocette)

Thruxton Bonneville 1965

Engine:	Air-cooled, ohv, vertical twin, alloy head and cast-iron barrel, 360-degree one-piece crankshaft, vertically split crankcases; unit construction
Bore:	71mm
Stroke:	82mm
Displacement:	649cc
Compression ratio:	8.8:1
Lubrication:	Double-plunger pump, dry sump
Ignition:	Twin coil system, with Lucas battery
Carburettor:	2 × Amal Monobloc 1⅛in; chopped off with single, rubber-mounted, top feed, central float chamber
Primary drive:	Duplex chain
Final drive:	Chain
Gearbox:	Four-speed, Triumph close-ratio
Frame:	Brazed and lugged tubular loop-type with single front down-tube and bolted-up rear subframe; duplex lower rails
Front suspension:	Triumph telescopic forks, with two-way damping
Rear suspension:	Tubular swinging arm, with Girling shock absorbers
Front brake:	8in full-width drum, SLS
Rear brake:	7in single-sided drum, SLS
Tyres:	Front 3.00 × 19; Rear 3.50 × 19

General Specifications

Wheelbase:	
Ground clearance:	5in (127mm)
Seat height:	N/A
Fuel-tank capacity:	4gal (18ltr)
Dry weight:	N/A
Maximum power:	52bhp @ 6,700rpm
Top speed:	124mph (200kmph)

Peter Butler with the Boyer of Bromley 500 Daytona during the 1968 event, which was held at Brands Hatch; co-ridden by David Nixon, the machine won the race outright – a fantastic achievement.

Even the Triumph retirements were fewer than the previous year, with only two failing to finish, M. Andrew/C. Dixon's 490cc Triumph with engine trouble, and J. Hedger/D. Doyle's 649cc Bonneville, whose engine seized.

The 1968 500 Miler: Triumph Wins Again

Brands Hatch was again the venue for the 500 Miler in 1968, and it had a surprise in store: all the leading large-capacity machines dropped out one by one, leaving victory to the Triumph Daytona 500 of Dave Nixon and Peter Butler. This was quite a result, considering the opposition included the 745cc Dunstall Dominator of Ray Pickrell/Dave Croxford, plus several works entries from both BSA and Triumph.

BELOW: The 1968 500-Miler winner in the pits at Brands Hatch. The Boyer T100T Daytona was a superbly prepared motorcycle, featuring every permissible extra. Note the Thruxton pipes and 'silencers', the 2LS front brake, alloy rims, alloy tank (of larger capacity), Girling racing shocks, ace bars and rear-set footrests.

As outlined in Chapter 8, the twin-carb T100T (Daytona) had arrived in time for the 1967 season, and this was a considerably more competitive motorcycle for production class racing than had been the single-carb T100SS (although this continued to be available) – a road test of the day recorded a maximum speed of almost 105mph (169kmph) in full road-going trim. Also, with its uprated braking compared to its single-carb brother the Daytona could now take on and beat the other British five-hundreds – *and* mount an effective challenge against the new crop of Japanese models, such as the Suzuki T500, the Honda CB450/500 and the Kawasaki Mach 3 triple, which were beginning to arrive in Europe.

1969: A Return to Thruxton

A return to Thruxton was made in time for the 1969 event, and Triumph machines dominated both the 750 and 500cc classes, besides the overall result that year.

In their 14th May issue, *The Motor Cycle* reported as follows:

> TRIUMPHS SET THE PACE
>
> Thruxton sizzled with speed on Sunday when *Motor Cycle*'s international 500-mile Grand Prix

ABOVE: Percy Tait during the 1968 Brands Hatch 500 Miler, with his 'works' T120 Thruxton Bonneville.

More pit action, but this time during the 1967 Barcelona 24 Hours, which together with the French Bol d'Or and the British 500 Miler were the big annual endurance events during the 1960s.

> d'Endurance returned to the Hampshire circuit. Overcast skies and a spattering of rain midway through the race did not stop Percy Tait and Malcolm Uphill on the winning 650cc Triumph Bonneville from shattering all previous records with a searing average of 84.3mph [135.6kmph]. It was the first time in the fifteen-year history of the event that it had been won at over the 80mph [130kmph] mark.

Interviewed after the race, Welsh star Uphill said 'at one stage I abandoned all hope of victory', going on to reveal: 'The engine seized and locked the back wheel, I pulled the clutch in and coasted for a while, and my heart sank. I thought we were out of the race.' After coasting almost to a standstill, Uphill had dropped the clutch, the engine had then been fired, and he toured back to the pits. There, under the eye of Triumph chief development engineer, Doug Hele, the spark plugs were changed, the bike refuelled, and Percy Tait took over. After a couple of cautious laps, Tait opened up, and from then on the Bonneville ran faultlessly to the end.

Humbled by the five-hundreds the previous year, the big bikes completely dominated the race, taking the first five places, with Triumph first, second and third. Sixth home and winner of the 500cc Class was yet another Triumph, the Daytona entered by Hughes and ridden by Ray Knight and Martin Carney.

1969 Thruxton 500-Mile Race Overall Result

1st P. Tait/M. Uphill
(649cc Triumph Bonneville)
2nd J. Cooper/S. Jolly
(649cc Triumph Bonneville)
3rd L. Phelps/C. Carr
(649cc Triumph Bonneville)
4th A. Smith/P. Mahoney
(654cc BSA)
5th K. Buckmaster/G. Collis
(649cc Triumph Bonneville)
6th R. Knight/M. Carney
(490cc Triumph Daytona)

The Trident Takes Over

Of the fifteen Triumphs entered for the 750cc Class of the 1970 Thruxton 500 Miler, most were the new Trident seven-fifty triples, rather than the Bonneville 650 twin. But even such a capacity increase didn't advantage the Meriden factory, because this year the winner was a Norton Commando, ridden by Peter Williams and Charlie Sanby; this was Norton's first win since 1964 at the event. Their works-prepared model was the biggest capacity bike up to that time to win the race. The 500cc class went to Suzuki, and the 250cc to Ducati. Most of the race was held in monsoon-like conditions (I should know, as I took part, finishing seventh on a Ducati in the 250cc Class).

In 1971 Triumph got their revenge for the Norton victory the previous year: a momentary loss of concentration cost the same Norton team certain victory when with just a few laps to go, Peter Williams slid off the factory 750 Commando and handed victory to the Triumph Trident pairing of Percy Tait and Dave Croxford. Tridents also came home sixth, seventh and eighth. Tait and Croxford managed 212 laps to win in a record 5hr 54min 26.8sec, at an average speed of 84.7mph (136.3kmph).

The Thruxton Event is Dropped

By this time the new Formula 1 for 750cc production-based bikes had been started, and the Thruxton event seemed to deteriote over the next few years; first, a change in the rules reduced the race to 400 miles (644km), and finally during the late 1970s it was dropped from the calendar altogether. In any case, Triumph participation had waned after the BSA Group financial woes, and for the remaining years of the race Norton and then the Japanese took over the limelight. Nevertheless, this is not to overlook Triumph, who for many years were a formidable Thruxton competitor – and as we have seen, even named a model after the event, the limited production Thruxton Bonneville.

12 Specials

The Triton (Triumph engine – Norton frame) was the most popular of all Triumph-engined specials for both road and racing. This Triton is unusual, however, as it features a genuine Manx Norton chassis with a pukka Triumph Grand Prix 498cc twin-cylinder engine.

BELOW: Close-up of the twin Amal carburettors, single float bowl and Manx central oil tank from the Manx Grand Prix special.

Without any question more Triumph engines have been used to construct specials than any other marque. This trend began not long after World War II, and such bikes have been built by everyone from the garden-shed amateur right through to specialists such as Dresda, who were able to get full type approval and thus take part in Production racing events as a separate manufacturer. To record all the various specials using Triumph power would take an entire book in itself, so the following is a selection of the most successful examples of the genre.

The Triton

The Triton was, and still is, the best known of all Triumph specials. First of all, the powerful, reliable, and low-cost maintenance Triumph twin-

ABOVE: JBS (Jones Brothers Special) with near-horizontally mounted all-alloy Tiger 100 pre-unit engine in a specially constructed frame. Brakes are Manx Norton, a 2LS at the front.

This Triumph special (at Cadwell Park during the late 1950s) is a mixture of several makes and models, and several home-made components. Many cycle parts are of BSA origin, whilst the front brake is a one-off dual affair, achieved by welding two drums back-to-back.

cylinder engine, combined with the equally legendary Norton Featherbed chassis, was an easy-to-build project. The first such machine came about largely because, during the 1950s, Norton would only sell a complete motorcycle, and there was a glut of Manx Norton frames and cycle parts from the many Formula 3 500cc racing cars that had been constructed. And

ABOVE: G. Clark's 498cc GCT sidecar special at Crystal Palace on 2 July 1960. It was basically a pre-unit Tiger 100 engine, with Norton Dominator brake hubs and home-made chassis. The other outfit (52) is a Featherbed Manx Norton single.

Former racer Stan Cooper of Boston, Lincolnshire, built this Triton, essentially a pre-unit Bonneville engine, Norton gearbox, Amal Concentric carburettors and various Norton Dominator cycle parts; the rear hub is a conical Triumph assembly.

although other engines were used (notably the Vincent V-twin), the Triumph was by far the most popular choice. For racing, this combination was ideal, because not only were genuine Manx Nortons expensive, but they were only available to those with a proven competition record.

The success of the original Manx-framed Triton led to a shortage of frames, once the word got around. This was solved by using components from the road-going Featherbed models that had arrived during the mid-1950s, first with the wideline and later with the slimline frame type.

Tritons have been built with both pre-unit and unit-construction engines, in capacities ranging from 350cc right up to the larger 650 and 750cc twins; and then the eight-valve Westlake engine conversion has even meant some 850cc Tritons!

LEF

The initials 'LEF' stood for Lewis, Ellis and Foster, who ran a motorcycle workshop in Watford, Hertfordshire, during the immediate post-war period. Their first attempt at building a racing motorcycle of their own design came in the late 1940s, when D.W.J. (John) Harrowell rode a superbly prepared 248cc-engined (a modified 350cc Triumph 3T) LEF at various British short circuits during 1948, 1949 and 1950, including an appearance in the TT in the two latter years.

The cycle parts were largely of LEF's own creation, and the specifications included a full duplex cradle frame, telescopic front forks and swinging-arm rear suspension. The front brake was a Triumph assembly from the Speed Twin/ Tiger 100 of the era. The LEF received considerable publicity at the time, and this led to several other Triumph 3T racing conversions for the 250cc class. Later in 1954 a twin-cam 124cc LEF racing single appeared, and this, too, was widely campaigned.

The 1964 Barcelona 24-Hour race, where Welshman Mick Manley rode this Manx-framed ex-works Triumph pre-unit twin-engined bike for the final twelve hours after his co-rider was injured.

Several Triumph 3T 350cc twins were converted to 250cc displacement for the lightweight class during the late 1940s and early 1950s. Here is just such a machine at Brough airfield, East Yorkshire, ca. 1954.

Both the 250 Triumph-based twin and the dohc single have survived, and the author was able to study them in considerable detail when they made an appearance at the CRMC (Classic Racing Motorcycle Club) 'Classicfest' at Donington Park in July 1986.

The Monard

The Monard (derived from '*Mon*ty & W*ard*') series of 500 and 650cc pre-unit Triumph-engined machines was largely the work of Geoff Monty, then a partner with Allen Dudley-Ward in a specialist motorcycle sports and racing dealership and tuning business based in Twickenham, Middlesex.

The two men had first met during the final stages of World War II, and the first of the Monty specials appeared soon after the end of hostilities. This was a souped-up Triumph Tiger 100 of 1939 vintage, to which Geoff had fitted a pair of telescopic front forks, whilst the engine was tuned and fitted with a supercharger using a cabin compressor from a German Messerschmitt Bf 109 fighter! Ridden by Geoff at Blandford, it proved faster than the recently introduced Triumph Grand Prix (*see* Chapter 13); but soon the FIM banned supercharging, and that was the end of the blown Tiger 100. However, with its innovative Monty and Ward pivoted rear fork, it did act as a test rig for the company's own suspension units. During the late 1940s, together with the similar McCandless system, the swinging-arm conversion became all the rage, both for racing and fast road work.

During the 1950s Geoff Monty built a succession of racing specials powered by AJS 7R, Velocette, and BSA Gold Star engines. Into the 1960s, and the Monty & Ward business expanded, including becoming the original Yamaha racing agents for the UK. Geoff then turned his considerable talent to the bigger classes, which coincided with the demise of the larger British four-stroke singles, the Manx Norton and Matchless G50 five-hundreds.

The result was the Monard, which put up some excellent performances during 1964, ridden by future world champion Bill Ivy. Powered by a tuned pre-unit Tiger 100 and T120 Bonneville engines, the Monard was essentially the GMS – the Geoff Monty Special, which had used a 250cc BSA Gold Star engine. The frame was notable because it had no rails under the engine or gearbox assemblies; brakes and forks were Manx Norton, whilst the swinging arm employed square tubing.

After Ivy was signed up by Yamaha in 1965, various riders raced the Monard Triumph-engined racers, including Rex Butcher and Ray Pickrell (later, Ray was a TT winner with the three-cylinder Triumph Trident).

Geoff Monty (seen here talking to his rider Bill Ivy) built the Monard (Monty & Ward) in both 500 and 650cc engine sizes – both used pre-unit Triumph engines. The frame did not have bottom rails, and was otherwise based on the Featherbed Norton design; brakes and suspension were genuine Manx components.

Ray Pickrell testing the 500 Monard at a deserted Silverstone during the closed season 1966/67.

This photograph of a unit 350 or 500cc Triumph twin-engined/ Greeves-framed special was taken at the Wirral 100 Club's New Brighton road races in 1966. Note the Norton Dominator front brake, and the home-made combined oil and fuel tank.

The Dresda Metisse

Dave Degens founded Dresda Autos in 1959; originally he specialized in Tritons for both track and road. Together with business partner Dick Boone, the fledgling concern soon found that they had a steady stream of customers wanting their services. Degens' name no doubt helped, as he was already a racer of considerable note.

During the 1960s the firm produced tuning and customizing parts, and even complete motorcycles, often with Triumph engines. A later development, in 1966, was the Dresda Metisse, using a 649cc unit Bonneville engine. At first the prototype machine employed a half fairing and massive German Münch front brakes, but the customer run of Dresda Bonneville-Metisse racers featured Italian Fontana brakes front and rear, plus a full dolphin fairing. Degens also built a number of Tritons, and again, the power unit was usually a suitably tuned Bonneville engine, with unit rather than pre-unit components.

In 1970 the by now Dresda-framed models gained a notable victory on the gruelling

At Mallory Park on 21 August 1966, Dave Degens of Dresda Autos introduced his prototype Dresda Metisse, fitted with a unit construction T120 Bonneville engine. At that time the front brake was a massive German Münich unit; later it was planned to fit Italian Fontana units. Dave Degens is sitting in the rear of his Ford Thames van on the right.

One of the production Dresda Metisse machines, with Fontana front and rear brakes. The main difference between the Dresda and the standard Metisse frames was the 'bent' triangle at the rear, and some slight modifications around the rear swinging-arm pivot point.

Barcelona 24 Hours, ridden by Degens himself and Ian Goddard. The Dresda frame was more compact than the Metisse one, because the Dresda assembly had been created primarily for a unit-construction power unit, whereas the Metisse had been produced for a wide range of engines, including many with separate engines and gearboxes (for example, the Matchless G50). Later still during the 1970s, Dresda used four-cylinder Honda engines (usually enlarged CB750s, displacing around 900cc), and these were successful in the French Bol d'Or 24-Hour endurance race on more than one occasion.

When the classic scene arrived, Dave Degens made a racing comeback using both 500 and 650cc unit Triumphs in Dresda cycle parts – the exact formula he had used to win events such as the Barcelona 24-Hour race during the late 1960s.

BELOW: Degens negotiating Mallory Park's hairpin on his 500 Dresda, at a CRMC race meeting in the summer of 1984.

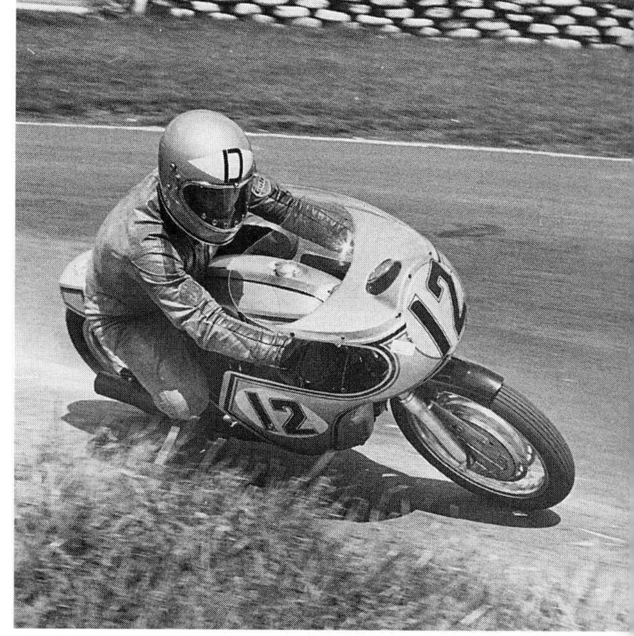

During the 1980s, Dave Degens and his Dresda Triumph (in both five-hundred and six-fifty guises) were a regular at classic race meetings, allowing enthusiasts to see once again one of the most competitive of all racing Triumph specials in action.

The Rickman Brothers

The Rickman story began a long time before World War II when Ernie Rickman, father of the brothers Don and Derek, owned a garage on the fringe of the New Forest in the small Hampshire town of New Milton. Following their father's death in 1947, the brothers, who had both served engineering apprenticeships, ran the family business until 1956 when they sold it to concentrate on their sporting interests: off-road (scrambling) racing, rather than on the tarmac. In 1958 they opened a small retail shop, again in New Milton. But as far as their racing was concerned, it soon became apparent that they were in need of machines that handled better, as they were often beaten by continental riders due to superior machinery, rather than superior talent. This led them to abandon the production motorcycles of the era, and to build their own special – and certainly their background meant they had the expertise to build hybrid bikes, utilizing the best components available.

The Rickmans called their special 'Metisse' (French for a 'mongrel bitch'). It featured a pre-unit Triumph Tiger 100 engine, a BSA Gold Star frame and Norton Roadholder forks; the tank, seat and mudguards were of

The Rickman brothers, Don and Derek, had already built up a formidable reputation off-road when they entered the road-race field with Metisse frame kits for a variety of engines, notably for the Matchless G50 and the range of Triumph twins. This Tiger 100 pre-unit-engined Metisse was photographed at a Brands Hatch practice day in the summer of 1966.

ABOVE: The Rickman Metisse, 1966 specifications, with high level exhaust, nickel-plated frame and 650 Bonneville unit engine …

ABOVE RIGHT: … the same basic kit, but for a pre-unit engine. Customers could purchase either a complete bike, or, as was more commonly the case, fit their own engine and transmission. Hi-level exhaust pipes without megaphones were considered by the Rickmans to be more suitable for short circuit events, at least with the six-fifty engine.

From 1967 onwards the Rickman Metisse racers were often equipped with disc brakes – usually Lockheed, as seen here on both wheels.

their own design. In performance, the newcomer enjoyed a debut victory at Bulbarrow Hill in 1959 with Derek at the helm, and then continued unbeaten for some fifty races – itself something of a record – which included no less than Grand Prix victories in Belgium and France. This unparalleled success led to a surge of requests for replicas, and it was then that Rickman Engineering was formed to cope with this demand. This also led to the replacement of the relatively heavyweight BSA chassis with a new one of virtually half the weight.

By 1964, half of Britain's off-road racers were campaigning Rickman-built Metisse motorcycles. There was also a lucrative association with the Spanish Bultaco marque, which was to spawn several worthwhile ventures, including the importation of the 125 and 250 TSS racing models. This surge of activity led to the construction of a new purpose-built factory that allowed much larger production runs.

The next stage came in December 1965 when Rickmans announced that they were branching out into road racing – and in February 1966, just six weeks later, the company had completed not one, but the first two bikes. These first machines were built in close cooperation with the Hornchurch, Essex, dealer/entrant Tom Kirby (six of whose 7R and G50 machines were to be rebuilt into new Rickman Metisse racers); they were to be raced by Bill Ivy at Mallory Park on Sunday 6 March 1966, the opening round of the British Championship season. And what a debut it was, too, Ivy not only winning the race, but also breaking the outright lap record of the Leicestershire circuit in the process.

Ivy's winning machine was equipped with a disc front brake that had been developed in conjunction with the Lockheed concern. But, as with the Dresda-Metisse, for the most part the first customer Rickman Metisse racers that year still used drum brakes front and rear. Eventually, hydraulically operated disc brakes were fitted on both wheels, setting a new trend that spread right across the industry.

As well as complete motorcycles, frame kits were offered, allowing owners to build their own bikes. Besides the ever popular, Triumph-engined, Metisse-framed machinery, there were versions fitted with Velocette singles, BSA unit twins and, of course, the AMC racing singles (the AJS 7R and Matchless G50). Later still, Rickman used Japanese engines, including Kawasaki and Honda.

Weslake

Originally another Rickman project, the eight-valve Weslake was a bolt-on kit for the 649cc Triumph engine (usually in unit form). This also pushed the displacement up to 700cc. Although it was a promising concept, in the early years it never really caught on; however, when the classic era began at the end of the 1970s, the Weslake gained a new life and is now commonly used, often in capacities up to 850cc. Another popular conversion is to a Morgo oil pump, replacing the 1930s Triumph plunger type for serious racing work.

The Chuck Special

Bill Chuck of Basildon, Essex, produced a range of customizing and tuning components for the Triumph twins during the mid/late 1960s; these included fuel and oil tanks, exhaust systems, clip-ons, rear sets and fairings. The original Triumph frame was retained. For the engine, the Chuck list was quite comprehensive, with camshafts, pistons, valves, valve springs and the like. Although the Chuck Triumph was fast enough for club events, and also the Manx Grand Prix, at national and international level the five-hundred and six-fifty Chuck unit twins were outclassed.

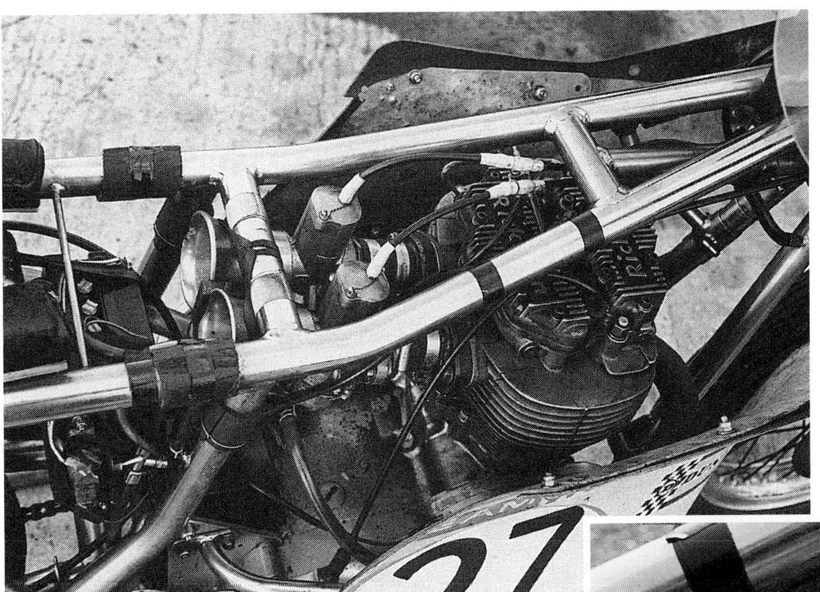

Next came the eight-valve Rickman top end for the unit six-fifty Triumph engine, ca. 1969.

BELOW: A close-up of the Rickman eight-valve top end.

The Magnum

This Triumph special was created by Anthony Hilder and Roger Northcote-Smith, who had a background in the car-racing world, as consultants. The pair then decided to apply their technological knowledge to the motorcycle world, and came up with the Deeprose-Magnum: this made its first appearance in 1971, ridden by Peter Cockram.

The frame was built up from magnesium alloy castings and tubing. The main spine ran back horizontally from the steering head to form the fuel tank and seat, and to support the rear shock absorbers; it could also act as the rear number-plate support in a bike constructed for road use. A pair of tubes ran down to support the swinging arm, which was also of magnesium alloy; to help keep costs down, it was triangulated in tubes rather than cast. The controlling suspension units were hydraulically linked. Motive power was provided by the unit construction T120 Bonneville engine, the capacity increased to around 750cc and quite high tuned. The front brake was a hydraulically operated disc in a drum hub. The wide use of magnesium, and a severe weight-pruning exercise, meant that the Magnum weighed no more than a machine of half its cubic capacity.

After the test programme was completed, the rear suspension was modified and the oil was relocated in a low-slung tank in front of the crankcase. The bike's weight ready to race with fuel and oil was an incredibly low 258lb (117kg). This, combined with the 60+ bhp of the big bore Triumph twin, meant outstanding acceleration – and this was undoubtedly one of the factors that made it virtually unbeatable over the short Brands Hatch 'Indy' circuit during the early 1970s.

Home Brewed Efforts

The home-brewed list of Triumph-powered racing specials is an almost endless one. A few of the more popular specials include the Tribsa, Tricati, Trimax, Trigusta, Tridot, Trinelli, Trihonda and Greenumph, which resulted from the matching of the Triumph engine with, respectively, BSA, Ducati, NSU, MV Agusta, DoT, Benelli, Honda and Greeves frames. The only one of these to be 'factory approved' was the DoT effort (but this was as a dirt bike, not a road racer). The favourite engine was usually a 500 or 650cc unit, whilst the most popular of all Triumph-powered specials, the Triton, used pre-unit and unit assemblies by equal measure.

The Ramotak Triumph: this is the pre-unit Tiger 100-engined version; a 200 Cub was also built. This is typical of the many home-made machines raced by their enthusiast owners.

Jon Minonno's Triumph eight-valve 'Battle of the Twins' racer at Daytona in 1981.

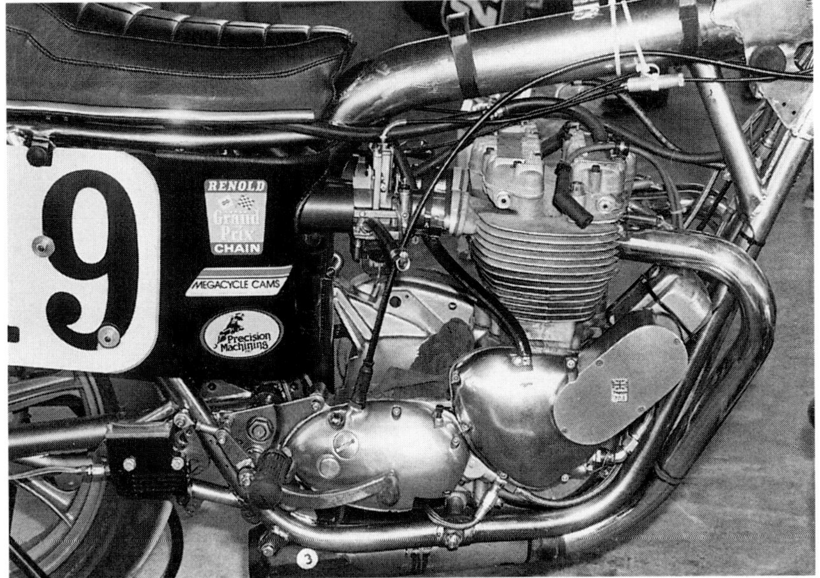

Close-up of the Minonno eight-valve Triumph; much work has been put into creating a competitive and technically interesting bike.

The Sidecar-Racing Boys

Besides the wide use of Triumph twins to power racing solo specials, the Triumph was also a popular choice with the sidecar-racing boys – though again, a full account of this part of the Triumph racing story would take far more space than is possible here. Owen Greenwood was one man who did exceptionally well when Triumph-powered. Later, Owen was to cause much controversy by racing the Mini tricar in sidecar events during the mid-1960s; but before this the Leicestershire star mainly used Triumphs. The hallmark of a Greenwood-prepared machine was its standard of workmanship. Before he joined the kneeler brigade, Greenwood's Triumph sidecars were built in the 'sit-up-and-beg' riding position; they could be fitted with either 500 or 650cc engines, these always being of the pre-unit variety.

Another notable Triumph-powered, sidecar-racing outfit was constructed by Ian Johnson in the mid-1960s. He decided to build his Tiger 110 pre-unit engine using a 180-degree crankshaft formation instead of the normal Triumph 360-degree one. The crank, of three-piece design, was reasonably easy to modify, but the camshafts were the real headache, each having to be cut between the cams and then rewelded with one lobe advanced 90 degrees on. Ignition was a Japanese Honda component, giving the necessary firing intervals.

A distinctive feature of the Johnson 180-degree conversion was that its exhaust (a 2 into 1 type) sounded exceptionally flat – it almost gave the impression that the engine was running on only one cylinder. However, performance was good, and favourable results encouraged other sidecar racers to attempt a similar conversion – though with differing levels of success.

ABOVE: Brid Caveney's very special 1968 Triumph 500 Daytona racer at De Land, Florida, March 2002: Gary Cotterell frame, Works Performance rear shocks, Yamaha rear hub, Grimeca front and close-ratio gearbox. Now resident in California, Brid had previously lived in the Isle of Man for fifteen years.

Brid Caveney's 490cc Daytona engine, with 32mm Japanese Mikuni carburettors and Bob Newby belt-drive conversion.

13 Triples

The Triumph Trident and its near brother the BSA Rocket 3 took almost half a decade to transfer from drawing board to metal. Work on the new design began at Triumph's Meriden works, near Coventry, during the spring of 1964, with Doug Hele, Bert Hopwood and Jack Wicks all being involved. The original idea was to create a 750cc class machine from, in effect, 1½ Triumph Speed Twin five-hundreds – and an excellent concept it was too, both as a motorcycle and from a production point of view, as many existing Triumph design features were utilized.

It could be argued that the BSA group, who owned Triumph at that time, were slow to react, because they did not in fact authorize production until as late as 1967. Had the Trident (and its Rocket 3 brother) been built earlier – say, in the mid-1960s – a march would certainly have been stolen over its main commercial competitor, the Honda CB750, which arrived in 1969; however, it was the Americans and Formula 750 that ensured the British triple racing successes, and this did not happen until the early 1970s.

Three-Cylinder Engine Design

The new three-cylinder engine followed existing Triumph practice, in effect adding a third cylinder to the existing twin. Valve gear copied the pattern set by Edward Turner, with two camshafts front and rear of the cylinder block, driven by gears and operating pushrods encased by vertical tubes lying between the cylinders.

Canadian Roger Beaumont racing one of the very first production T150 Tridents during the autumn of 1968. In standard 'ex-showroom' guise the 740cc (67 × 70mm) triple put out 58bhp at 7,250rpm. Note the original 'raygun' silencers and drum front brake.

A forged crankshaft was specified: after its original manufacturing operation, this was reheated and twisted to provide a 120-degree operation. Balance was achieved by integral webs, there being no conventional flywheel. With a stroke of 70mm and bore size of 67mm, the engine was slightly over-square (short-stroke), giving a displacement of 740.4cc.

The big-end bearings were plain, as were the two inner main bearings, whereas the ends of the crankshaft ran in ball (drive-side) and roller (timing-side) bearings. The crank was carried in a three-piece, vertically split crankcase, this assembly comprising a central section, to which were bolted two outer pieces. As with the early pre-unit Triumph twins, these cases carried the two camshafts in plain bearings, with an intermediate gear, driven by the crankshaft gear, meshing with gears attached to the ends of the two camshafts. But the three-cylinder was a unit-construction design, which meant that the rear of the main section doubled up as the gearbox shell, which was closed on the left (nearside) to carry the main and layshaft bearings. The underside of the crankshaft carried a finned oil sump in which was retained a gauze filter of the type employed on the existing twin-cylinder machines.

The design team provided a single-cylinder block of aluminium alloy cast with pressed-in austenitic liners. The three-ring pistons had two compression and one oil scraper rings, with the gudgeon pins running directly in the forged, light-alloy connecting rods, the latter featuring steel-backed, white-metal-lined big-end shells. The big-end caps for these were retained by special bolts that located the caps and were sealed by locknuts.

The cylinder block casting also carried pressed-in alloy tappet guides, one being located between each cylinder at front and rear; the two on the right each contained a pair of tappets, that on the left only one. Each tappet operated an alloy pushrod featuring hardened-steel end-sections.

The cylinder head was also a one-piece aluminium casting. Bolted to this were two separate rocker boxes, one containing the trio of exhaust rockers, the other the matching ones for the inlet. The head featured three separate inlet stubs bolted to it, whereas the exhaust stubs were screwed in.

The valves, two per cylinder, each had two coil-valve springs, the latter held by a conventional collar and collet set-up. The rockers were adjusted by means of simple locknuts at their outer ends, and pivoted on shafts lubricated by an external oil pipe branching from the scavenge pump feed to the oil cooler.

The Lubrication System

On the series-production Trident the oil cooler was fitted just below the steering head and was a standard fitment. Otherwise the lubrication system was the conventional Triumph/BSA dry-sump type, with a separate oil tank that fed a gear pump located in the nearside (left) crankcase and gear driven by spurs from the crankshaft. The lubricating oil passed through a second filter in the centre crankcase casting behind the engine and below the gearbox; from there the oil was supplied to the two central main bearings, which then transferred to the other crankshaft bearings. In the early engines the main bearing caps carried feed pipes to the tappets and camshafts, but this method was soon discarded as these components were lubricated by splash, as were the timing gears and pistons. In addition, the removal of the oil pipes was found to actually extend crankshaft life.

Oil drained into the crankcase assembly from where it was scavenged by the second oil pump, the lubricant passing through the oil cooler prior to its return to the oil tank. This was vented to the primary chaincase, whilst the return in the tank incorporated a drip feed adjuster and supply pipe for final-drive chain lubrication. The engine lubrication system was also responsible for maintaining the primary chaincase oil at its correct level.

The tachometer drive housing was bolted onto the top centre of the crankcase, whilst the drive spindle for this was skew-gear driven from the exhaust cam. This also drove the contact breaker mechanism from its offside (right) end, the back plate supporting the three sets of points located within a small circular housing with a chrome cover providing access for maintenance purposes.

The Ignition System

Initially, ignition was by battery and three separate coils mounted in series underneath the saddle. However, some bikes used a Lucas capacitor system, which relied on the generator to provide the power, thus allowing the 12-volt battery to be dispensed with if needed, but retaining the contact breakers to act as a trigger. But many Tridents have been used for racing and road use with aftermarket electronic ignition, a favourite being the Boyer Branden type. With electronic ignition the mechanical advance and contact breaker points are discarded, and are replaced by an electromagnetic trigger that connects to an electronic box incorporating ignition advance circuits.

Triumph and BSA Triples' Differences

At this stage it should be pointed out that the Triumph and BSA triples were not exactly the same. The original Trident (including those raced by Triumph in Formula 750 events in 1969–72) had vertical (upright) cylinders. But right from the start the BSA version had its cylinders inclined forwards by some 15 degrees. Later, during the NVT era, Tridents were offered with the BSA layout.

The crankcases of the two engines were different, as were the timing side and gearbox covers – the two latter components being designed to appear as a 'single flowering shape', as Roy Bacon described in his book *Triumph Twins and Triples*, on the BSA, and two distinct covers as on the original Trident.

The Transmission

In standard road-going guise the engine produced 58bhp at 7,250rpm (with silencers). The power was transmitted by a triplex primary chain from a sprocket mounted outboard of the oil-pump drive. To save space on that side of the engine and also to avoid excess shaft overhang, the alternator was fitted to the opposite end of the crankshaft, in the timing case. The primary chain was tensioned by a blade fitted in the base of the chaincase and adjusted from the front. It drove a shock-absorber unit that in turn was coupled to a single-plate diaphragm clutch, designed by Doug Hele with a single Borg and Beck plate. This lay within a casting fitted between the inner primary chaincase and the gearbox housing. The clutch was lifted by a ball and ramp device carried in the outer chaincase, and operated a conventional four-speed, direct-top gearbox (five speeds were usually specified in the racers).

The gearbox consisted of the traditional main and lay shafts, with the latter running on needle races and featuring gear-selector forks operated by a circular cam plate geared to a quadrant worked by the positive stop mechanism. As on the six-fifty Triumph twins, the quadrant pivot lay in the front-and-back direction within the inner cover. As previously outlined, alternative outer covers were fitted to the two engines, but both supported the outer ends of the gear pedal and kickstart lever shafts. The kickstart quadrant (needed for Production racing events) operated in the conventional manner of the mainshaft-mounted gear driving through a face ratchet. The gearbox sprocket was fitted inboard of the clutch in the normal British fashion, and drove the rear wheel by a ⅝ × ⅜ (530) final drive chain on the motorcycle's nearside (left).

The Cycle Parts

The cycle parts were considerably different from the series-production roadster compared to the factory racing threes – and the many replicas constructed afterwards. Although the basic engine assembly proved capable of being transformed from roadster to racer, the running gear did not; hence the original street-bike's frame, front forks and brakes (all based on existing T120 Bonneville components) were largely dumped in favour of purpose-built racing components. But it is worth noting that in standard form the Triumph triples featured a single front down-tube, whereas the BSA had duplex tubes.

The Racing Conversion

The well-known Triumph factory tester and veteran road racer Percy Tait was the first to campaign a racerized version of the three-cylinder Triumph (or for that matter one of the BSA versions), when he won sixth place at the international Hutchinson 100 meeting at Brands Hatch in the summer of 1969.

In November that year, the BSA/Triumph competition department was given official authorization to prepare works racing versions of the Triumph Trident (and the BSA Rocket 3) for the American Daytona 200 the following March. In a mere three months the race bikes were designed, built and tested for this prestigious event. Whilst Doug Hele oversaw the preparation of the engine units, a totally new frame was commissioned by chassis specialist Rob North. And right from the first test session it was obvious that both men had done their respective tasks superbly, the machinery being fast and having excellent handling and braking.

So why had the normally conservative BSA Group board given the go-ahead? First, it badly needed some positive publicity, as it was then entering a period of what ultimately would prove a terminal decline. There was also a rapidly growing interest in Formula 750 racing, encouraged by the new friendship between the international sports governing body the European-based FIM and the American AMA authorities. This meant that the Daytona 200 was now open to any bike (production based) up to and including 750cc; previously the Americans had restricted it to ohv engines up to 500cc and side-valves up to 750cc.

The giant American market took some 75 per cent of the BSA Group's production at this time, so the value to the British company was truly great. Finally, unlike Grand Prix racing, Formula 750 meant that although quite extensive modifications were allowed, it was still production based as far as the engine unit was concerned, so there was also the advantage of racing being a way of testing new ideas and finding solutions, which in normal use might only surface years later.

1969 T150 Trident

Engine:	Air-cooled ohv across-the-frame three, alloy head and barrel, 120-degree forged one-piece crankshaft, three-piece crankcase; unit construction
Bore:	67mm
Stroke:	70mm
Displacement:	740cc
Compression ratio:	9.5:1
Lubrication:	Double gear pump, dry sump, oil cooler
Ignition:	12-volt battery and three separate coils
Carburettor:	3 × Amal 626 Concentric Mark 1, 26mm 150mm jets
Primary drive:	Triplex chain
Final drive:	Chain
Gearbox:	Four-speed
Frame:	Brazed and lugged tubular loop-type with single front down-tube and bolted-up rear subframe; duplex lower rails
Front suspension:	Telescopic forks, oil-damped with rubber gaiters
Rear suspension:	Swinging arm, twin shocks
Front brake:	8in drum, SLS
Rear brake:	7in drum, SLS
Tyres:	Front 3.25 × 19; rear 4.10 × 19

General Specifications

Wheelbase:	58in (1,473mm)
Ground clearance:	6.5in (165mm)
Seat height:	32in (813mm)
Fuel-tank capacity:	4.25gal (19ltr)
Dry weight:	468lb (212kg)
Maximum power:	58bhp @ 7,250rpm
Top speed:	130mph (209kmph)

At Daytona

Across the Atlantic the early promise evident during the test programme was shown to be real when Gene Romero set Daytona alight during the official practising period: he was speed-trapped on one of the works Triumph Tridents at 165.44mph (266.19kmph), and he also set the fastest qualifying lap at 157.36mph (253.19kmph) (57.2 seconds) on the Daytona banking. Not only this, but the great Mike Hailwood had come out of retirement to race a BSA triple at Daytona, and actually led the race at one stage. But racing at Daytona revealed one small, but ultimately serious problem – one that all the testing in the winter months of a cold British climate had failed to throw up: the distinctive 'letterbox' air scoops at the front of the fairings in the Triumph and BSA machines did not allow sufficient cool air to reach the engine in the heat of the flaming Florida sunshine, with the result that it overheated.

So one by one the British triples lost ground, first Hailwood's machine, then Romero's. Hailwood was forced out when a valve dropped, but Romero struggled on to finish second, with Don Castro third on another triple. Victory went to Dick Mann's works Honda CB750 four. Interestingly, the Japanese design also suffered a weakness – stretched cam chains, and this resulted in all the other Hondas having to quit before full distance.

Success at Last

But the Daytona setback was only temporary, and soon the Triumph (and BSA) three-cylinder racers were winning just about everything in sight on both sides of the Atlantic. Bert Hopwood wanted to build the production roadsters more closely in line to the works racing models, but unfortunately for him, Triumph customers and the marque itself, this never happened because management never gave the necessary authorization. And sadly, the British motorcycle industry did this over and over again, thus stunting its full potential. Regarding the Triumph Trident this was particularly annoying, considering its undoubted sales potential, with the era of the Superbike just round the corner.

Percy Tait (centre) in the Triumph race shop whilst mechanics prepare one of the 1970 Daytona Tridents. Note details such as the massive Italian 4LS drum front brake, oil cooler, the ignition coils at the front of the crankcase, and the Rob North-designed chassis.

As well as in Formula 750, the Triumph and BSA triples were also the machines to beat in the 1970 series of long-distance endurance races for series-production sports bikes. In June 1970, Welshman Malcolm Uphill won the Production TT in the Isle of Man on a Trident, averaging 97.71mph (157.21kmph); whilst another Triumph three ridden by Paul Smart and Tom Dickie took the Bol d'Or 24 Hour race in France, at an average speed of 76.51mph (123.1kmph) for the 1,828 miles (2,941km) race distance. When one realizes that this was achieved against considerable opposition from rival firms such as Honda, Kawasaki, BMW Laverda and Norton, these were considerable victories.

The 1971 Season: Fantastic Success for Triumph

With Daytona as the main spur, more development work took place in the closed season prior to the start of the 1971 season. Besides the existing bikes, two Tridents and two Rocket 3s were constructed, and by February 1971 details were released. With the power output now up to 84bhp (the 1970 model was 80bhp) at 8,500rpm, the latest machines were even quicker than the previous year, capable of at least 170mph (273kmph) on optimum gearing.

The changes included twin Lockheed hydraulically operated discs with two-piston calipers in place of the giant 10.8in (250mm) Italian Fontana four leading shoe drum brakes at the front; a single Lockheed disc (again using a two-piston caliper) at the rear; and Amal concentric carburettors of 1 3/16in (30mm) replacing the GP instruments from the same source. Wider front forks were also needed to accommodate the disc brake set-up. Rob North had also designed a lower frame that dropped the overall height of the machine by some 2in (5cm); this, together with modified fairings, helped improve high speed front penetration. Because of the lower frame, the oil cooler was transferred to the nose of the fairing. All four machines were built at Triumph's Meriden factory under the supervision of Doug Hele. Engine modifications for 1971 were relatively minor: the rockers and pushrods were heavier, changes were made to the rocker-arm geometry, and there was an improved camshaft oil supply.

1971 Formula 750 Trident

Engine:	Air-cooled, ohv across-the-frame three, alloy head and barrel, 120-degree forged one-piece crankshaft, three-piece crankcase; unit construction
Bore:	67mm
Stroke:	70mm
Displacement:	740cc
Compression ratio:	12:1
Lubrication:	Double gear pump, dry sump, oil cooler
Ignition:	Triple contact breakers, coils and battery
Carburettor:	Three × Amal Concentric Mark 1
Primary drive:	Triplex chain
Final drive:	Chain
Gearbox:	Five-speed, Quife
Frame:	Rob North steel tubing; hydraulic steering damper
Front suspension:	Telescopic forks, oil-damped
Rear suspension:	Tubular swinging-arm, twin rear shock absorbers
Front brake:	Dual Lockheed hydraulically operated discs, with two-piston calipers
Rear brake:	Single Lockhead hydraulically operated discs, with two-piston calipers
Tyres:	N/A

General Specifications

Wheelbase:	N/A
Ground clearance:	N/A
Seat height:	N/A
Fuel-tank capacity:	5.7gal (26ltr)*
Dry weight:	364lb (165.1kg)
Maximum power:	84bhp @ 8,500rpm
Top speed:	170mph (273kmph)

* For Isle of Man TT

The 1971 Daytona 200

Besides several leading American riders, the Triumph and BSA triples were to be ridden at Daytona in March 1971 by Paul Smart (Triumph) and Mike Hailwood (BSA). A notable signing was the 1970 Daytona 200 winner Dick Mann, who would ride a Rocket 3. There were no fewer than ten riders in all on the British threes. The race itself was to be virtually a carbon copy of the 1970 event, with Hailwood leading until once again sidelined with valve troubles. Paul Smart took over and led for a considerable distance, but with a mere thirteen laps to go, his Trident retired with a holed piston. This left that wily old Daytona campaigner Dick Mann to sneak yet another famous victory in America's premier race – and although it was with a BSA, rather than Triumph, the winning bike had been built at Meriden. Gene Romero repeated his 1970 result with runner-up slot on his Trident, whilst twenty-year-old Don Emde was third on another Rocket 3. So for 1971 it was an all-British rostrum.

In fact the Daytona result was to be just the start of a fantastic year for the Triumph and BSA triples, as they went on to sweep everything else aside.

Percy Tait and mechanic Fred Swift at Mallory Park, 14 March 1971, with one of the latest Trident Formula 750 machines.

The Anglo-American Match Race Series

The next big event in the 1971 race calender was the three-meeting Anglo-American match race series, in which the entire British and American teams rode either Triumph Tridents or BSA Rocket 3s! The idea for the series was originally Peter Thornton's, president of BSA Incorporated of America. Then Peter Deverall, marketing director of the BSA Group's motorcycle division back in the UK, negotiated with circuit owners MCD (Motor Circuit Developments), who agreed to host the series at their Brands Hatch, Mallory Park and Oulton Park circuits on 9, 11 and 12 April 1971.

The project was given huge impetus when American Gary Nixon came home fourth on a works Triumph Trident at Mallory Park's international 'Race of the Year' in September 1970. Nixon put up a terrific display in what *The Motor Cycle* described as 'a scintillating battle'. He was the first top-class American to contest a British event for some sixty years. Ironically Gary Nixon was unable to take part in either the Daytona 200 or the new match races in the spring of 1971, having broken his leg in a crash during pre-season training on a road bike.

The BSA/Triumph-sponsored American team was originally to have consisted of the first five men in the 1970 American Championship series: Gene Romero (Triumph), Jim Rice (BSA), Dave Aldana (BSA), Dick Mann (BSA) and Don Castro (Triumph). But Romero decided not to come because 'the financial rewards were not great enough', and he was replaced by Don Emde. Gary Nixon (still suffering the effects of his broken leg, which had been pinned) also came over to Britain as honorary team captain. The British team consisted of Percy Tait (Triumph), Ray Pickrell (BSA), Paul Smart (Triumph), Tony Jefferies (Triumph) and, having his first ride on one of the triples, John Cooper (BSA).

But there was drama before the Anglo-American race series even began, when four of the riders in the six-strong American team were involved in crashes at Oulton Park a few days earlier, which nearly put paid to their attending the start of the series the following Easter weekend! The first occurred even before the Americans climbed onto their bikes: Jim Rice was driving a hired Ford Zodiac car, accompanied by Daytona winner Dick Mann and Don Castro. They had covered several laps of Oulton Park when Rice lost control and the car finished up on its roof at Lodge Corner. Undeterred and fortunately unhurt, they clambered out, righted the car, and within an hour were all practising on their race bikes. The second crash occurred when Dave Aldana hit oil left by the car and slid off, as one newspaper report said, 'in spectacular style'. But he, too, was uninjured, and his BSA only superficially damaged.

On race day Mann and Gary Nixon – the latter showing that he was fitter than anyone had imagined – set the pace for the Americans, and British teamster Paul Smart observed that it would be 'a lot closer than most people seem to think'. American Champion Gene Romero had flown over for the pre-race press conference at The Royal Lancaster Hotel, London, even though he was not racing. At this same event Paul Smart received cheques to the value of $US 3,750.00 (£1,700.00), his reward for

ABOVE: For 1971, dual Lockheed hydraulically operated discs replaced the Fontana drum brake at the front of the F750 works racers. Calipers were two-piston affairs, the discs being of solid, undrilled form.

Installation of the three Amal Concentric Mark 1 carburettors on the Triumph (and BSA) triples.

The Easter 1971 Triumph/BSA-mounted American match race team. Left to right: Don Castro, Gary Nixon, Jim Rice, Dave Aldana, Dick Mann and Don Emde.

American teamster Don Castro approaches the fearsome Paddock Hill Bend at Brands Hatch during the first meeting of the 1971 Anglo-American match races.

Gary Nixon (right) and Dick Mann at Oulton Park, Cheshire, at the Easter match races in 1971.

setting the fastest practice lap at Daytona and for leading the race for thirty-one laps.

The score after the six races (two at each venue) was Great Britain 183, and the United States of America 137. So by a massive forty-six-point margin the home team won the first Anglo-American match race series at Brands Hatch, Mallory Park and Oulton Park. Joint top scorers were Paul Smart and Ray Pickrell. The top-scoring American was the consistent Dick Mann. John Cooper, who scored the fourth highest points was probably the most impressive, as it was the Derby man's debut on one of the big triples.

'Race Gossip'

But it was the high costs of staging this whole exercise that really made the headlines – particularly in a historic context, as the whole BSA Group was only months from financial disaster. And because of this I make no excuses for reproducing in full my friend Mick Woolett's piece from his 'Race Gossip' section in *The Motor Cycle* dated 14 April 1971; with the heading 'Will the BSA's bubble burst?' it went on to say:

> Strange how times change – and stranger still how quickly we accept new situations. And surely the most striking change in the motorcycle scene over the past few years has been the emergence of the BSA-Triumph group as a major force in road racing. It wasn't so long ago that there was rarely even talk of road racing at Small Heath (BSA's headquarters): the powers-that-be simply would not hear of it. Now, with the American corporation making the running, the group are spending more money this year on this branch of the sport than any other factory in the world. Rumours in the States speak of a million dollar race budget for 1971. This covers all types of contest, from short-track to road racing, but the major slice of the money is going to the latter and the development of road-race machinery. Of course, the million-dollar tag is probably a pretty wild exaggeration, but you can get some idea of the vast sums to be spent if you take a brief look at the finances of the weekend's match race series. For example, when American champion Gene Romero made it clear that he didn't want to take part, this was agreed, but he was asked to travel to England to be present while the series was on. He flew first class from California, stayed at the Dorchester, travelled in a chauffeur-driven car, and had an expenses allowance. Cost to the group? I guess about £1,200! Multiply that by twelve (six riders, plus team manager, two mechanics, and two or three executives) and you get some idea of what the actual match-race series cost: £14,400. Add a few inevitable extras, and BSA-Triumph won't get much change out of £20,000 [at 2004 figures, this represents over £200,000].
>
> As a racing enthusiast and firm believer in the value of publicity gained through racing and record breaking, I'm delighted that BSA-Triumph are making such a flat-out effort, but I must admit that the cost frightens me – it seems like a wonderful dream that will end with a bang!

And how right Woolett's comments were to prove in the coming months.

The Three-Cylinder Racer is Put to Test

In May 1971 *The Motor Cycle* staffman David Dixon was able to test one of the works three-cylinder racers. Dixon began by saying:

> Exotic sounds and big names have for long been the successful recipe for spectators, but the mixture has been synonymous with the foreign machinery usually ridden by British riders. Until Easter: then the Anglo-American match race series called a halt, and for that we have to thank our American cousins and the BSA-Triumph group.

Of the fourteen three-cylinder factory racers built up to that time, David Dixon was able to sample two over the 2.78 mile (4.47km) circuit at Snetterton in Norfolk shortly after the extremely successful match races (some 66,000 spectators viewed the series). Most of his riding was on John Cooper's BSA Rocket 3, but he also used Paul Smart's Triumph for comparison purposes. Although blisteringly fast, Dixon's main concern was the handling:

> This was my only real criticism of last year's equivalent – Percy Tait's Daytona seven-fifty, which I galloped at Snetterton in August 1970. This model showed a tendency for the front wheel to chop out when cornering over ripples. However, although the effort to chuck this model from one side to the other is considerable, now the handling is so good that one can concentrate entirely on the purely physical effort.

The difference was thanks to the modified frame: not only was this 2in (5cm) lower, but the fork angle had been made steeper, from 62 to 64 degrees. David Dixon also discovered that:

> Stiffer rear suspension has cut weaving but gives a harsher ride, and I found I was being thrown out of the seat over the more severe of Snetterton's bumps. But the bike really does stick on line. Although mechanically similar to the BSA, Smart's Triumph pointed up variations between the pair.

Externally the major difference was, of course, the BSA's sloping cylinder block. Theoretically this should have given marginally better handling, because the weight was a trifle lower and further forward. But as Dixon discovered, 'the handling discrepancies came from Smart's opting for softer rear suspension, while Cooper chose hard springing.' Dixon found that 'where the Triumph was inclined to wallow over undulations, the BSA's rear wheel pattered, in the process transmitting shocks to my bottom.' Unlike the 1970 bikes, the latest models featured movable seats and alternative footrests to suit individual riders. Vibration on both machines was felt mainly through the seat, but Dixon found that it 'was not at all troublesome, and was less than that normally experienced on a standard roadster three'.

Snetterton was much wider and more open than the majority of the British short circuits, but even here David Dixon said that 'without question, they are men's machines – big, hairy monsters so powerfully quick that they must soon require a race of big, hairy men to handle them.' Nevertheless, he also concluded that:

> The new bikes are wonderfully satisfying to ride! I restrained myself from yanking open the throttles when coming out of the hairpin – just as well! The steering went light as the revs rocketed to 8,500 in first, second and third, and only when I snicked into fourth did the airborne feeling disappear; the acceleration is guaranteed to make your heart go thumpity-thump. They are terrific. All we need now are more Formula 750 races to keep them exercised.

But to anyone who had worked alongside Doug Hele throughout his career, the success of these machines was no real surprise, knowing his methodical, realistic approach to technical issues and racing alike. His development team had included the likes of Norman Hyde (later to set up his own tuning business) and John Woodward, and the results spoke for themselves.

The Boyer Racing 750 Trident racer, ca. 1971: Seeley frame, Paghlin brakes, alloy tank, hydraulic steering damper, 19in Dunlop KR racing tyres, and race-kitted engine.

Detail Improvements for 1971

Essentially as originally constructed for the 1970 Daytona 200, the Triumph (and BSA) triples were 95 per cent right. But what Hele and his team did for the 1971 Trident racer was largely attention to detail. Besides the frame changes already charted (and looked after by Rob North) and also the disc brakes, the main thrust of the detail improvements concerned the engine and streamlining.

Besides the modified valve gear (the rocker details have already been described), the engines were modified from standard production and provided with new camshafts (giving increased lift and longer opening), reworked combustion chambers to suit the specialist 12:1 Hepolite pistons, cleaned up porting, polished (standard) crankshaft and connecting rods, larger carburettors, and a three-into-one exhaust with single megaphone.

Design and construction of the three-piece fairing for the 1971 bikes was a team effort involving the development team, group engineering staff and the BSA-Triumph research establishment at Humberslade Hall, and Ray Lloyd and his colleagues from the specialist Screen and Plastics company.

'Reduction of drag' was the main purpose, combined with cooling. As already mentioned, the lower frame had made it possible to transfer the oil cooler from its original home (ahead of and slightly above the exhaust rocker box) to the nose of the fairing. The first trials of the forward-mounted oil cooler took place in May 1970, but at that time no provision was made for leading away heated air that had passed the cooler. Later a new system was adopted to do just that, so that cooling air now reached the oil cooler through a narrow horizontal slot, just below the front racing number plate. From a box at the rear of the cooler, the heated air was transferred via a nose pipe at each side to an exit louvre in the fairing side.

To the casual onlooker, one aspect of the 1971 Triumph and BSA works racers was somewhat puzzling: why did the aluminium

Besides its widespread use in Formula 750 and Production machine events, the Trident was even used as a power source on three wheels, as this kneeler sidecar outfit shows.

fuel tanks have two filler caps? The following is the answer given by Doug Hele when interviewed by Bob Currie in March 1971:

> A Daytona refuelling stop has to be seen to be believed. They have these huge, quick-filler devices, with a 2in diameter butterfly valve, and ... woosh! The tank is full in six to eight seconds! But obviously, for that much fuel to go into the tank in that few seconds, the same amount of air must be displaced in the same period. I am keen to try an aircraft refuelling system, too, with a hose connected to a valve in the side of the tank and the supply cutting off automatically when the tank is full. In addition, the machines used in British short-circuit events had a much smaller tank – all with only a single filler cap.

Continuing Successes

Thruxton 500 Victory

A momentary loss of concentration cost Norton an almost certain victory in the Thruxton 500 race for series-production machines in May 1971. In 1970, Peter Williams and co-rider Charlie Sanby won in what *The Motor Cycle* called 'appalling weather' (I can testify for the conditions, having also taken part on a Ducati 250 Mark 3). But in 1971 the sun shone, and the same two Norton riders built up a two-lap lead over their closest rivals. But in a momentary lapse of concentration Williams made a mistake and dropped the bike after locking up the front wheel. So with the Norton out, the lone works Triumph Trident in the race came through to win in a record-breaking 5hr 54min 26.8sec, and an average speed of 84.7mph (136.3kmph). This was the fourth success in the Southampton Club's long-distance event by veteran Percy Tait, partnered by Dave Croxford. In second place, a lap astern, came a 750 Rocket 3 piloted by Bob Heath (who then worked at BSA's Small Heath factory) and John Barton (employed by Triumph at their Meriden works).

Superbike Victories

The first ever Superbike race was staged at Brands Hatch on Monday 31 May 1971 – and Percy Tait roared to victory, thus adding another page in the success story of the Triumph/BSA three-cylinder racing machines.

Then came the annual Isle of Man TT races, and even before the event it was felt that, given good weather, the new Formula 750 race was bound to set at least one record. As reported by

The Motor Cycle: 'It must be the first new event to go into the annals of the Isle of Man series with lap speeds over the magic ton.' And the commentators were absolutely correct, Tony Jefferies taking his factory Triumph Trident to victory at an average speed of 102.85mph (165.48kmph) – *The Motor Cycle* headline in their 9 June 1971 issue shouting 'Wow, What a Race!'. Jefferies also established a lap record for the class at 103.21mph (166.06kmph). Ray Pickrell (BSA Rocket 3) was runner-up, with Peter Williams (Norton Commando) third.

The Formula 750 wasn't the only Triumph TT victory in 1971, because five days later, Jefferies with Ray Pickrell stormed home ahead of the field in the four-lap Production race, riding another Trident. Actually, three of the top six finishers were mounted on Triumph triples. The works Triumph and BSA three-cylinder bikes had special 5.7gal (26ltr) fuel tanks to enable them to complete the race non-stop. Ray Pickrell averaged 100.07mph (161.01kmph) – and it was the first time in TT history that a race restricted to catalogue sports machines in full road-going trim had been won at over the magic ton. Pickrell had switched from his BSA to Paul Smart's Triumph after trying both in practice, and he said after the race that 'the Triumph seemed a little smoother, with less vibration'. Through *The Motor Cycle*'s speed trap Pickrell's machine recorded 142.3mph (229kmph). As a point of interest, the first six finishers were:

1st	R. Pickrell (Triumph Trident)
2nd	A. Jefferies (Triumph Trident)
3rd	R. Heath (BSA Rocket 3)
4th	H.O. Butenuth (BMW R75/5)
5th	D. Nixon (Triumph Trident)
6th	B. Clark (Norton Commando)

Pickrell's bike was subsequently nicknamed 'Slippery Sam', and was destined to be used by various riders to win the Production TT for the following four years, making a record-breaking five wins in all. Lovingly maintained by Les Williams after it finally retired, it ended up in the National Motorcycle Museum, Birmingham.

More Technical Details

At the 1971 TT more technical details of the Triumph and BSA triples were revealed. First, two of the Formula 750 engines were given overhead rockers – where the ball-end adjusting screw was switched from the valve end to the pushrod end. This made it possible to grind the rocker arm for line contact with the flat valve top, rather than point contact, so vastly increasing the contact area (at the other end, contact form was unaffected). This change was made by Hele and his team to eliminate indentation of the valve tip, which not only made it impossible to check the running clearance with a feeler gauge, but much more seriously, it led to failure once the indent extended through the case hardening. This happened to Mike Hailwood's BSA when he was leading the 1970 Daytona 200. The new rocker was lighter, and the inertia of the adjuster was reduced because its travel was shortened. Access holes for the repositioned adjusters had to be provided in the rocker boxes by the engineering team.

Another important, but as yet unreported change, was made to the steering-head bearing, necessary because of the increased braking power since the introduction of the twin discs at the front. The original cup-and-cone steering-head bearings had been replaced by a four-bearing layout that Hele considered was much better suited to the increased loadings. Conventional taper roller bearings were passed over because, though they were thought to be entirely satisfactory for ordinary usage, their included angle of some 30 degrees was considered too small for the 570lb (258.5kg) that the Formula 750 Trident racer weighed, including bike, fuel, oil and rider, and when capable of speeds well in excess of 150mph (240kmph). Hele considered an angle of 70 to 80 degrees would be more appropriate.

Therefore a pair of crowded roller bearings looked after the braking loads, whilst two caged, radial-roller bearings looked after the axial loads. The margins were such that no provision for adjustment was deemed necessary, and this maintenance-free feature was an added bonus in machine preparation.

At the same time, Doug Hele revealed that on the sports production racing bikes (including Pickrell's TT winner), the increased power was 'largely attributable to a new cam form'. Compared with the standard cam shape there was some forfeit of torque in the lower part of the rev range, but the use of five speeds made light of this. Also the large capacity fuel tanks meant that the works production models were able to do the race non-stop. Argument had long raged in TT circles as to whether or not the time saved in cutting out a fuel stop was countered by impaired handling in the early laps, when the fuel load was greatest – but Doug Hele ensured that it wasn't by jacking up the front fork springs, thus making sure that the steering geometry was unaffected by the additional weight. Thicker oil in the fork legs gave the stiffer damping required.

Hele also revealed that the carburettors used by the team during the 1971 season were his own development of the Amal Concentric 930 instruments. His aim was 'to get as close as possible to the peak power and peak torque (at 7,000rpm) obtained when using Amal GP carbs, whilst retaining the advantages of the Concentric.' Chief of these was obviating fuel-height variations in the jet when cornering – a centrifugal effect encountered when using the separate float chambers with the GPs. Also, the linkage employed with the modified Concentric cluster retained the synchronization of the throttle slides better than did three cables.

The deficit in peak torque with standard Concentrics was in fact due to the diameter of the trumpet being considerably bigger than that of the induction tract proper, and offset to it, to accommodate the primary air-bleed holes, the excess diameter reducing air speed, whilst the offset disturbed the flow. A smaller diameter trumpet, in line with the main tract, put this right, but naturally masked the air bleeds. As a result there was insufficient mixture compensation for snap throttle opening from three-quarters to flat out.

Hele found the solution was to turn the air-bleed passages through 90 degrees, bringing them out at the bottom of the trumpet boss. He also maintained that it was an advantage that the right-angle turn also trapped blow-back droplets of fuel.

The net outcome was that Hele's Concentric modifications resulted in a peak power figure to within 1bhp of that provided by the GPs, whilst acceleration out of corners was much improved, the engine being, as he put it, 'so tractable that there is virtually no meggaphonitis'.

Financial Difficulties

Amidst the glory accrued from its race victories with its three-cylinder racers, the parent BSA group announced a massive economy drive at the beginning of July 1971 – in an attempt to stem the previous year's huge trading loss – and the need to increase prices as a result of rising material, component and production costs. Because of this latter move it was expected that demand for its motorcycles would fall and bring about production cuts.

At the same time they announced that they had 'parted company' with motorcycle division managing director Lionel Jofeh, and warned their 7,000 employees 'of impending redundancies'. In addition the BSA Group abandoned all its moto cross and trial plans, and closed its competition shop. The road-racing side, largely funded by BSA-Triumph's USA arm, 'would continue at present'; this being overseen by Doug Hele and his team from Triumph's Meriden works. The only good news of the entire week was Dick Mann's victory (on a BSA Rocket 3) at Kent, Washington, in the tenth round of the AMA National Championship, which he was already leading by a comfortable margin.

Back in Great Britain, Percy Tait and Ray Pickrell gave a 'high speed formation exhibition' on their triples at Snetterton during the third round of the Shell-sponsored Team Challenge championship.

The following week came reports that a proposed takeover bid by multi-millionaire Dr

Daniel McDonald, boss of the Bermuda-based investment company, Vision Enterprises, had stalled, awaiting reports from the BSA Group's auditors, Cooper Brothers. It was also reported that 850 workers had been made redundant. But one ray of sunshine in an otherwise gloomy BSA-Triumph scene was that the road-racing programme in both the UK and the USA would continue. Race chief Doug Hele had this to say: 'It is our intention to have three works machines at both the Hutchinson 100 at Brands Hatch on Sunday 8 August, and at Silverstone two weeks later.'

Triumph tester Percy Tait rode a Trident at Castle Coombe in mid-July, finishing runner-up in the 750cc race to Ken Redfern riding a Dunstall Norton twin. Paul Smart (Triumph) and Ray Pickrell (BSA) were to race the other machines at Brands Hatch and Silverstone, Smart being now recovered from the injuries that had kept him out of the TT.

At the end of July it was revealed that the BSA group had recorded a £3.3 million loss. Dr McDonald admitted that 'The size of the loss came as a surprise', and his interest cooled. These worse-than-expected losses were blamed on delays in designing new models, production problems, and a consequent low volume of output in the period leading to the beginning of the peak selling season.

Triumph Successes

The annual Hutchinson 100, held that year at Brands Hatch, saw Paul Smart win both fifteen-lap legs on his works Trident. He finished ahead of Ray Pickrell (BSA Rocket 3), Barry Sheene (500 Suzuki twin), Tony Jefferies (Triumph Trident), Percy Tait (Triumph Trident) and Rod Gould (350 Yamaha). A couple of weeks later, big-time bike racing made a return to Silverstone. *The Motor Cycle* race report in their 25 August 1971 issue picked up the atmosphere:

> Silverstone had seen nothing like it since the great days of the early 1950s, when Geoff Duke reigned supreme on the works Nortons. Every road to the 2.9 mile Northampton circuit was jammed two hours before the meeting was due to start, and programmes were sold out before racing got under way.

There were two main reasons for the crush. Mike Hailwood (riding a 350 Yamaha) was back in action on two wheels in Britain for the

Production racing was a happy hunting ground for the Triumph Trident triple. Works star Paul Smart puts one of the five-speed works bikes through its paces in the summer of 1971.

first time in nearly two years, and the international meeting sponsored by the John Player cigarette brand was the first major motorcycle event at Silverstone for six years.

Triumph and BSA triples dominated both the Formula 750 and Production races. In the F750 Paul Smart (Triumph) won, and in the process set a new motorcycle record for Silverstone at 104.95mph (168.86kmph), with Percy Tait (Triumph) second and Ray Pickrell (BSA) third. Behind these 750cc racers Hailwood and John Cooper (350 Yamsel) fought it out for fourth spot, with Hailwood eventually taking the flag first. Five of the first six finishers in the Production race were on the triples, the result being: 1st Ray Pickrell (BSA); 2nd Paul Smart (Triumph); 3rd Percy Tait (Triumph); 4th Peter Williams (Norton); 5th Pete Butler (Triumph); and 6th Dave Nixon (Triumph). Pickrell and Smart shared the fastest lap at 101.32mph (163.02kmph). As a comparison, when winning the 500cc race, World Champion Giacomo Agostini set the fastest lap at 102.7mph (165.24kmph) on his works three-cylinder Grand Prix machine.

Just a week after shattering the Silverstone lap record, Paul Smart and his works 750cc Triumph Trident scored another victory on Sunday 29 August 1971 at Snetterton. The 'Maidstone Flyer', as Smart was nicknamed, scorched round the 2.71 mile (4.36km) Norfolk course to victory in the main 'Race of Aces' event, and in the process pushed the absolute motorcycle lap record up to 96.98mph (156.04kmph). This was 1.15mph (1.85km) faster than the old record, set up by Rod Gould on a factory 350cc Yamaha, and over 3mph (4.8kmph) faster than Mike Hailwood's record on a 500cc Honda! These speeds prove just how quick the 1971 three-cylinder Triumphs really were.

And so it continued: the following weekend Paul Smart became the first man on a motorcycle to lap the South London 1.3 mile (2.09km) Crystal Palace circuit in under a minute (in fact he did it twice) (these speeds were achieved during his victory in the Sponsors Challenge race). The same weekend Percy Tait clinched the 750cc British Championship title at Castle Combe, Wiltshire; he also set the fastest lap, at 93.3mph (150.1kmph).

Triumph Triple Versus MV Agusta

By now, many people were wondering whether a works Triumph-BSA triple could beat Agostini and his five-hundred MV Agusta. It was a provocative question, and one that highlighted the significant progress made by Doug Hele and his team at the Triumph factory in developing the three-cylinder racers over the previous few months. As Mick Woolett said in his 'Race Gossip' column in *The Motor Cycle* dated 8 September 1971:

> Twelve months ago an ace rider on a good TR2 Yamaha was more than a match for the big British racers. In fact, at the Hutchinson 100 and the 'Race of the South' the best Paul Smart could do was to finish a well beaten fourth and fifth respectively. Now the tables were truly turned, and the Yamahas can't live with Smart or his BSA-mounted team-mate Ray Pickrell.

But at the forthcoming Mallory Park 'Race of the Year' the 750cc triples would have to beat not only the best of the Yamahas, but also Agostini and his MV. And Mallory, with a wide variation of corners packed into only 1.35 miles (2.17km), was a far cry from the wide, sweeping bends at Silverstone. Yet John Cooper had proved that the big British racer *could* go at Mallory, when he equalled the lap record in the Anglo-American match race series at Easter. And since then, Hele and his development team (even with BSA Group's financial crisis) had found more power and improved handling; Smart in particular had been in tremendous form (setting new lap records at Silverstone, Snetterton, Oulton Park and Crystal Palace), and was expected to be supported by Ray Pickrell, Percy Tait, and American star Gary Nixon who was flying over for the meeting.

Before Mallory, however, came the French Bol d'Or, where, riding superbly in heavy rain for the first ten hours of the twenty-four-hour marathon, forty-one-year old Percy Tait and thirty-three-year old Ray Pickrell took their BSA Rocket Three (prepared at the Triumph factory) to a brilliant last-to-first victory over the 2.8 mile (4.5km) circuit at Le Mans.

Mallory Park 1971: Cooper's Race of a Lifetime

The contest on Sunday 19 September 1971 at Mallory Park in Leicestershire, went down in motorcycle racing history as one of the greatest ever races, certainly to be held on the British short circuits. Many who were there that day still call it the 'race of a lifetime', and certainly, in many ways it was the Triumph/BSA triples' greatest day. *The Motor Cycle*'s headline said it all:

> British dreams came true at Mallory Park on Sunday when John Cooper on the latest 750cc three-cylinder BSA beat Italian World Champion Giacomo Agostini fair and square to win the 'Race of the Year'.

But his success only came about after the BSA Group's marking director Peter Deverall insisted that Cooper be lent the machine. Originally, Cooper's only previous ride on one of the three-cylinder bikes had been for the Easter Anglo-American match race series, as a 'one-off'. In fact, shortly after his death in 2002, Doug Hele revealed just how close a call Cooper's presence at Mallory Park had really been:

> I felt we had the team we needed for the 'Race of the Year', but Deverall said we must have John Cooper. I was a bit upset at him for interfering, but we knew Cooper was a potential winner and provided him with a bike.

Also Cooper's Rocket 3 was a second-string machine, with an earlier non-squish motor, previously used in TT practice and raced by Percy Tait and Bob Heath in minor events. Before the 'Race of the Year' event, this particular bike had been the subject of a weight-saving exercise, its weight reduced by some 14lb (6.5kg); to do this had involved the fitting of a compact Ferodo racing clutch and ultra-lightweight magnesium casings, incorporating a large breather unit in the outer inspection cover and a lighter crankshaft.

In the course of the race the two rivals exchanged places constantly, Agostini showing up best in the hairpin section, and Cooper around the sweeping Gerard's Bend. It was

Triumph works rider and tester Percy Tait taking the inside line at Mallory Park from John Cooper (BSA Rocket 3), 'Race of the Year' meeting, 19 September 1971.

Agostini's first defeat in a major event on the bigger MV since Mike Hailwood and Honda left the GP scene at the end of 1967. The remaining top six finishers in the race were: 3rd Ray Pickrell (Rocket 3); 4th Paul Smart (Trident); 5th Percy Tait (Trident); 6th Jarno Saarinen (350 Yamaha).

At Cadwell Park a week later the main race was dominated by local hero Derek Chatterton (350 Yamaha) and Agostini on the 500MV; the best of the big triples was Cooper, in third.

October 1971: Agostini versus Cooper Again

After Cadwell Park came the final big British meeting of the year, the 'Race of the South' at Brands Hatch on 3 October 1971, and in this year it was advertised as 'Agostini v. Cooper Again'. As if to emphasize that his earlier Mallory victory had been no fluke, Cooper beat Agostini by some 2.2 seconds in the ten-lap, 26.5 mile (42.6km) race. Shattering Mike Hailwood's lap record (set on a works 297cc six-cylinder Honda), Cooper broke the 91mph (146.4kmph) barrier with a round at 91.03mph (146.5kmph), to score an impressive victory. Interviewed after his Brands success, John Cooper said: 'I can't believe it. It's terrific winning races at any time, but particularly when you are up against real opposition.' The other top six finishers were: 3rd Ray Pickrell (Rocket 3); 4th Percy Tait (Trident); 5th Alan Barnett (350 Yamsel); 6th Charlie Sanby (750 Kuhn Norton).

More Financial Woes

In mid-October 1971, only a few days after Cooper's Brands Hatch victory, came the dramatic news that the huge and sprawling BSA factory at Small Heath, Birmingham was to cease motorcycle production by the end of the year when three-quarters of the 25-acre (10ha) site was to be sold (to Birmingham Corporation) for redevelopment. Starting with immediate effect, a rapid run-down of the plant could mean as many as 3,000 redundancies. This was in an attempt to stem the crippling losses that had been incurred over the previous few months. Under the planned re-organization, both BSA and Triumph models were to be built in the more modern factory at Meriden. With a greatly reduced workforce, Small Heath would concentrate on guns, the production of components and spares for BSA and Triumphs, and sub-contract engineering.

But the real problem still existed: how to pay off the outstanding debts to the bankers, and how to tide the group over the winter period (when stocks of machines are built in readiness for the peak buying season). And it was generally agreed that the BSA Group needed approximately £15 million. Some £10 million of this had been arranged by an overdraft with Barclays Bank secured against assets, but this still left the group having to find the remaining £5 million.

Having already resigned as the group's chief executive, Eric Turner (no relation to Edward) was to give up his chairmanship at an extraordinary general meeting called for 1 November 1971, though he was to remain as a consultant. The new chief executive was 49-year old Brian Eustace. Acting chairman during the transitional period, pending a permanent appointment, was Lord Shawcross, a BSA Group director since 1967.

The Big Race at the Ontario Speedway

Ontario, California was the setting of the richest prize fund in motorcycle racing history up to that time – a massive $US 102,000 (£41,000) for the whole meeting. But coming just after the Small Heath closure news, only two official factory bikes were able to take part: John Cooper's Rocket 3 and Gary Nixon's Trident.)

Arrangements to enter Cooper for Ontario were eventually confirmed after Vancouver's BSA agent, Trevor Deeley, had agreed to a factory suggestion that he should sponsor the Englishman. The decision was not received so enthusiastically by the group's regular teamsters, however, Paul Smart saying: 'I'm very disappointed. While I've had a run of bad luck in recent events, it was the bikes that let me down. Seems people have quickly forgotten the lap records I set at Silverstone, Snetterton and Oulton Park in August and early September.' In fact John Cooper sympathized with Smart, saying: 'I think I've earned the right to go, but I only wish the factory had sent Paul, too. I'd have thought that one BSA and one Triumph would have been ideal'.

In fact, a factory-prepared works Triumph *was* to be raced at Ontario, but by American Gary Nixon. It was flown to California together with Cooper's bike; a couple of days later, race chief Doug Hele followed, with two mechanics. Five other American-based riders were scheduled to use the bikes they rode at Daytona.

But what was Ontario? To most it identified a place in Canada, but in motorcycle racing during the early 1970s it meant a new event – in California. The Ontario Motor Speedway was completed in 1970; situated just a few miles east of Los Angeles, the speed centre cost 25 million US dollars. It featured a whole complex of circuits, but the one used for the big race in October 1971 was nothing like Daytona – instead, *The Motor Cycle* described it as 'a scratcher paradise'. Just over 3 miles (5km) in length, it featured twenty curves and corners. The big race was the final round of the American Motorcycle Association's championship that had started in Texas in January, and had taken contestants all over the States as they fought for points at more than twenty title meetings.

Victory for Cooper

The race was run in two 125-mile (200km) sections, with a 45min interval during which the bikes could be rebuilt with components taken into the pit area; only crankcases had to remain unchanged. In the first leg Cooper finished third (after qualifying eighth fastest), behind the winner Gary Nixon's Trident and French Canadian Kawasaki star Yvon du Hamel. For the second heat most teams switched wheels, because tyre wear was found to be high on the abrasive surface.

Nixon and Cooper shot ahead as the forty-three starters got away for the second leg. Relatively slow to start, du Hamel completed the initial lap back in eleventh spot, but he then fired his Kawasaki triple through the field and by the fifth lap, the French Canadian star was fourth and closing fast on the leaders. Then came disaster for five of the top runners: a large oil patch on a medium-fast left-hander caught out Nixon, du Hamel, Ron Grant, Dick Mann and Dave Aldana. Luckily no one was injured, and Nixon, Grant, Mann and Aldana were able to remount; but du Hamel's race was run, as his Kawasaki was too badly damaged to continue. This mêlée left Cooper in the lead, chased by Triumph Trident-mounted Gene Romero, who had been delayed in the first leg by a crash, and Kel Carruthers.

Romero then assumed the lead on lap fourteen, and held it until lap twenty-seven; but the American champion was then forced out with a throttle cable problem, caused by his earlier spill. Next, Carruthers led from Cooper – and it was now very much a case of whoever finished first would be declared the overall winner. With just two laps of the race left, Carruthers seemed to have things under control. But then came a decisive moment when the Australian Yamaha rider was baulked as he lapped slower riders, and Cooper, who admitted later that he had not realized that the race was so advanced, made a supreme effort. Coming out of the final turn and still several lengths astern, the Englishman screamed the triple to 9,500 rpm – 1,000 over the normal maximum – and in the process thundered into Carruthers' slipstream on the drag to the flag. He then pulled off an amazing victory by pulling out and taking the flag by – as reported by *The Motor Cycle* – 'no more than six inches'.

The fastest lap of the two-leg event was set by Gary Nixon, whose Triumph went around at an average speed of 90.54mph (145.68kmph).

Interviewed after the completion of the second race, Cooper said 'It's unbelievable! What can I say? I'm lost for words!' As he had every right to be, having just won a whole host of prizes: these included various bonus cheques, a huge silver cup, bottles of champagne and a gold wristwatch. His total prize money (not including bonuses) came to $14,500 (which at the exchange rate then in force came to nearly £6,000). Equally happy was BSA-Triumph race chief Doug Hele, who exclaimed: 'It was like a fairy story. I still can't believe it'.

But the Ontario race victory was also remembered for another, rather more unpleasant sequel, in which Californian Bob Bailey took advantage of a rule which then allowed anyone to buy the winning machine for $2,500 (£1,000) if they came up with a certified cheque for the full amount within thirty minutes of the race ending. The result was to cause great consternation in the BSA-Triumph camp, because Cooper's winning machine was the very latest model, and had obviously not only cost the BSA group a lot more to build, but also held Hele's secrets of the factory's latest race developments.

Cooper's BSA Rocket 3, and the Triumph Trident on which Nixon set the fastest lap, were updated machines with a modified clutch. This altered the chain line and allowed the three-cylinder engine to be mounted without offset, as on the earlier models raced by the other members of the BSA-Triumph line up. Nixon's bike was in fact the one raced so successfully by Paul Smart when he broke the lap records at Silverstone, Snetterton and Oulton Park within the space of just eight days a few weeks earlier in late August. Factory sources confirmed a power output of 'around 86bhp', whilst the engine repositioning provided 'easier handling, especially on fast right-handers'. Weight had been trimmed by some 14lb (6.35kg) to 350lb (158.8kg). It was also generally agreed that – as noted in *The Motor Cycle*, dated 27 October 1971 – 'acceleration is terrific, and gave Nixon a marked advantage over du Hamel's Kawasaki when they were fighting it out with almost frightening ferocity in the first leg.'

A few days after Cooper's Ontario success the international sports governing body gave the green light to the Formula 750 class – although not giving it full world championship status. Previously, the American AMA and British ACU had worked together to promote the new class. As finally 'approved' by the FIM, the F750 rules insisted upon machines of between 251 and 750cc, of which at least 200 had been built by manufacturers. Only frames, forks, wheels and brakes approved by the machine manufacturer could be used. A surprise stipulation by the FIM was that, because of fears over high tyre wear on very powerful machines, races were not to exceed 200 miles, unless there was provision for an interval to change tyres.

Team Cutbacks

In mid-December 1971 came news that the BSA Group was extending its economy drive to America, and had slashed the strength of its works teams from a total of eight riders in the United States to two. Men retained for 1972 were the recently crowned 1971 AMA champion Dick Mann (BSA) and 1970 champion Gene Romero (Triumph). The biggest surprise from amongst those axed was Gary Nixon, works rider for Triumph over the previous five years and twice national champion. However, during the 1971 season Nixon had been plagued by injuries – although he had proved at Ontario in October that he was still the best American-born road racer. The two other Triumph riders to lose works support were Don Castro and Tom Rockwood, and BSA men looking for new berths were Dave Aldana, Jim Rice and Don Emde.

In 1971, Mann had led a BSA-Triumph whitewash to win the first four places in the AMA's national championships, with Romero, Rice and Aldana in second, third and fourth places. Then just before Christmas in 1971, BSA-Triumph marketing director Peter Deverall was reported as saying that in the UK, during 1972, the group would 'contest all major events, but with their team riders cut from four to two'. Favourites appeared to be John Cooper (BSA) and Ray Pickrell (Triumph), with Tony Jefferies and Percy Tait having 'occasional outings'.

A New Company: Norton/Villiers/Triumph

If the international problems of 1971 had seemed bad, in 1972 they became even worse for the troubled BSA Group (which of course comprised Triumph!). Despite the efforts of the newly reorganized board of directors, a loss of £3,300,000 was recorded at the end of July 1972. Even so, the Triumph name was still to be seen in race results, the Isle of Man TT in particular, in June 1972 Ray Pickrell winning both the Production and Formula 750 events over the legendary 37.73 mile (60.71km) mountain circuit. But after these poor trading results became public, it was obvious that things could not go on as they were.

By this time the British government (with the Conservative Edward Heath as Prime Minister) had become involved via the DTI (Department of Trade and Industry), and after much prolonged discussion, a new company, NVT (Norton Villiers Triumph) was formed, essentially a joining together of the two remaining British motorcycling manufacturing groups, Norton and BSA (the latter, of course, meaning Triumph). This new organization came into being in July 1973. By a strange twist of fate, Triumph's famous designer Edward Turner, who had been ill for some time, was to die on the 15 August that year. And as Ivor Davies recalled in his book *Triumph, The Complete Story* (The Crowood Press):

> This was sad, but at least he did not live to see the total destruction of the company he had created, as well as his factory at Meriden, which was demolished in 1984 to make way for a housing estate.

NVT resulted in a two-factory industry: Norton at the old Villiers works in Wolverhampton, and BSA/Triumph at Small Heath, Birmingham. It was this latter location that led to the infamous Workers Co-operative, backed by Tony Benn, Industry Minister under the new Labour administration that had replaced the Tories at the 1974 election.

Ray Pickrell on his way to winning the 1972 Formula 750 TT in the Isle of Man. In doing so the Triumph star broke both the race and lap records at 104.23mph (167.7kmph) and 106.68mph (171.65kmph).

The proposed closure of Meriden was something the Triumph workforce wholly opposed (Triumph, it must be remembered, had been the profitable side of the former BSA Group's motorcycle arm). The result was a sit-in that went on for a long time. In the end, after endless arguments and the production of numerous plans by both sides (and much financial pain!), a co-operative was finally formed at Meriden in March 1975, with a government loan of £4.2 million. This ultimately led to the re-introduction of the twin-cylinder Bonneville, by now enlarged to 750cc (744cc – 76 × 82mm). By these means Triumph survived for a few more years, though these actions brought about the end for both BSA and ultimately Norton itself – and, unfortunately, the death of the three-cylinder Triumph Trident and BSA Rocket 3 models.

Tony Jefferies taking his Trident Formula 750 machine to fourth place in the 750cc race of the international Gold Cup at Scarborough in September 1972. He also shared the fastest lap (a record) with Norton works rider Peter Williams at 71.57mph (115.16kmph).

The Story of Slippery Sam

But before all this happened, there was one more fairytale ending for the three-cylinder racing saga. This was the story of 'Slippery Sam', the Trident on which Ray Pickrell had ridden to victory in the 1972 Production TT. Rescued from a cellar and subsequently prepared in the former race shop manager's home, it was subsequently purchased by Les Williams (himself part of the original BSA-Triumph development team at Meriden). Having already won in 1971 and 1972, this same bike then went on to a further hat-trick of TT victories (making five in total!). The latter wins were scored by Tony Jefferies in 1973; Mick Grant in 1974; and for the marathon ten-lap (377.30 mile) race in 1975, Slippery Sam was shared by Dave Croxford and Alex George.

So how did one bike dominate a single event for half a decade? Well, the 'Production' tag in Slippery Sam's case wasn't strictly true: it was, in fact, a specially built and tuned one-off. Not only was it exceedingly fast, but it was also extremely reliable, and besides the loving care that had gone into its preparation was a host of performance-enhancing extras. These included 11.5:1 pistons, special cams with fiercer lift, a five-speed close-ratio Quaife gearbox, and even a modified frame. In the braking department, at first a massive 240mm Fontana four leading shoe drum was employed at the front; but from 1974 twin Lockheed hydraulically operated discs were specified. With a full fairing, special seat and tank, Slippery Sam weighed in at under 400lb (182kg) dry. A number of replicas were constructed by Les Williams during the late 1970s and early 1980s, but from 1984 onwards, the original found a permanent home at the National Motorcycle Museum near Birmingham.

Meanwhile, with the break-up of the BSA-Triumph Group and its subsequent acquisition by NVT, many full works F750 racers were sold off. In addition, as with Slippery Sam, several more in the form of replicas were constructed

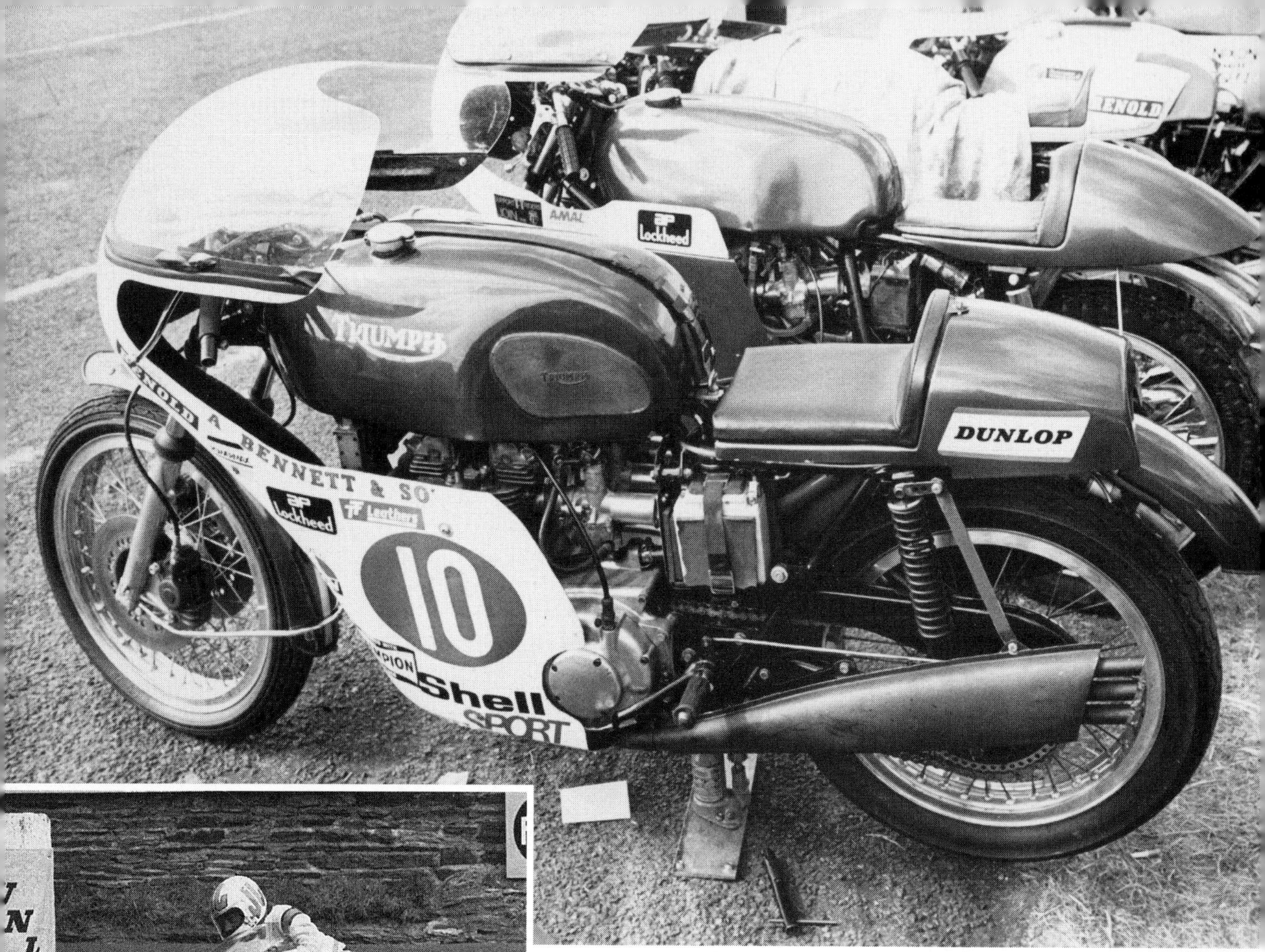

ABOVE: *Mick Grant's 1974 Production TT-winning Trident, 'Slippery Sam'. This famous mount was at the time entered via the Nuneaton-based Triumph specialist A. Bennett & Son.*

ABOVE: *Mick Grant winning the 1974 Production TT at 99.72mph (160.45kmph); he also set the fastest lap at a speed of 100.74mph (162.09kmph).*

RIGHT: *The class winners of the 1974 Production TT. Left to right: Keith Martin (Kawasaki, 47); Mick Grant (Triumph, 10) and Martin Sharpe (Yamaha, 67).*

ABOVE: Alex George with Trident 'Slippery Sam' at Governor's Bridge during his record-breaking 102.82mph (165.44kmph) lap and subsequent victory in the 1975 Production TT.

RIGHT: National Motorcycle Museum mid-1980s: Mick Grant shakes hands with the museum's founding trustee, Roy Richards. The bike is the five-times winning 'Slippery Sam'.

BELOW: The most famous Trident of all, the Les Williams-prepared 'Slippery Sam' production bike.

'Slippery Sam' on display at the National Motorcycle Museum, Birmingham. Sadly in September 2003 a fire destroyed this, and many other priceless examples of British motorcycle heritage.

from standard machines. So at least when you visit a classic event for historic racing bikes, the odds are that you will be treated to the sight and sound of these magnificent British racing motorcycles. In many ways the Trident and its sister the BSA Rocket 3 were, if one discounts the Norton Rotary and the modern day Bloor Triumphs, the last of the really great motorcycles made within the confines of the British Isles.

Fred Huggett, the CRMC Formula 750 champion on more than one occasion during the 1980s, with his works replica Trident.

14 The Bloor Era

The infamous Meriden worker co-operative came into being as a direct result of Triumph being 'conscripted', as one journalist described the July 1973 BSA Group merger with Norton-Villiers, to form NVT (Norton Villiers Triumph). Norton-Villiers had its origins in the collapse, in 1966, of AMC (Associated Motor Cycles) who themselves comprised at that time AJS, Matchless, Norton, Francis-Barnett and James. Manganese Bronze was headed by the industrialist Denis Poore, the man who had taken on the mantle of attempting to save the remains of the British motorcycle industry by combining the remains of AMC, Villiers and the BSA Group. In mid-1973 the Conservatives were in government, and with their backing Poore decided to streamline the NVT operation by backing the BSA Small Heath plant in Birmingham, rather than the Triumph Meriden works near Coventry. By this time BSA had stopped producing its own motorcycles, and instead of its own Rocket 3, was building Triumph's T150V and, later, T160V Trident models.

And so faced with mass redundancies – or in popular terminology 'the chop' – the Meriden

The national Triumph Speed Triple Challenge run in the mid-1990s was a successful and well contested one-model race series in Great Britain. This machine is seen at Donington Park in July 1994; the race was one of the support events at the British Grand Prix that year.

ABOVE LEFT: Engine cutaway of the 900cc triple on the factory stand at the NEC Show, Birmingham, in November 1994.

ABOVE: Speed Triple radiator and racing exhaust header pipes.

LEFT: Speed Triple engine, with revised clutch cover for the racing series.

Clutch removed to show the internal details of the clutch plates and primary drive gears.

Drive side of the Speed Triple engine.

force rebelled, and in September 1973, in place of the intended shutdown, the gates were padlocked from the inside, and the workers began what was to turn out to be an eighteen-month sit-in. During this period the Conservatives were defeated in a general election, and with a new Labour government in power, official government backing switched from Poore and NVT to what was to become known around the world as the 'workers co-operative'. With trade minister Tony Benn's help, and with the title of Meriden Motorcycles, the new enterprise became a reality in the spring of 1975 when the government gave the co-op a £4.2 million loan and the factory's gates were opened once more.

But this 'investment' was to prove a commercial disaster, as the co-op never made money, and instead chalked up major losses. In 1977 it received a £1 million lifeline from GEC, then four years later, in 1981, it had its debt mountain wiped out by the then Conservative government. But even then it couldn't balance the books, and by mid-1983 Meriden hit the rocks; with no money forthcoming, the liquidators auctioned off the plant and machinery. As for the famous Meriden site, this was bulldozed to make way for a housing estate!

John Bloor Saves the Triumph Name

The Triumph name – the only valuable asset left – was purchased by John Bloor, who had made his fortune building houses all over the Midlands area of Great Britain. As Bloor has proved many times over since then, he is an astute entrepreneur, and knows how to run a business successfully. He is also a patient man, so instead of telling the press anything, he simply kept quiet and got on with the job of making full use of his new purchase. In 1985, the Devon-based Les Harris concern began producing the T140V Bonneville seven-fifty under licence (from John Bloor) – although this project was to have a relatively short life-span, because in September 1990 the first of the all-new Bloor Triumphs were launched at the German Cologne Show.

The New Model Range

The bikes were really new – in fact in many ways they owed more to the then current Japanese industry than to anything seen from Triumph before – except for model names. The range was headed by the mighty Trophy 1200 four, and three pairs of bikes were listed: the Trophy, the Daytona and the Trident. By September 1991 the entire six-model line-up was in production at the newly constructed Bloor Triumph factory complex at Hinckley, Leicestershire: the unfaired Trident three-cylinder in 750 and 900cc guises, the fully-faired Daytona in 750 three-cylinder and 1,000 four-cylinder versions, and the fully-faired touring-oriented Trophy 900 triple and 1200 four. By 1996 a new bike was rolling off the Hinckley production line every six minutes, giving an annual figure of 15,000 units. But by this time new models had appeared, including the Tiger 900 Trail (1993) and the Trident Sprint roadster.

Triumph had also gone racing, its first efforts through dealer-backed efforts, notably south London-based Jack Lilley, an enterprise run by Jack's son Steven and partner George Hallam. There was also the highly popular Speed Triple Challenge race series. Backed by the factory, rounds were held at all the major circuits, and even included a support race at the 1994 British Grand Prix, held at Donington Park. The Speed Triple café racer had been launched for the 1994 model year, and was based on the Daytona chassis (soon to be phased out) with a minimal tail fairing and powered by the latest 900 three-cylinder engine.

The T595 and T509

In October 1996 the Bloor Triumph works unveiled a pair of significantly improved motorcycles: the T595 Daytona sportster and the T509 Speed Triple. The sportster had a new 955cc (79 × 65mm), liquid-cooled, three-cylinder engine, which in standard form put out 128bhp at 10,200rpm, giving a maximum speed of 160mph (260kmph). Designed by Chris Hennegan, it benefited from the following features: a curved oval-tube aluminium frame; engine casings cast in magnesium for lightness; an electronic fuel-injection system; and a six-speed gearbox in place of the five-speed box used on earlier Bloor Triumphs. Other notable aspects of the T595's specification included inverted Japanese Showa front forks, and a monoshock rear suspension from the same source. So at last Triumph had a machine capable of taking on the very best in the world – at that time the Ducati 916 and Honda FireBlade – both in the showroom and the race circuits.

The T509 Speed Triple was essentially a naked version of the T595. It was notable for its two small chrome round headlamps.

The TT600

But it was the arrival in November 1999 of Triumph's first modern six-hundred which really set the marque back on the road to a major racing comeback. By the late 1990s the most important class, at least for mainstream mass sales, had become the ultra-competitive 600cc Super Sports class, and for over a decade the Japanese, led by the benchmark Honda CBR600, had dominated. But now at last there was a British challenger. This achievement showed in the Triumph sales figures, and by 2000 the Hinkley company's production had reached 100 motorcycles a day, the maximum capacity at the original Hinkley factory.

The Shirlaws of Aberdeen Speed Triple racer during the 1994 series.

For some time it had been evident that a new factory was needed so that production could cope, and construction of the new plant began in May 1999 on a nearby industrial site. However, a major fire at the beginning of 2001 placed the marque, its workforce and dealer network under an unwanted pressure.

Nevertheless, the arrival of the TT600 had given Triumph an extra dimension, and without that disastrous fire there is no doubt Triumph would have gone racing earlier with its new six-hundred. As it was, in the TT600's first few seasons it was left to the Jack Lilley-backed effort to provide a challenge in the British Super Sport 600 series, with riders who included the promising youngsters Guy Etherington and Howie Mainwaring. But from the beginning of 2003 the Triumph factory took up the challenge themselves: a new era was about to be born.

The Valmoto Daytona 600

As my friend Alan Cathcart said in the November 2003 issue of *Motorcycle Racer* magazine:

> 2003 has been a momentous season for Triumph, the world's oldest and arguably most historic motorcycle marque, because for the first time since being rescued from the scrapheap of history two decades ago by the millionaire property developer John Bloor, Britain's finest is back in racing officially with a works team, something which last happened twenty-eight years ago when the late, great Slippery Sam – tragically destroyed in the recent National Motorcycle Museum fire – won the last of its five Isle of Man Production TT victories in the dying days of the Meriden factory operation.

V&M (Valentine & Mellor) was formed by Jack Valentine and Steve Mellor in 1983, and from then on, the two men built up an enviable reputation as probably the biggest British name in the engine-tuning business. In fact Alan Cathcart went as far as saying:

> They turned V&M into the exact British equivalent of America's famed Vance & Hines tuning duo – and not just because V&M were for many years V&H's British distributors. For like Byron Hines, Mellor is an engine wizard adept at extracting unlikely amounts of horsepower from four-stroke engines – a skill that found due reward with the three European drag-racing titles and several British crowns that his partner Valentine won riding V&M bikes during numerous years in the Euro drag leagues, just as Terry Vance was doing Stateside!

It wasn't until 2003 that the Triumph factory in Hinkley, Leicestershire, finally took the step that (Alan Cathcart) 'seemed inevitable' from the time the British marque entered the racing-driven 600 Super Sport market sector four years before, with the fuel-injected (a first for the class) TT600. However, my own feeling is that Triumph did not feel that they had a potentially competitive bike until the new, sharper-styled, totally re-engineered Daytona 600 arrived for the 2003 model year.

Triumph gave the Valmoto race team, owned by Jack Valentine and his wife Doris, a two-year contract to run their official factory-backed effort. This has seen the veteran Jim Moodie (twice British Super Sport champion) and the promising young star Craig Jones (the 2002 British Junior Superstock Champion) race the bikes in the 2003 British Super Sport Championship, whilst New Zealander Bruce Anstey defeated a hotly contested Junior TT to give the team its first major victory in no lesser venue than the Isle of Man. This achievement was made even sweeter because team-mates Jim Moodie and John McGuinness also finished the race, thus helping Triumph win the Manufacturer's Team Prize.

Technical Development

The Daytona 600 has the shortest stroke measurements of any engine in the Super Sport field, at 68 × 41.3mm. However, this has been something of a mixed blessing, as Steve Mellor observes:

> We used to run 14.2:1 on our R6 Yamaha, the one that we won the British title with, so we tried an

Opening the new Jack Lilley Triumph showroom, Shepperton, on 25 July 1992. The company was the first to become involved in racing the new Bloor range. The bike is a 900 Trident triple. Left to right: George Hallam, Jack Lilley, and 8-times world champion Phil Read.

Guy Etherington on the Jack Lilley 600 Daytona racer during a round of the 2002 British Junior Supersport at Rockingham.

The 2003 Valmoto Daytona 600

Engine:	Liquid-cooled, four-valve per cylinder, dohc, across-the-frame four cylinder
Bore:	68mm
Stroke:	41.3mm
Displacement:	598cc
Compression ratio:	13:1
Lubrication:	Wet sump; oil cooler
Ignition:	EFI (electronic fuel injection)
Carburettor:	Fuel injection
Frame:	Triple-cell aluminium perimeter type; aluminium swinging arm
Gearbox:	Six-speed close ratio
Front suspension:	Kayaba 43mm cartridge telescopic forks, with k-Tech internals and stiffer fork springs
Rear suspension:	Penske single shock, multi-adjustable
Front brake:	Twin 308mm Sunstar discs, with four-piston Nissin calipers
Rear brake:	Single disc, with two-piston calipers
Tyres:	17in front and rear
Exhaust:	Micron stainless steel, with titanium can
Wheels:	Standard Triumph three-spoke
Brake hoses:	Goodridge braided steel
Brake pads:	Carbon Lorraine
Steering damper:	Öhlins hydraulic
Engine oil:	Morris
Final-drive chain:	Regina
Wheelbase:	54.72in (1,390mm)
Steering-head angle:	24.6 degrees
Trail:	0.35in (89mm)
Dry weight:	368lb (167kg)
Maximum torque:	48ft/lb @ 12,000rpm
Maximum power:	126bhp @ 14,500rpm (rev limiter activated at 15,500rpm)
Top speed:	176mph (283kmph) – electronically timed Isle of Man June 2003

engine with a lot more compression, which isn't easy to do with big valves on the short-stroke layout. But it actually made less power, which was quite a blow because we were counting on that to help overcome the biggest handicap we have with the bike at present, which is missing that jump out of a turn. The problem may be the full-dome piston masking the bigger valves, so till we sort this out we've mainly worked on camshaft and valve timing to put us on the pace.

In the opening round of the British championship series at Silverstone in spring 2003, Craig Jones finished in the top ten, a mere ten weeks after the first engine was received by Valmoto from the Triumph works. In fact it was Jones who put the Triumph 'on pole' in the qualifying sessions for the mid-season round at Knockhill in Fife, Scotland. But as Jack Valentine later revealed:

> Winning the TT was important for Triumph, but racing there and in the North-West 200 a couple of weeks beforehand was a real distraction from the British Super Sport, because the requirements of the two forms of racing are so different. To be honest, it set us back on the short circuits, because it took six weeks out of the season at a crucial time when we were just getting on the pace. What's more, we had to suspend development to concentrate on building the bikes for the TT, whilst all the time our rivals were working on improving their bikes. We're glad we did it, especially as we won, but it did mean we've spent the rest of the season trying to play 'catch up' again.

As sold in the showrooms, the 600 Daytona puts out around 98bhp at the rear wheel, at 12,400rpm. By the time the team went to Silverstone the engine in race guise was putting out some 120bhp, and by mid-season this had gone up to 126bhp at 14,500rpm – again at the rear wheel, with 48ft/lb of torque at 12,000rpm.

Though the Daytona 600's sharp-edged bodywork does not appear particularly aerodynamic, the Valmoto machine was clocked in the Isle of Man at a hugely impressive 176mph

Scot Jim Moodie riding the Valmoto Daytona 600 at Donington Park in the October 2003 British Super Sports.

(283kmph). When asked why so quick, Steve Mellor replied:

> I think the chassis is very good, and the characteristics of the engine make it a very confidence-inspiring bike on the road circuits. It's on slower circuits in the British series that it's not at its best, because of the lack of jump out of turns, and the way it backs into corners under heavy braking. That's okay up to a point, but then it starts being uncontrollable. A slipper clutch would be a big help in fixing that.

There is no doubt that with all the four Japanese factory bikes heavily involved, the 600 Super Sport class is the most competitive of racing classes, certainly in Britain. Triumph's problems have been compounded because in qualifying, the team was usually faced in 2003 with the fact that it was the first time at each circuit with the bike, and so no data existed at all. As Steve Mellor said: 'We're working on development at the races, and sometimes we try something and it doesn't work, which loses us time, whereas we should really be qualifying the bike on at least

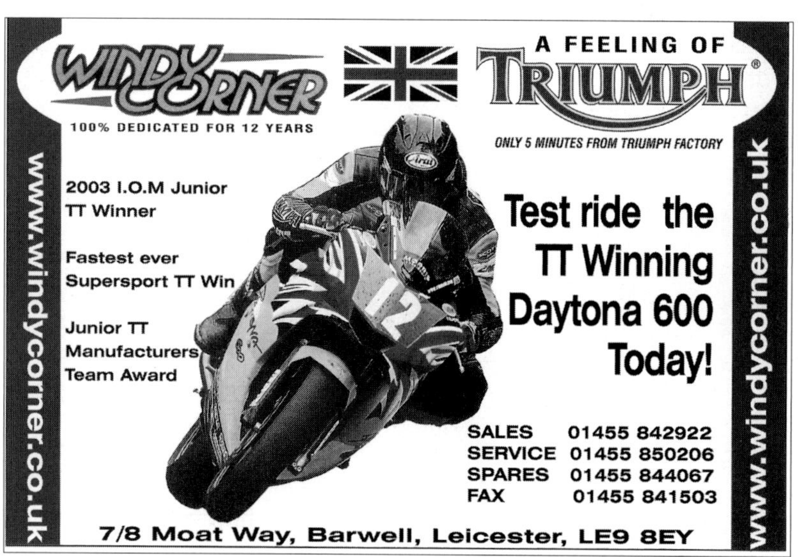

A 2003 advertisement proclaiming the Valmoto-prepared, factory-backed Daytona 600TT racing success that year.

the second row for every round.' So it was very much avoid a case of development as the season unfolded.

To experiment constantly with different cam profiles, duration and valve timing, Valmoto were provided with a supply of unmachined billet camshafts by the Triumph factory's R&D department. Once a different camshaft design has been arrived at, specialists Kent Cams manufacture a supply from the Valmoto master for the team to employ. There is also a Micron stainless steel exhaust with a single titanium end can, made to the team's own specification. As Steve Mellor revealed: 'It's a good engine that's also extremely strong and reliable.'

So most of the work was concerned with blueprinting components such as the crankshaft, connecting rods, and pistons – all parts that could not be changed under Super Sport regulations. Porting and gas flowing were improved through the already free-flowing cylinder head. The compression ratio was increased from the standard 12.5:1 to 13:1 but, as explained earlier, the short-stroke dimensions have proved a problem in this area.

Electronic Fuel Injection

EFI (electronic fuel injection) is a feature of the Triumph six-hundred, in fact it has been a feature since the first 600 TT models made their debut for the 1999 model year. Steve Mellor again: 'It's the first time we worked on this system in Super Sport competition.' But he does agree it makes setting up the engine 'so much easier'. Valmoto retained the stock Keihin ECU fitted to the street bike, which they progressively modified to raise the rev limiter; by mid-season 2003, this had been set at 15,500rpm.

The team has also used a Dynojet Power Commander to alter fuel mapping for the EFI, although another problem has been how to alter ignition in 'real time'. So far this can only be achieved by requesting a different ignition map from the Triumph factory. The upper one of the dual throttle butterflies in each 37.5mm Keihin throttle body had to be disconnected after tests proved it had no effect above 7,000rpm – lower than the bike was ever revved in short-circuit events, and the intakes were later shortened to a uniform length, unlike on the road-going model where the two central ones are longer than the two outer ones. Steve Mellor commented: 'This moves peak power higher up the rev range – though to be honest, the one big drawback we had at first was getting the engine to keep on revving hard without the power dropping off. That's the opposite of what you'd expect with a short-stroke bike.'

The Frame is Retained Unmodified

The standard Daytona 600 triple-cell aluminium frame was retained in unmodified form as per the Super Sport regulations, with a 54.7in (1,390mm) wheelbase, 24.6-degree head angle and 3.5in (89mm) of trail as the original numbers that the rules call for. The swinging arm also is of aluminium, and for racing features a Penske monoshock: this has the advantage of providing both high- and low-speed compression damper adjustment, whilst 'up front' the standard-fit 43mm Kayaba telescopic cartridge forks were equipped with K-Tech internals and stiffer fork springs to optimize damping. An Öhlins steering damper is useful, particularly on bumpy surfaces or 'road-going' such as in the Isle of Man.

The stock three-spoke Triumph wheels were another item that the rules said could not be changed. Braking was taken care of by the street bike's 308mm Sunstar discs, with four-pot Nissin calipers equipped with Goodridge braided steel hoses and Carbon Lorraine pads.

The Evo Motor

By the end of the 2003 season Valmoto had developed what they called the 'Evo motor'. This, it claimed, would provide much-improved acceleration out of the corners, with enough power to hoist the front wheel well clear of the ground out of slower turns in second gear. So it's hoped that it will be just a matter of time before the Triumph Super Sport racer is truly competitive. The 2004 season will be an important one for both Valmoto and the factory. As a Triumph enthusiast I hope the two parties are successful in this quest.

Index